A MEMOIR

In memory of my beloved wife Phyllis
and for
my daughters Síle and Jane
and
my grandson David.

# A MEMOIR

Terry de Valera

CURRACH
PRESS

First published in 2004 by
CURRACH PRESS
55A Spruce Avenue, Stillorgan Industrial Park, Blackrock, Co Dublin

www.currach.ie

1 3 5 7 9 10 8 6 4 2

Cover by Currach Press
Cover photograph by Máirín de Valera
Author photograph inside back flap by Lorcan Brereton
Origination by Currach Press
Printed in Ireland by ColourBooks Ltd, Dublin

ISBN 1-85607-911-2

# CONTENTS

# LIST OF ILLUSTRATIONS

23. Jimmy O'Dea and Seán O'Sullivan RHA at the Áras
24. Bust of Father (by Albert Power RHA)
25. Portrait of Mother (by Seán O'Sullivan RHA, courtesy National Gallery)
26. Self with pianist Charles Lynch DMus, c.1978
27. With Yann Renard-Goulet RHA, 1951
28. Frank McKelvey RHA and his wife Elizabeth
29. Leslie Mellon
30. Presenting Cathal Brugha's .45 Smith & Wesson to the National Museum, together with Christy Cruise's .45 Webley (courtesy National Museum)
31. Self with Phyllis (Lorcan Brereton)

# PROLOGUE

The two primary reasons which prompted me to write this memoir were, firstly, the detailed record which my mother wrote specially for me at my request and which sets out many aspects of her anxious, stressful and exceptionally long life. I felt that these precious recollections should be available for posterity. Many writings about her to date do not reveal her true character. Too often the impression left is of a gentle little woman, who stayed in the background and held few opinions. In essence a number of these writers show her as little more that the devoted wife of her famous husband. While it is true that she was a gentle, loving wife and devoted mother, there still lay within her small frame, the heart of a lioness, a truly determined and strong character, unswerving dedication to her strongly-held principles, both political and moral, her deep sense of patriotism, and her absolute commitment to her religious faith. Although she herself would not easily admit it, she showed herself to be so brave in many adverse, dangerous and difficult circumstances. She had many talents, artistic and otherwise.

When I came to ask her to commit her memories to paper, she was at first hesitant for she opens her memoirs with the following: 'In the nature of things an autobiography must be egotistical. Self-love is strong in most of us. Our estimate of our character and of our achievements is hardly likely to be a very low one. I shall try to write a true and accurate account.' For my own part I hope that my effort, will reveal more of the real Sinéad de Valera and of her closest friends, her true devotion to her husband, her family, her country, her talents, her life in moments of sunshine, but also in the deep gloomy shadows which were so often her lot.

My second reason, and equally important, is to deal with events in my father's life, a number of which have not hitherto been recorded, but also to refute many false and salacious allegations, which have, of late and in the past, been laid against him. I have corrected a number of errors which have appeared from time to time. The reader will see that I have in many instances challenged unjust and untrue allegations or impressions suggested by unproven innuendo.

For the remainder of my work I am sure that it could appear, in parts, to be somewhat egotistical, but as my mother remarked, all autobiographical work must, of necessity, contain something of that element.

I was anxious, however, to name and to treat or mention the lives of several who had touched my life, believing, as I do, that their lives and their achievements are worthy of remembrance and that recognition be given for the services they rendered, whether in politics, the arts or other pursuits. Many of those I mention were in one way or another important threads in the fabric of Irish society of their time. I hope too that the information I have supplied, may be a source and of some use to future writers and biographers.

It is a matter of sorrow and deep regret that my good friend, the late Professor Thomas P. O'Neill did not live to see this work completed. It had been my hope that he would write a preface to this work, which he had agreed to do prior to his untimely demise. For very many years I had relied upon his skill and great expertise as a renowned historian, very much so when I first undertook this work. He had been equally helpful to me in historical research (mostly on subjects concerning art) which I carried out and published in the past. He had been, in many ways, my mentor, always there to guide me from as far back as the early 1950s. His loss to scholarship is, in many ways, irreplaceable.

I wish to express my thanks to Prof. O'Neill's widow, Marie, herself a historian in her own right, for her help and encouragement during the course of my writing this memoir. We had been law students together in the early 1940s.

There are many others to whom I feel indebted for their assistance and advice, and the encouragement they gave me in the course of my writing. There are, however, several who deserve special recognition. My warmest thanks go to my good friend Tony Behan and his son Paul for so generously giving me the use of their efficiently run office and its equipment and for allowing me to have the typing service of initial drafts.

All this assistance greatly eased my task.

I wish to acknowledge and to express my thanks to the Franciscan Friars for permission to use letters and other material relating to both my father and my mother, which material has been left to them in trust and is now in University College, Dublin.

My warm thanks, too, to my friend Breandán Mac Giolla Choille, the eminent archivist for his help and expert advice. In a special way I wish to express my gratitude to Luis Enrique Valera, the Marques de Aunon, for his ever-willing and useful assistance when tracing my father's Spanish connection. Without his help, so generously given, my task would have been that much more difficult. I would also like to thank William F. O'Grady, solicitor, and his partner, Mr Kirbby Tarrant, solicitor, for highly-valued and useful advice.

I would also like to express my gratitude to surgeon James M. Sheehan, the present owner of The Hermitage, Cross Avenue, Blackrock, for making the title deeds of the premises available for my perusal and in particular a copy of the will of Lt Col Henry Lucas St. George.

There are so many other friends who through their encouragement and interest, have, each in their own way, helped me along in what turned out to be a mammoth undertaking. To all of them my sincere thanks.

I wish to record my special gratitude to my friend, the Rev. Dudley Levistone Cooney, the highly-respected president of the Old Dublin Society (of which I have been a member for almost twenty-two years), for his kind introduction to Currach Press. In particular I wish to thank Brian Lynch, my publisher, for his ever-present co-operation in the production of this memoir.

I wish to give special acknowledgement and heartfelt thanks to my good friend, Theo Mortimer, (Hon. Editor of the Old Dublin Society's *Dublin Historical Record*) for all the hard work which he put into the task of editing this memoir, to say nothing of his expert and valuable advice, as he himself is an expert researcher and biographer in certain matters musical.

I am particularly grateful to Joseph M. Silinonte of New York, a professional genealogist and researcher of many years standing, for vital and important information he so kindly supplied to me in relation to the marriage of my paternal grandparents.

My special thanks too to Lorcan Brereton, a professional photographer (son of Mrs Ruby Brereton, one of Phyllis' closest and dearest friends), for supplying a number of excellent photographs and for making copies of others, which it is hoped, will add considerable interest to my work.

Finally, but by no means least, I wish to record my thanks to my beloved late wife, Phyllis, my daughters Síle and Jane and to my grandson David for their long suffering patience, encouragement and practical help during the countless hours I laboured on this work.

I have made great effort to be accurate, truthful and fair in my reporting. I have also endeavored to record, as best I could, something of the atmosphere and standards of the time covered in my work.

If, in the end, I have at all added to or have advanced knowledge by providing useful and reliable information of an historical nature, which covers a long period of time, my task will have been well worthwhile.

Terry de Valera
Charton
Foxrock
Co. Dublin

# CHAPTER I

*Earliest Recollections*

I was born at 10.00a.m. on Whit Sunday, 4 June 1922, the youngest of seven children. It was a tragic year in the history of Ireland, for within weeks of my birth, the Civil War had begun. When I was but a few weeks old, my mother said to my father 'I think that there is going to be a wave in Terry's hair.' When he showed no interest, she rebuked him. She tried to attract his attention again, and he replied 'How can I mind about the wave in Terry's hair when they are fighting in the Four Courts?'

Many years later, Father told me that he often regretted having visited the nursing home on the day I was born. In so doing, he had missed a meeting, which in retrospect he thought might have helped to avert the ever-growing conflict between pro- and anti-Treaty factions. For my part I only hope that my arrival in no way contributed further to the course of the Civil War.

I was named after Terence MacSwiney, the Cork patriot who had died in 1920 on hunger strike in Brixton Prison in England. I am proud to bear his name and indeed, I possess a souvenir of this great Irish man – his watch. I believe he wore it during the brave and terrible ordeal he suffered as he passed to his heroic end. Terence MacSwiney's sister, Mary, gave me her brother's book *Principles of Freedom* in which she wrote the following inscription:

To Terence de Valera on his first birthday.
From the sister of the Terence whose name he bears, who can wish him nothing better than that he may grow up as noble a character as the martyr Terence, and live to worthily perfect and enjoy the fruits of that freedom for which all our martyrs died.

Máire Mac Shuibhne
June 4th, 1923

Although she addresses these elegant words to 'Terence', this is not my real name. MacSwiney used the name 'Terence', although the Irish form is 'Traleach'. I was christened Toirdhealbhach, but was known as Terry, never Terence. When I grew up, at my father's suggestion, I changed this woeful spelling and abbreviated it to 'Toirleach'. I confess that I do not care for Toirleach, despite its fame in Irish history and much prefer Terry. It is not uncommon for people to dislike the name they are given. My mother did not care for her own Christian name, Jane, which she changed to Sinéad in her later life.

At the time of my birth the family was living in Greystones, Co. Wicklow, a beautiful county which would have a profound influence on me for the remainder of my life. In August 1924, however, weary and hard-pressed by the tragic events which had taken place in her life since the 1916 Rising, my mother took a house known as Ellistrim Lodge in Roundstone, Co. Galway for a holiday with the family. Here she hoped to find some peace, as well as a place in which the older members of the family could perfect their knowledge of the Irish language.

Galway is the scene of my earliest childhood memory – standing beside a turf fire with a group of old women in black shawls and also the deep blue mountains in the distance.

The family had left Greystones only months after my birth, first to 18 Claremount Road in Sandymount and then, in 1925 to nearby Elm Villa. The house was owned by a friend of my mother, Miss Delahunt, who let it to her. Elm Villa was then about fifty to sixty years old and in a rather dilapidated condition. It had been designed as a mock castle finished in poor cement compo-work. Its style of architecture was not uncommon for the period in which Elm Villa had been built in the middle part of the Victorian era, with turrets at the rear. Through years of neglect, the turrets had filled with water which caused dampness and mould in parts of the basement. In our time the entrance to the turrets was blocked up.

Elm Villa stood on about three-quarters of an acre and was surrounded by a somewhat neglected garden and a small field. At the end of the field, adjoining the neighbouring property, Mother kept poultry as well as two pet goats. The driveway ran straight from the hall door to the entrance gate on Serpentine Avenue. There was a gate lodge at the entrance but it, too, was in a poor condition and remained unoccupied during our tenancy.

The owner of Elm Villa, Miss Delahunt, was a rather stout lady who dressed mostly in black. On one of her visits she put me on her knee where

I was fascinated by the large white collar on her dress. I remember saying 'That's a bit of curtain', much to my mother's embarrassment. Miss Delahunt was quick to reply 'Oh no my dear, that's Carrickmacross lace!'

By then all my brothers and sisters were at school. I remained at home with Mother and the maid Agnes Devaney. Although I played with my sister Emer, I was a loner, save for the company of my brother Ruairi to whom I formed a strong attachment. Almost six years my senior, Ruairi had a deep influence upon me throughout my life.

I spent many weary hours with Mother as she received numerous visitors. My only companion was the dog, Nessa, a Kerry Blue. At times even she tired of being confined as the visitors talked on and on. Most of these people had connections with the 1916 Rising and other major historical events, some went back to my mother's day in the Gaelic League at the turn of the century. I still wonder how Mother bore these endless, no doubt well-meaning visits. In spite of her otherwise robust health, she suffered frequent and painful attacks of migraine. There were times when she was confined to bed in a darkened room, her only companion the faithful Nessa who refused to leave her side. Nessa lived until the autumn of 1938, after which my mother resolved that she would never have another dog. Dinny the cat died when he was about eleven, in the same year as Nessa. By this time we had moved to Bellevue and I buried them both in the rose garden and I tended their grave until we left the house in 1940. These two animals played significant part in my childhood and boyhood days.

The family seldom saw my father during this time. Mother told me that he hardly saw me for the first two years of my life. He was frequently away from home, including his many tours in the United States. When he returned from America, he told us of his voyages on the great ocean liners of the time, ships like the *Leviathan* and the *Majestic*, then the largest passenger ships in the world – and he gave us balloons with the ships' names written on them. Although he travelled thousands of miles by sea, he dreaded these voyages as he was so often seasick. Travelling by train across America, he visited every one of the forty-eight states, surviving no fewer than three rail accidents without injury. One was particularly serious, involving a head-on collision between two express trains. He spoke graphically of how the two great engines were locked together, standing at an angle of 45 degrees, which he demonstrated with his two index fingers. There were a number of fatalities and he and his companions did what they could to assist the many injured. He and his friends were lucky, travelling at the rear of one of the trains.

Father sometimes brought back mementoes from his trips, but the ones we loved the most were the real Native American head-dress and bow. He had been presented with these during his last tour of America when he had been made an honorary chief of the Chippewa tribe. My brothers and I were delighted: we could play Cowboys and Indians with real things. Ruairi always insisted that we took the Indians' side.

In later years Father spoke again of his time with the Chippewa in Wisconsin. As part of the initiation ritual, the chief of the tribe and the chief-elect had to draw a little blood, then to mix the blood to signify their brotherhood. This did not appeal to my father, so he somehow managed to avoid this part of the ceremony without causing offence. Although my brothers and I derived many years of pleasure from these souvenirs, in later times we regretted that the beautiful head-dress became tattered and torn until it finally disintegrated. The bow, too, was broken and eventually lost.

A much less pleasant childhood memory of my father involved being forced to take an extremely disagreeable medicine. Amid much struggling and protest, he managed to pour the slimy substance down my throat. I was furious at losing the battle and well remember climbing the stairs and shouting 'Dirty fellow, filthy fellow. I wish he would go back to jail again!' Father enjoyed my words of protest so much that he told this story in many parts of the world. My sister Emer remembers that she thought that jail was a place where any self-respecting father might find himself from time to time. Little wonder, for Father had been in such institutions no less than fourteen times.

Although I was too young to remember most of the times my father had been incarcerated, or indeed was not born for much of it, I do recall the last time he was in jail. It was February 1929, and he had set out for Belfast intending to deliver a lecture. Unknown to him, the British Government had issued an Exclusion Order and he was arrested at Goraghwood Railway Station by the RUC and sentenced to a month in prison.

Mother's sister, Bridget, was with us that day, no doubt quite deliberately, since father knew the danger of being arrested and had warned my mother. When the phone rang, Bridget answered it. As she listened, she burst out with her characteristic loud and sharp laugh. Mother began to laugh too. I could not possibly understand what was happening, so I too joined in the laughter. It is that they both had anticipated what would happen and therefore were not in the least surprised at the news.

When Father was not at home, which was very often, life went on as usual, with my mother in charge of home matters and her children's education. Lessons could be interrupted at any time by a constant stream of visitors, many of whom I remember. There were people like Seoirse (George) Irvine whom Mother had known from her days in the Gaelic League. He had taken part in the 1916 Rising and had been imprisoned as a result. Irvine was a devout Protestant and when Father was drafting the Constitution, he had an argument with him as to the use of the word 'Catholic'. Irvine contended that he too was a Catholic, although not in the Roman tradition. I remember him as a small dark man who seldom smiled, but he was a true friend to my mother at a time when she needed friends.

Another of Mother's Protestant friends was Nora Cunningham, a matron in a nursing home who always brought sweets. Other loyal friends included Miss McKeown and her niece, Francie Sullivan, both of whom had rendered valiant and brave service during the time of the Black and Tans and the Civil War.

A most welcome visitor was my mother's childhood friend, Lil Saurin, a little grey-haired lady with a sweet and smiling face. Although she and her family took the pro-Treaty side in the Civil War, this never affected the bond between her and my mother. She called Mother 'Doll', a nickname given to her by her father when Mother was a baby. She played the piano and I still have some of her music.

Another Protestant friend, Sinéad (Jane) Wilson, had also known Mother since their days in the Gaelic League. Their friendship began in Tourmakeady, Co. Mayo, where they had gone to study Irish. Both my mother and her sister Bridget had won scholarships to Tourmakeady and Mother continued to go there until her marriage in 1910. When I knew Sinéad Wilson, she was a handsome lady, then in her late sixties, with well groomed silky grey-hair, a distinctly aquiline nose, with deep-set sparkling blue eyes. When she spoke Irish, she did so with a rather grand and semi-English accent.

Our visits to her charming and historic house in Rathfarnham were always special occasions. As we ate her lovely teas, a pet cockatoo perched on her shoulder. One day she brought me into the hall and pointed to a blunderbuss hanging on the wall. 'Do you see that gun?' she asked. 'Many, many years ago [this must have been at the end of the eighteenth century] my grandmother saw a burglar in her house. As he stood in the moonlight, my grandmother seized the gun, fired and shot him dead!' For a young boy, little could compare with visits to a house with a cockatoo, the deadly blunderbuss and in summer her lovely garden full of flowers.

Our journeys home from Miss Wilson's involved the long walk to Rathfarnham village, past open countryside. We rode the open-topped tram to the kiosk in Pembroke Road and another tram to the top of Serpentine Avenue, followed by another good walk to Elm Villa. After we moved to Springville in Blackrock, Miss Wilson visited us only once. She died shortly afterwards from a stroke at the age of seventy-three. Mother felt her loss deeply and always spoke of her with affection for many years to come.

My mother's varied circle of friends included the eccentric Viviene Butler-Bourke. An American citizen of Irish ancestry, she had a great love of Ireland but would not give up her American citizenship, something which meant nothing to me at the time. She was passionate about animals, violently anti-vivisectionist and a strict vegetarian. Her dog Fionn, a beautiful, highly-bred and groomed Airedale, always accompanied her. He got on remarkably well with Nessa, but barely tolerated me. I have noticed that some highly bred dogs can be off-putting and indeed downright snobs, if dogs can be such!

Despite her doting care, Fionn eventually died and she gave him a formal funeral to which she invited Mother and other close friends. Mother felt embarrassed about having to attend such a ceremony, yet did not want to hurt her friend. Fionn was buried at the foot of Douce Mountain in Co. Wicklow, complete with specially-made coffin in which Vivienne had put semi-precious stones. As she placed the coffin in the grave, skylarks were singing loudly as one would expect on a glorious June day and in such an idyllic setting. When Vivienne heard their song, she exclaimed 'Now I know his little soul is happy.'

Viviene finally settled in Canada where she died in the mid-1930s. In her will she directed that her body be cremated and that her dog Conla, be put down, and his body be likewise cremated. Their ashes were then to be mingled and scattered in a Canadian river. Mother on hearing the news of her death remarked, 'Poor Viviene, she was always looking for something in life which she never found.'

Another couple and their children were frequent visitors from even before my earliest childhood. They were Frank Hughes and his wife Kitty. My mother had a special affection for the pair, especially Kitty, a handsome lady who dressed particularly well. Frank had been the best man at my parents' wedding and a close friend of my father's since their youth.

Two other visitors, Agnes and Gertrude Cullhane, lived in considerable comfort in Rathgar. Their family's unlikely source of wealth came from the sale of feathers. The two ladies were very fashion conscious, as they could well afford to be, and I remember them arriving once in those awful 'coal scuttle' hats. Gertie asked if she might take her's off: it squeezed so tight that it was giving her a headache. My mother freely admitted that woman's fashions did not interest her. She was no seamstress, nor did she knit, although she said that at times she regretted not having these talents.

When Father was at home, he too had many visitors. I have particular memories of Dorothy Macardle and her 'Baby' Austin 7. I believe it was one of the very early models. Father boasted that he could knock fifty-five miles per hour out of the little car, and Dorothy herself told this story of this truly diminutive car. One day she was driving in College Green. There was a well-known garda on point duty. If he was an inch, he was some six foot six inches tall and in a typical Dublin way had earned himself the nickname 'Tiny'. He was well-known to be somewhat cranky. Tiny signalled Miss Macardle to come on and as she did she accidentally drove over his foot. He was furious and shouted at her 'If you do that again I'll kick you and your flea to the other side of College Green!'

One of the main reasons for Dorothy Macardle's visit was to talk to Father about her book, *The Irish Republic*, which was first published in 1937. Not long before her death, she confided to Father that she had given the best years of her life to the book, devoting some ten years to researching and writing this monumental work. She begged him 'Do not let it die.' I was in my teens when the first edition appeared and soon became very interested in its contents. Miss Macardle noticed this and was sufficiently impressed to leave me the rights of this work in her will. This scholarly undertaking has been attacked by latter day 'revisionists' whose principle motive appears to be to wish away or water down many aspects of modern Irish history and cast aspersions or doubts on ideals and simple patriotism. Speaking of revisionists reminds me of the late Vinny May, a prominent member of the S Branch (of which we will hear more in chapter four). He had a distinguished career when fighting the Black and Tans in Dublin and had taken part in several successful actions. He remarked scornfully about revisionists and their ilk: 'They are just the kind of people who if there was real trouble again, would have the bed shot from OVER them!'

Frank Aiken, Father's close friend and colleague, was a frequent visitor. He drove an 'A Model' Ford, which he once showed off by driving up the slag heaps at the Avoca Mines in Co. Wicklow. Included in the astonished audience were Dr Jim Ryan and his wife Máirín. We were certain that he would turn over or come crashing down on us, but he was quite fearless and continued this experiment to see how far he could force the car up the steep incline.

I have memories too of Máirín being dressed as bridesmaid for the wedding of Tom Derrig and Mother's close friend, Jenny Mason, who had done secretarial work for Michael Collins.

We were also very close friends with the Coughlan family. There were six of them to seven of us, almost one-to-one. Emer, the youngest, was my boyhood sweetheart: very pretty and attractive. The Coughlans had two cars (a rarity in the 1920s), a 1927 Dodge and a 1921 Citroen. Mrs Coughlan loved driving and was among the earliest lady drivers in Ireland. Her son Éamonn was a terror who would never had survived in the traffic of today.

The Coughlans lived in a very attractive home in Bray, Co. Wicklow. Our journeys there were so different from such a journey today. Once we left home, we first passed through Deansgrange, an isolated village with little to see except the cemetery. Then there were the isolated villages of Cabinteely, Loughlinstown and Little Bray, until we reached Bray itself. Once, as we attempted to pass the Old Courthouse in the Main Street in Bray, Éamonn Coughlan was forced to stop, then cautiously make his way through the cattle on a fair day when the entire street was crowded with livestock.

Perhaps because I was the youngest, Mrs Coughlan was very fond of me. It was she who gave me my first pedal-car (in those days called a 'pedal motor'). I still can remember its light brown bodywork, finished with a smart yellow stripe.

Two other callers of the period were my godparents, both of whom lived nearby. My godmother was Mother's friend, Eleanor Butler, the well-known geographer. She was completely deaf and had to use an ear trumpet, but I always found her kind and affectionate. My godfather, John O'Connor Cox, was known to us as Sean Athair (grandfather). He gave me presents which were far too grown up for a youngster, such as fountain pens and tie pins. I hated when he put me on his knee and kissed me, at the same time being pricked by his stubby moustache.

Ever since my boyhood, there was a strong bond between me and my elder sister Máirín. She was almost ten years older and in ways became, to some little extent, a second mother. At bedtime she read to me in a dark room with a horrid smelly oil lamp, which acted as a night lamp, which cast eerie shadows over the dismal surroundings. Máirín read to me from Robert Louis Stevenson's *A Child's Garden of Verses* which delighted me and 'made my childhood days rejoice'. I have read those same beautiful little Stevenson poems to my own children and my grandson David. She also read rhymes from A. A. Milne's *When We Were Very Young*. She told me stories of Robert Emmet and Sarah Curran, beginning an interest in Emmet which has lasted to this day.

In later years Máirín often talked of our time at both Elm Villa and Springville. Like Ruairi and Vivion, she provided the details which I did not then fully understand about life in the 1920s and early '30s.

Elm Villa had electric light which was supplied by the far-from-reliable Pembroke Power Station in Ringsend. This was prior to the foundation of the Electricity Supply Board and there were frequent blackouts, malfunctions and general failures of the system, especially in winter time. Many hours, perhaps a whole day or night, could pass when candles and oil lamps had to be used. These long blackouts added to the strange atmosphere which seemed to pervade the house.

There was a room at the back known to us as the playroom, which was where we generally took our meals. One evening, Father came in and was enjoying a quick snack of tea, a boiled egg and my mother's home-made brown bread, one of her specialities and much-liked by my father. While he ate, Ruairi and I played with lead soldiers in the corner of the room. At first, Father took little notice, but then looked up and asked 'Ruairi, what are you playing?' 'Soldiers, Dad,' was the reply. 'We are attacking the English.' Father replied: 'Not the English, Ruairi … just play they're the enemy.' He did not wish us to have any enmity towards the English people.

When Father left the table, he took up the empty eggshell and, with a broad grin, threw it across the room where it landed neatly on 'the enemy'. As he walked out of the room, he announced: 'And there's a shell on them.'

Elm Villa was not a lucky house as far as health was concerned. Vivion could scarcely stay a night there without an attack of asthma. He was then a boarder in Blackrock College which is where he spent most of his time. Brian was also an asthmatic, and my father developed a severe dose of pleurisy shortly after we came to live there. Emer too had a serious illness. I contracted double pneumonia from which I nearly died. Although I was only just three, I had vivid memories of this illness, especially the visits of Dr McCarville. For political reasons, other doctors were not as sympathetic or willing to treat me because the bitterness of the Civil War was still very strong. Dr Patrick McCarville had taken part in the War of Independence and had been sentenced to six years penal servitude for operating in what his court martial called a 'Flying Squadron'. He was a close friend and supporter of my father. In the 1920s he was a specialist in Temple Street Childrens' Hospital and he later practised as a dermatologist at 38 Upper Fitzwilliam Street. My brother Brian became very ill with asthma in the mid-twenties and Father sent for McCarville who said the boy must be admitted to Temple Street Hospital immediately. Father was doubtful if this was necessary but McCarville retorted 'I'll leave the politics to you, Chief, but leave the medicine to me!'

The treatment for my illness was very crude by today's standards, and quite painful. I screamed with pain as my mother held me over her knee while the doctor slapped red-hot poultices across the upper part of my back. I can remember lying in my cot and hearing the word 'crisis', although of course I had not the slightest idea what it meant. In those days they could do little but wait for the crisis to pass. If the patient came through this vital time of some nine days, the chances of recovery were good; if not, there was no hope.

I still can see Dr McCarville's striped trousers as I looked around while he examined me. In those days, all top rate specialists did their daily rounds in morning dress, a practice which continued well into the early thirties.

Among the many friends of my parents a special place must be given to Dr Robert Farnan, his wife Lora, her sisters Mary Macken and Margaret Keady. Perhaps of all my father's friends and colleagues none were so close, nor had his trust as had Robert Farnan. At that time Dr Farnan was at the top of his profession as a gynaecologist. He had made a great deal of money and owned No. 5 Merrion Square, a charming bungalow in Howth which I was told cost as much as £8,000 to build in the 1920s, due among other things to vast excavation of solid rock. He also owned beautiful Bolton Castle with its many acres in Co. Kildare. The doctor himself was a native of Kildare and very proud of this. He was widely acknowledged to be an expert on breeding cattle and kept some famous bulls. He sheltered my father many times when he was on the run. He gave financial support to Father in his political and other undertakings and, according to my mother, also to the family. Father had the greatest respect for his astute judgement and confided in him in relation to many political and personal matters too. They spent a great deal of time together. Farnan absolutely revered my father and always addressed him as 'the Chief,' as did so many of Father's other colleagues.

Sadly Robert and Lora Farnan's marriage was childless but following the tragic death of Lora in 1938 the doctor remarried. By this second marriage he had a son, Patrick, who afterwards was ordained and has become a priest of considerable prominence in the Archdiocese of Dublin.

Father made Dr Farnan a director of the *Irish Press* and later appointed him a senator. In sickness he proved himself to be truly knowledgeable and sympathetic especially when Emer had a serious illness in 1930. My recollections of this outstanding Irishman are of a very large man, well over six feet in height with a full figure and a somewhat ruddy complexion. As a child I found him a little aloof and serious. He himself enjoyed good health living to a great age despite the fact he smoked no less than sixty cigarettes a day. He died on 7 January 1963. Father never really quite got over his death, for Dr Farnan was one of his dearest and most loyal friends. Mother was equally fond of him and his wife Lora and repeatedly spoke of their countless kindnesses to the family.

Lora was very direct in her manner and fearlessly spoke her mind in her characteristic rather deep-throated voice. We all loved her especially the four youngest. One great treat was when she and her elder sister Marie took us to town at Christmas. There they bought us lots of expensive toys a number of which I still have. This annual treat continued for at least six Christmases from 1927 to 1932.

I have vivid memories of Christmas of 1930. As usual Mrs Farnan and Marie Macken brought us to Laurences' which was then the leading toy shop in Dublin. This firm had two shops, one in Grafton Street, later to become part of Brown Thomas and still later Marks and Spencer. The other shop was in Lower O'Connell Street on the western side. The four youngest arrived at the O'Connell Street shop having been driven there with Mrs Farnan and her sister by their chauffeur Tommy in their giant 40 hp Cadillac.

We were only a short while in the shop when my eye lighted upon a beautiful pedal car. At once Lora said that I should try it out. By then I was an experienced pedal car driver thanks to the car which Mrs Coughlan had given me years earlier. Without the slightest difficulty I manoeuvred it through other cars, tricycles and toys on the shop floor. Mrs Farnan was very impressed and no doubt saw my joy as I showed off my skill. She called the lady assistant enquiring as to the price to which she received the answer 'Two guineas, Madam, and I would point out that this model is the very latest with balloon tyres.' 'Right,' said Lora, 'we'll take it.' Having purchased other toys for Brian, Ruairi and Emer, Lora was waiting for the bill to be made up. She turned to her sister and said 'these balloon tyres are something which Bob's cars have not,' although at that time Dr Farnan had the Cadillac, and in addition, a beautiful Dickie Rolls Royce. When we arrived home that evening Laurences' had already delivered the pedal car to our home. We had by then moved to Springville in Blackrock.

Dr Farnan took an exceptional interest in Éamon who followed in his footsteps specialising in gynaecology and with such distinction. The elder man had been truly Éamon's mentor and Éamon felt in his debt to the end of his life.

My father loved driving, but as the 1930s progressed, he could no longer trust his eyesight. Still I remember being with him as he drove a variety of cars, including a 1925 Chevrolet, a Dickie, an A Model Ford and an A Model Saloon. A cautious but by no means slow driver, he purchased his first Dodge in 1934 but drove it very little. The last time he drove was in 1938, after he bought the beautiful seven-seater Dodge. He only drove it for a few hundred yards before saying to Christy Cruise, his senior driver: 'Ah, no Christy I cannot see properly.' He never drove again.

Father believed that he should not accept a car provided by the State. His cars were his own, so that he felt free to use them as he wished for family purposes. It was only when he became President that he used the State's Rolls Royce. Even then, he sometimes used his own car which is now in the de Valera Museum in Ennis, Co. Clare.

While I remember Elm Villa in bright summer days, I seem to remember it most in the rain and winter time and those awful dense fogs which were very much part of Sandymount of that period. Before I went to school at the age of six I was the only child at home. I remember one day when I had just past six years of age I was playing in the basement with my pedal car, the one Mrs Coughlan had given me. My mother and the maid Agnes Devaney were the only other people in the house. I tired of my game and according to the strict instructions given to me by my father I put the car away under the stairs. He insisted on this for one night he had fallen over it. I turned to join Mother in an upstairs bedroom. I could hear Agnes at work in the kitchen and the sound of running water, but even more the distinct sound of the squelch of clothes being washed. As I was about to mount the stairs I was facing a passage at the end of which was Agnes' bedroom. As one came out of that room (which was on ground floor level) there was a bathroom (in fact the only one in the house) to the right. It was mid-morning somewhere half-way between the time I had got up and lunchtime. Quite slowly the door of Agnes' room opened and there stood a woman dressed in a creamy white night-dress which came down well below her knees. She was wearing slippers with red lining, her black hair cut short with a fringe, her face seemed a pale yellow and she had deep set eyes. Even more extraordinary she was wearing Brian's dressing gown around her shoulders. She was low-sized and somewhat stout. Remembering her appearance, as I do, she would have been around fifty years of age. I had a completely uninterrupted view of her. I have since calculated that she could not have been more than twenty to twenty-five feet from where I stood.

She stared straight ahead and then walked a few paces slowly in my direction, turned, put her hand on the handle of the bathroom door and went inside. I fled upstairs in panic and told my mother what I had seen but she did not believe me. In my childish way later I called her 'dirty Agda', for Agda was the name which I gave Agnes Devanney. The trauma of this weird experience still haunts me so much so that I still have nightmares of this event.

Worse however was soon to follow. One evening it was still light, I was in bed looking at the pictures in A. A. Milne's book *When We Were Very*

*Young.* I was alone in the room. Suddenly the door opened and looking up I saw the head of a woman peer through the door with a terrifying face and fiendish grin. She was wearing a tea towel over her head. Almost as soon as she appeared however she vanished and the door closed. This was certainly no nightmare – I was still awake – for I must admit that I had been rather naughtily scribbling on the book which I still have in its battered condition and which bears the scrawls of that evening. While my mother did not believe my experiences, she strictly forbid me to say anything.

Nessa often slept in the day time on a mat in the passage leading to Agnes' room. By nature she was a quiet gentle dog, despite the reputation of her breed, but one day she suddenly jumped up and became highly agitated, barking angrily and baring her teeth, while at the same time she backed away from the door of Agnes' room. I remember Vivion, Máirín, Brian and Ruairi trying in vain to pull her away, but nothing would pacify her as she continued to face Agnes' room and the bathroom. No one saw anything on this occasion but apparently Nessa did. It is well established that animals can and do react violently and show fear or anger when faced with the occult or in a paranormal situation.

These happenings so fascinated me that I was determined to follow them up in later years, in an effort to produce evidence which would substantiate my story. I discovered that a woman who had lived in Elm Villa some years before I was born, was said to have been a woman of ill-repute who entertained the Black and Tans and other British troops. She was once seen walking around the house wearing a steel helmet and is said to have committed suicide, some said in the bathroom. My mother-in-law, who then lived in Sandymount, said that she had heard of the woman's reputation and even knew her to see, although she could give me no details of her facial appearance.

I found out more information from the local boot-maker in Sandymount when I called on him especially for this purpose on 1 June 1948 and then made a written record of my interview. He was a man named Hayes who had had his business there from the early part of the century. He confirmed that there had been such a woman and that he too believed that she committed suicide, saying 'She did herself in.' Hayes said that she had married three times, although he was sure that they were not true marriages but merely co-habitations. He said she had once called into his shop and his description of her fitted the figure I had seen. Other elderly residents of Sandymount agreed with his story that the house was supposed to be haunted.

In more recent times, I decided to take my investigations still further and have established that this woman had indeed lived in Elm Villa prior to 1922; her name corresponding exactly to that given to me by Mr Hayes. She died on 28 December 1922 – some six months after my birth – not in Elm Villa itself but at an address close by, which at that time was a kind of nursing home, for and run by two ex-soldiers, one of whom had been killed in the First World War. As to the cause of death, I have been advised by two independent experts – one a doctor, the other a former senior official of the Registry of Births, Deaths and Marriages – that the information on her death certificate can be interpreted as consistent with a self-administered substance. In those days it was common for the cause of death to be disguised where a suicide was suspected or known to be the case.

One day in the mid-1950s while I was in practice as a solicitor, a man called to my office in connection with some business. In the course of our conversation, he mentioned that he too had once lived in Elm Villa. I immediately connected his name with the family who had occupied the house for a short time immediately before our family arrived in 1925. We chatted about the old place and then I asked him if he had any experiences there, not of course mentioning mine. He said that one day, when he and his brother George were in their teens, they were horse-playing in a room we had used as Máirín's and Emer's bedroom. Suddenly his brother cried out 'What's that?' claiming that a figure had passed beside them. My informant said that he had seen nothing, but his brother was adamant that he saw a figure which he continued to claim for years to come. This brother had long since emigrated to Australia.

Yet another corroboration of my story was when a friend of my eldest brother, Vivion, was a student in UCD in the early 1930s. This girl and her sister took a flat in Elm Villa, which when we left was converted into a number of flats. The girl claimed to have seen the self same woman as I have described. She later emigrated to America and is now dead.

Following further research, I found a death notice in a well-known Dublin newspaper dated the 30 December 1922 which described her as a 'widow', the funeral was 'strictly private'. There was no mention of any form of religious service, nor did the notice disclose a place of burial. Further enquiries revealed that her remains had been taken from the nursing home for immediate burial in one of Dublin's better-known cemeteries. Only three other females are buried in this grave which was opened in 1912, so they may well have been relations.

The death certificate refers to a 'husband', yet the notice in the newspaper describes her as a 'widow'. I found reference to this husband as late as 1923. The mention of 'husband' and 'widow' at first seems confusing, but we should bear in mind what Hayes had said to me of her 'marriages'. I do not propose to disclose the woman's name and some other details in deference to any relations or next-of-kin who may still be living.

From many years of reading, collecting material and the study of the occult and psychical research, I found that it seems that some acknowledged experts in this field have put forward a plausible theory which could, perhaps, explain many ghostly phenomena. These experts claim that in certain circumstances, not yet fully understood, 'flakes of personality' shed away and linger in the ether long after death. These can be picked up at some future time. These 'flakes', they contend, remain and can convert into the visual or auditory or both. They further contend that certain events, most usually violent ones, leave such a deep impression as to materialise to even quite unsuspecting recipients. They go further by claiming that these 'flakes' can defeat time itself and transport the recipient instantly to the moment of the happening of past events, even a very distant one. Time, therefore, as we know it, becomes temporarily suspended. Those who hold this theory argue that this process is something akin to a kind of super television, but they further submit that wonderful as television is, it is naught compared to the capacity and complexity of the human brain and so they say why cannot the brain receive and transmit messages even beyond, across or outside the usual accepted concept of time. They do not, however, claim to know nor do they attempt to explain the actual mechanics as to how or why these phenomena occur.

It is of particular interest to note that the above theory does not depend on the traditional notion of 'appearance after death' where a person is said to return from some spiritual state or existence or that the deceased himself actually re-appears after death. They claim that in essence apparitions are purely a *physical phenomenon* not necessarily coupled with spiritual connotations. Interesting as this latter theory may be, it does not satisfactorily render invalid the earlier one, nor is it sufficient to eliminate an essential spiritual content. Clever as this 'agnostic' view appears, the traditional one held over centuries seems to be the more probable and therefore the spiritual content remains an imperative.

It has been long since established by experts in the study of the occult or paranormal happenings that children are the frequent recipients of manifestations. To my knowledge no satisfactory or conclusive reason has been suggested why this should be so.

I have told my story factually, but freely accept that in the final analysis, it is for readers to form their own judgements on the circumstances set out and draw their own conclusions, depending upon whether or not they believe in, or accept, the existence of matters relating to the occult or other psychic phenomena.

As my mother had forbidden me to tell anyone of my experiences, I kept my silence until we had left Elm Villa. But one Sunday morning when we had moved to Springville, I related my story to the assembled family. Mother immediately confessed that if she had believed me when I first told her, she would have left Elm Villa at the first opportunity. My elder brothers and eldest sister always believed that I had a truly paranormal experience. So did my mother, but she was greatly disturbed by it.

This story leads me to another, not perhaps unconnected. Dinny (Denis) Coffey came to help Mother in the garden and do odd jobs for her. He had given the cat to Mother, hence the cat was called after him. One afternoon he was digging in the garden close to the house. As his work progressed he unearthed a small package, the paper of which had almost completely disintegrated. To his great surprise he came across several rounds of .303 ammunition. Vivion was at home and at once took charge. At that period he knew well the significance of ammunition being found in the garden of Eamon de Valera's house. I remember him pushing me out of the way but did not succeed in preventing me from seeing the find. Arrangements were made immediately to dispose of the ammunition. Dinny Coffey was a cranes man, living in Ringsend and working in the Port of Dublin. I saw him put the ammunition in an old piece of sacking and carefully binding it with twine. I distinctly remember this, as Vivion again tried in vain to push me away. This was a Saturday for Dinny most frequently came to us then. The following Monday morning Coffey was at work as usual. He carefully attached the package to the hook of his crane, swung the machine round and dumped the package, watching it carefully as it went to the bottom of the Liffey. Dinny Coffey was in every way politically sympathetic and so he could be completely trusted. Then and in later years there was much speculation in the family as to how the ammunition came to be there but all agreed that it must date from the time when the Black and Tans came to pay their 'compliments' to the woman I had seen.

My mother was particularly close to her two surviving sisters, Catherine and Bridget, known to us as Auntie Kitty and Auntie Bee. They were both younger than Mother, their eldest sister Mary having died of a painful cancer in 1917. My mother was also fond of her brother Laurence who lived with Bee. Our family had a great devotion to our aunts and uncles as they all showed us much kindness, especially from 1916 onwards. Kitty's husband Andrew (Uncle Andy to us) was very jolly, always full of fun and jokes. It became a tradition that our families met for a reunion in our house each 29 June known in the family as 'the 29th'. These happy reunions soon turned to tragedy when Bee's husband, Richard Cotter, contracted tuberculosis and died on the 4 January 1929 at the age of thirty-six, leaving his widow with five children.

I have few recollections of Dick Cotter, although I remember him saying to Mother: 'I'm not at all well.' He was particularly good-looking, had a great interest in photography and wireless sets, and loved and owned some old motor cars. Auntie Bee could have a sharp tongue at times and remarked that his cars always broke down before they reached the end of the street.

Dick Cotter remained a loyal friend of the family although he had taken the Pro-Treaty side in the Civil War and was rewarded with a senior post in the civil service. He too had fought in 1916 and had been imprisoned. There was a deep gloom in our family when he died so young. I was only six-and-a-half and this was my first experience of death.

Especially after Dick's death, Mother visited Aunt Bee in the old home in Munster Street on the north side of the city. We changed trams at Nelson's Pillar and many of the trams which ran north of the pillar were open-topped. Looking down from these trams we could see into the burnt-out ruins in Upper O'Connell Street destroyed in the Civil War. I have distinct memories of this.

When we returned home from such a visit, our favourite game was to take off our shoes and socks, get hold of some newspapers and pretend we were the unfortunate newspaper boys who sold newspapers at Nelson's

Pillar and in all weathers. They often entered the trams to do so, dressed in ragged clothes and were bare-footed. I can still see their pathetic little figures as they boarded a tram and called out 'Herl-a-Mail, Herl-a-Mail.' We imitated this pleading cry, their names for the papers *Evening Herald* and *Evening Mail*.

In those far-off days, where there was no instant news service, we relied on the battery-operated wireless set made by Dick Cotter and even an old crystal set with its own earphones. We listened to the Irish radio station 2RN, and on the larger set we could hear the English broadcasters saying 'Coventry calling, Coventry calling'. One day Ruairi called me and handed me one side of the earphones while he listened with the other. 'Listen,' he said, 'that is the greatest tenor in the world!' It was John McCormack.

My brother Éamon once accompanied my father to Moore Abbey, Monasterevan, then the Irish home of McCormack. He remembered the tenor standing in the drawing room with one arm resting on the mantelpiece while he sang for Father. Father told me that McCormack fell out with him later, quite unreasonably he thought, when McCormack sought the use of the Aula Maxima in Newman House, part of the then National University. Father explained that although he was chancellor of the university, its use was not in his gift, but McCormack would not accept this.

I last saw Count McCormack as I was passing the Shelbourne Hotel not long before his death. I stood back to let him pass as he came out of the foyer with a number of people. As he was about to enter a taxi, I heard him say goodbye to his friends, but his voice was hoarse and feeble. He obviously found great difficulty in speaking.

My first school was the national school in Sandymount to which I was sent in September 1928. Strangely, I have few recollections of the place, save two companions, Billy and Harry Barriscale. Harry died while he was still a boy, but I met Billy again in later years when we both served in the Local Defence Force during World War II. I have better memories of Star of the Sea Church where, from the age of five, I was brought to mass either by my mother or elder members of the family. It was there that I first heard the organ, the sound of which would later hold such a special attraction for me.

Both motor cars and aviation played a part in my early childhood. There was great excitement with the news that Charles Lindbergh had made his successful solo flight across the Atlantic – Máirín and Ruairi explained the wonder of crossing the great ocean all the way from America as we awaited the news of his safe arrival in Europe. Little did I know then that some ten years later, I would have the privilege of hearing the story of his epic flight from the aviator's own lips.

There was further fascination when the ill-fated airship, the R101, came over Dublin. The huge cigar-shaped craft lingered in the air, first over Ringsend and then directly over Sandymount. Its roaring engines looked ridiculously small compared with its vast grey bulk. When the engines stopped, the R101 hung silently in the morning air and remained quite stationary and almost straight overhead at a height which could not have been more than five hundred feet. We could even see the crew in the gondola mounted beneath the great airship. My mother warned me that if I saw it again on my way to school, I was to stand still on the footpath and under no circumstances to continue walking lest I wander into the roadway.

The fate of the R101 was tragic. On 5 October 1930 it crashed in France. There were fifty-four people on board and only six survived, the British Air Minister being one of those who perished.

It was about this time that I heard of the death of the British racing driver Sir Henry Seagrave. He held the land-speed record in his famous 'Golden Arrow' but lost his life trying to attain a new record on water.

In another aviation recollection, Ruairi pointed out Captain Macintosh's aircraft (a Fokker monoplane named *Princess Xensa*) as it flew over Elm Villa. The captain, together with Colonel Fitzmaurice, was preparing to make the first east-west crossing of the Atlantic which they subsequently had to abort due to vile weather conditions. A little later, Colonel Fitzmaurice, then the commanding officer of the Air Corps, made a successful flight with his German companions Baron Von Hunefeld and Captain Kohl. In my view Fitzmaurice had not been as well remembered as he deserves.

In recent years I became friendly with the barrister the late Oliver D. Gogarty, the son of Oliver St John Gogarty. The latter was violently opposed to my father and said many bitter and vitriolic things about him but this never prevented the friendship between his son and me. He told me many stories of great interest so much so that I begged him to record them but alas I do not think that he did so. He was a marvellous raconteur. He accompanied his father, who himself was an experienced pilot, to Baldonnell on 12 April 1928, the day Fitzmaurice and his colleagues took off. He described far better than I can, the tense atmosphere and excitement, with many people of importance present. Included in the large awaiting crowd was a chaplain to the Air Corps whom Gogarty described as a typical very gildy Free State Officer and strict disciplinarian. Amid all the fuss awaiting the momentous take-off the chaplain became concerned about the spiritual well-being of the crew and insisted that they go to confession. It seems that they had no option and they and the chaplain disappeared into a hanger. Weight, with the heavy fuel load required for the vast journey, was a great problem. The mechanic in charge of preparing the plane was so particular in saving weight that he even went so far as to skin the oranges to be taken on the journey. The crowd awaited the reappearance of the air crew. At last they came out looking rather sheepish to which Gogarty Senior quipped 'Well that should make the load considerably lighter!'

Oliver D. Gogarty, known to his friends as Noll, also spoke to me about Sir William Orpen. He had sat for the artist when he was a boy and he went on to tell me of a visit to Orpen in Howth. The artist was playing with balloons filled with gas ignited with methylated spirits but when the supply ran out Orpen used whiskey, fuel which he would have much preferred to have consumed himself.

In the latter part of the 1920s a military tattoo was held annually in the rugby grounds in Lansdowne Road, accompanied by a marvellous display of fireworks which we could enjoy from nearby Elm Villa. One day Emer and I were out for a walk and we passed the grounds where soldiers were dismounting from lorries. I stopped to look, fascinated by their smart appearance and their rifles. Emer thought otherwise and caught hold of my arm. 'Come on,' she said, 'don't look! They're Staters' – a none too complimentary name for the Free State army used by those who were anti-Treaty. Emer, some four years my senior, was the last in the family who could recall the raids on our home by the Free State army during the Civil War.

By the end of the 1920s, my parents became anxious to leave Sandymount. Vivion simply could not stay long at home and Brian's asthma was also affected. It seemed that the air in Blackrock suited Vivion better, and besides, Father himself had happy associations with the district.

The hunt for a suitable new home accelerated. The days in Elm Villa were numbered. Miss Delahunt also died about this time, and according to my mother, she had given instructions to her solicitors to draw up a will in which she left Elm Villa to my mother. The instructions were given on a Friday and she was to execute the will the following Monday, but she died suddenly at the weekend. Mother often said that the loss of this bequest was in fact a blessing in disguise, for had she become the owner of Elm Villa, she would have been tempted to remain in spite of its obvious drawbacks.

In 1938 Elm Villa was sold, demolished and some sixteen houses were built on the site. The very last of the elm trees which grew around the boundary with Serpentine Avenue disappeared some years ago. I saw the house for the last time while it was in the course of demolition. I can still picture its broken outer walls silhouetted against the afternoon sky, its paneless windows like the eye-sockets of a skull. It looked a sorry sight, a gaunt and pathetic ruin. Its days were over and with its passing, the end of an era, and with the exception of Emer, with no regrets for the rest of the family.

# CHAPTER II

## *A Growing Awareness*

On 12 March 1930, the day we left Elm Villa, Mrs Coughlan looked after Emer and I for the day, and that evening Eamonn Coughlan drove us to our new house, Springville, in Blackrock. As usual, my mother was in charge of all the arrangements and had negotiated the purchase. Father always had complete confidence in her and left such arrangements in her capable hands. When necessary, she displayed considerable business acumen.

Springville required a good deal of work, both decoration and repair. Electricity also had to be installed as it was still lit by gas. (The ESB supply had only reached Blackrock and Booterstown some two years previously.) Since Springville had no garage and needed an extra toilet and other accommodation, Mother had the difficult and delicate task of negotiating the purchase of a small strip of land from our neighbour, Canon Northridge, the owner of Chesterfield, with its eleven acres. Canon Northridge drove a hard bargain, but eventually sold us the required piece of land. Although he differed in both his political and religious beliefs, in time he became a good neighbour.

The land around Springville was small, compared with Elm Villa, but Mother was glad to be rid of the responsibility and cost of keeping a large garden. With five active sons, however, she soon came to see the disadvantage of so small an amount of land. She never had an interest in gardening as such, although she loved flowers, especially violets, and often quoted Keats' lines: 'Fast fading Violets covered up in leaves'.

Our first morning in Springville was a Sunday and Mother sent the four youngest to ten o'clock mass in Booterstown church, the family's parish church for many years to come. This was my first connection with that beautiful church which I have since looked upon with great affection.

By the time we moved to Springville, Vivion and Máirín were doing splendidly in university, winning valuable scholarships, soon to be followed by Éamon and Ruairi. Likewise, Brian was progressing well at his studies. Emer, like Máirín, had been at school in Loreto Convent in Stephen's Green but she was sent to Zion Hill once we moved to Blackrock. She returned to Loreto some years later and left with considerable academic distinction. For a while I was sent to the convent school in Booterstown and made my First Communion in Booterstown church on 14 June 1930. Later I went to the local national school where the master was James Divine, known to generations as 'Bookie' Divine and very much in the mould and style of the old-fashioned school master. Although he looked severe with his Edwardian moustache, at heart he was a kindly man. He was then coming to the end of his long career and had tired of teaching, so I fear he somewhat neglected us.

If Divine was not as attentive as he should have been, his assistant, Miss Farrell, was quite the opposite. We all loved this little barrel of a woman with lively eyes which sparkled over her diminutive spectacles. Her great interest was music, and she spent more time than the curriculum provided at singing lessons. It was not long before she discovered I had a good voice and gave me solo parts in the school choir. She frequently drilled me up and down, using the old-fashioned tonic sol-fa chart which hung on the wall.

My mother also kept one of these charts in the playroom, and if a proper pointer was not to hand, she grabbed the poker from the fireplace! Mother herself had a limited musical training but she had an excellent ear and sang with a sweet clear voice. Had she received more formal tuition, she would have been a good singer for she had considerable expression in her voice, a wide range and remarkably good diction. She often sang old ballads which she had heard from her mother, along with Victorian love songs, songs of Stephen Foster, national airs and hymns. She knew almost all of Tom Moore's 'Irish Melodies' which were very dear to her.

When Mother lived in Greystones, she had a Protestant friend, Annie K. Hawkes, who was very much her senior. According to my mother, Miss Hawkes was almost blind and one of the most saintly people she had ever known. Annie Hawkes was the author of a famous hymn 'I need Thee every hour', which was one of Mother's favourites. It can be found as hymn number 692 in the Church of Ireland hymn book. Annie Hawkes left my mother her ring which, as was the custom in the nineteenth century, was made of her own hair with her initials set in gold. Mother gave this ring to my wife Phyllis.

The weather during the summer of 1931 turned out to be particularly fine, and as the season approached, Mother grew concerned about how the younger members of the family would spend the holidays. Brian and Ruairi occasionally went to Blackrock College to play tennis and cricket, but there was less scope for Emer and I. Mother had a strong faith in prayer, so she prayed earnestly for a solution. She did not have long to wait for an answer. Towards the end of June, her friend, Máirín Ryan called unexpectedly. A native of Kerry, she always spent her holidays there with her husband and family. Since her house at Kendleston near Delgany, Co. Wicklow would be vacant for the month of August she graciously offered it to Mother.

Towards the end of July, the family made preparations for the forthcoming holiday. Father did not participate in these plans as he was so involved in his political work, as well as with the launch of the *Irish Press*.

On the morning of 1 August, Máirín and Emer went ahead of the rest of us and were driven to Kendleston. It was a glorious summer evening and at 8.00 p.m. my brother Éamon took the driver's seat in the Ford saloon. My mother, Brian, Ruairi and I climbed into the car and commenced our journey reaching Kendleston some forty-five minutes later.

As we left the village of Delgany, we proceeded along the narrow, untarred road, the wheels of the car throwing up clouds of dust on the grass verge. We reached the entrance gate and drove up the winding avenue to be greeted by Máirín and Emer. I looked up at the house and its lofty tower, standing proud against the late evening sky, then dashed into the house with Emer leading the way. She made straight for a staircase to the first floor, and then to a flight of spiral steps which brought us to the top room in the tower. There, I had my first sight of a panoramic scene which I came to know and to love so well.

Kendleston was a 'fine gentleman's residence' built at the end of the nineteenth century by a Dr Thompson for his bride, Miss Orpin. Alas, this family was soon to know sorrow with the death of their infant child. Neither did Dr Thompson himself live all that long. There is a fine memorial to him and his family in the local Church of Ireland church in Delgany.

Dr Jim Ryan purchased Kendleston in 1925. Since the vendor knew of Dr Ryan's political background, he refused to sell the house with its original hundred acres. Instead a compromise was reached and Dr Ryan succeeded in buying the house with some thirty-seven acres. From the beginning, Kendleston was a working farm and continued to be so during the Ryan family's time there. The house itself was spacious, with a fine square hall, and a large elegant drawing room with an attractive bay window. The dining room was well-proportioned, while off the hall was a cosy study. The bedrooms were likewise spacious. The kitchen was located in a sunken basement and included a dairy leading out to a spacious yard in which there were several out-offices, including stables, garage and kennels.

The evening we arrived, all Brian wanted to do was see the horses, but it was so late that he had to wait until the morning. Mother and Éamon returned to Springville, leaving Máirín in charge of the four youngest. In later years, she confessed that these duties were not to her liking as she found the cooking and household chores rather irksome.

Although Mrs Ryan's maids were on holiday, Barney, who worked in the house, had remained behind. He was then in his mid-twenties and his duties including the daily routine of cleaning and refilling the oil lamps. Kendleston had no electricity and would not for some years to come. Barney also tended to the garden near the house, including the enchanting little rose garden which sloped off to the south.

It did not take us long to discover that Barney was rather fond of practical jokes. One evening, he told us to look out for Dr Thompson's ghost which could be seen gliding down the main staircase. (He, of course, intended faking the ghost himself.) But Brian was too quick for him and saw the frightened reaction of the younger members of the family. 'Right, Barney,' Brian said. 'I'll be waiting for him at the foot of the stairs with a loaded shotgun!' That was enough. We heard no more of such ghostly yarns.

On our first morning at Kendleston, we were all up at 7.00 a.m., preparing to attend mass in the Carmelite chapel in Delgany. John, the foreman, lived in a cottage in the farmyard with his wife, Maggie. At about midday, we saw him coming up the avenue leading Billy, a gentle pony, all saddled and ready. Sixteen-year-old Brian mounted the animal, and from that moment, he knew what he loved most in life. I too had my first ride that morning, the first of many which I enjoyed there.

There was a tennis court at one side of the avenue where Ruairi, Brian and Emer played; I tried my hand too but did not make much of it. I was happier playing on the swing which hung from a giant Scots pine tree. Thinking back, I recall Hood's lovely lines which my mother often recited:

Where I used to swing
And thought the air must rush as fresh
Two swallows on the wing

An archery bank in the small field adjoining the lawn was overlooked by the windows of the drawing and dining rooms. On the walls in the hall hung various bows, and Brian, Ruairi and I soon learned to shoot arrows at home-made targets.

Within a day or so, we had settled in and become friends with Barney, John, Maggie and Bill, the other farm worker. They all gave us a warm welcome. Brian spent most of his time riding Billy, and John sometimes let us have Captain as a second mount. Captain was a docile, grey farm horse and a particular favourite of John's. I managed to get poor Captain to gallop, although the animal was not used to this. How beautiful it was to sit astride Billy or Captain and to look across the vista, especially towards the evening with the distant sea to the east, the Hill of Downs to the west, and the Great and Little Sugarloaf Mountains to the north. It was a delight to look across the unspoilt fields and hedgerows to the tower of Delgany church and to hear the sound of its bell come floating across the still air as the twilight gathered where 'Drowsy tinklings lull the distant folds'.

Emer was quick to make friends with Sal, the cocker spaniel. She was always a great reader, and I can still see her sitting on a deck chair and reading in the midday sun with Sal crouched beneath the shadow cast by the chair.

To me, Kendleston was a place of wonder, adventure and delight. It was then in wide open, unspoilt country, as rural as any other part of Ireland. Delgany, the nearest village, was small, neat and attractive while northwards was Blacklion, a mere hamlet in which could still be seen the remains of mud-walled cabins. A number of the cottages were thatched. My mother said she prayed best in Blacklion church, but this I doubt, as Booterstown would have been its rival. Greystones, about a mile to the east, was then an isolated large village which held mixed memories for my mother. Other large houses were scattered about the district, including Uplands, the home of the O'Neill family who were very friendly with the Ryans and with my parents.

About half-way down the avenue there was a path through a wood leading down to a cart track which in turn led to the farmyard. I loved being alone in this wood, playing games of make-believe. The canopy of thick leaves almost defied the shafts of warm sunlight which pierced through here and there to the ivy-covered undergrowth. Among the great trees stood a beech which 'wreathes its old fantastic roots so high'. It was my joy to climb the steep, winding path to the rose garden, full of its sweet scent of roses 'where my sense of their deliciousness was spell'd', the sight of brightly coloured begonias and neatly clipped box hedge.

Another favourite game was playing cowboys, made so popular by the films at the time, many of which were still silent. Brian and Ruairi also joined in the fun. Ruairi cleverly converted Emer's school Panama hat for me to wear as my cowboy hat. Armed with six-penny cap guns, it was thrilling to gallop across the fields, then hide in the wood, dismount and lie in ambush.

On the way down to the farmyard was the gate of the large walled kitchen garden which was Bill's domain. Here the air was filled with the perfume of sweet pea. I can seldom smell sweet pea now without being transported to Kendleston and all its tender memories.

On the far side of the farmyard was a little stream which ran into a pond where farmyard ducks swam in the company of water hen. Towards evening, I delighted in watching the procession of ducks headed by the senior drake as he led them from the pond to their house in the farmyard. Traffic, except for the occasional horse-drawn vehicle and a neighbour's car – Dr Eccles in his old bullnosed Morris Dickie – was almost non existent. During all my time at Kendleston, I never heard or saw a tractor. To my knowledge there were none for miles around. In those days, I only saw one aeroplane, an Air Corps Avro.

Our stay at Kendleston coincided with harvest time, and we were expected to join in the cutting of the corn. Although this was hard work, it was also a pleasure. Our neighbours, the Deverauxs, provided an additional horse so that Captain and his two companions could pull the great binder driven by John. We sometimes saw an unfortunate corncrake – such an uncommon sight now – running helplessly at its approach.

Bill was from Co. Wexford and he took charge of us as the sheaves fell from the binder. John was a Wicklow man, so arguments were bound to occur. John insisted that we put seven sheaves in a stook, while Bill wanted nine. The disagreement became quite heated, but John's idea prevailed. It's likely that there was a greater yield in the more fertile land of Wexford, hence Bill's plea for the greater number.

We were also pressed into service to harvest the potatoes and sugar beet and took part in other farm activities, including milking the cows which like everything else, was done by hand. Emer became such a great milker that even Maggie was a little jealous of her skill. I tried my hand too, but Maggie nearly always had to finish off the cow. This task done, we carried the milk up to the dairy in shiny buckets. I turned the handle as Maggie skimmed the milk. I loved the cream, even when it was still quite warm and could drink as much as a tumbler full. We also helped Maggie when she made butter to her own special recipe, not quite a 'country butter' but much milder, something with special lasting memories.

When John went out for a message, he yoked Captain to the orange-coloured farm cart. He took his little five-year-old son, Patsy, and I went along for the ride and John sometimes let me drive Captain. One day he stopped in Delgany, went into one of the little shops and came out with sweets, aniseed balls which could be purchased sixteen for an old penny. They were a delicious treat as we bumped along the rough, dusty road as the blazing sun beamed down upon us.

Indoors we enjoyed the old clockwork or 'wind-up' gramophone with its limited number of records. There were fine recordings of McCormack and Kreisler playing 'Angels Guard Thee' and Schubert's 'Ave Maria'. Another recording was an instrumental version of Toselli's 'Serenade', and there was a collection of old sea shanties and a few Jimmy O'Dea sketches. Whenever I hear Toselli's 'Serenade' it revives memories of perhaps the happiest part of my childhood.

When each long, happy day had ended, we came in for supper and then went down to the kitchen where Barney entertained us by playing the mandolin which he played rather well. We sang all sorts of songs, including the popular airs of the day. Too soon, it was time for bed, we climbed the steep, dark stairs to the hall where the old grandfather clock ticked away the quiet hours, as though reluctant to let each pass. By the light of an oil lamp, we climbed the main stairs to our rooms, slipped into bed, to dream of the morrow, until the raucous rooks in the nearby trees awakened us to the bright morning light and another day in that earthly paradise.

Such joy could not last, for too soon the month drew towards its close. On the Sunday we left, Father and Mother came to collect us. I spent the latter part of that day going around and saying goodbye to all I had known and came to love. We packed our things, got into the car and drove away. It was like Robert Louis Stevenson's poem 'Farewell to the Farm': 'As last round the bend, "Goodbye, goodbye to everything."' It was time to return to school with no real break until the end of the year. Mother resumed her usual duties while Father continued in his ever-anxious work.

All these memories are not the gilded ones of an old man, for we were particularly blessed with the weather of that year. August 1931 was one of continuous sunshine, not rivalled until the glorious August of 1947 and latterly by the extraordinary fine summer of 1995. The countryside in north-east Wicklow was indeed beautiful and quite unspoiled, remaining so up to the mid-1960s. I seldom travel to those parts now; it breaks my heart to see the enormous changes which have taken place. So much of the area has been heavily built-up and is in many ways almost unrecognisable as the place I had known in my youth. The population pressure on this part of the east coast has ruined the rural beauty, solitude and peace which we once loved and treasured so much.

# CHAPTER III

*Brighter Horizons*

The general election of February 1932, following a campaign conducted in the most dreadful snowy weather, brought my father to power with the support of the Labour Party. Ruairi was then fourteen, and it was he who explained to me the significance of the election and the change it would make in our lives.

There had been great excitement in the house for weeks, as nothing but the election seemed to matter. As the results started to come in, my mother was occupied with phone calls. Although she was delighted when it became clear that the anti-Treaty side were making such progress, she was also apprehensive: she did not look forward to becoming the wife of the President of the Executive Council, then the title for the head of the government. Mother never faltered in her strong and deeply held Republican political views, but she held no bitterness against Father's opponents and retained a friendship with several who had opposed him in the Civil War.

An episode from this period remains most vivid in my memory. Vivion had just returned from Blackrock College and was in his room with Éamon, Brian and Ruairi when he sent for me and said he was about to tell me a secret which I must not divulge to anyone. He then showed me a revolver, a Smith & Wesson .45, which had a curious and chequered history. Fr Bertie O'Farrell CSSp, a great friend of the family, had hidden the weapon under an altar stone in a side chapel of Blackrock College after the Civil War. There it had remained until Vivion brought it to Springville in 1932. Fr O'Farrell had quipped that, unknown to the other members of his community, many masses had been said over this revolver and it was truly well blessed. Years later, and indeed not long before Vivion's death, he told me who the gun had belonged to – none other than Cathal Brugha.

Shortly after this, a lorry-load of soldiers drove into Cross Avenue. They got out, and formed a semi-circle in the road in front of our house and stood with fixed bayonets while I watched from my sisters' bedroom. Vivion had raced to his room, grabbed the Smith & Wesson and dashed for the back garden, vaulting the wall and hiding himself in the grounds of Chesterfield. The soldiers, however, did not approach the house itself. After about five minutes, they boarded the lorry and drove away. Vivion was given the all-clear to return to the house. We were all greatly puzzled by this event, especially as Father was not at home at the time. No explanation was ever discovered, although Mother suspected it was yet another raid by the Free State army. She was clearly relieved when the lorry drove away, as was Vivion. I never heard any more of this strange occurrence.

Vivion escorted Father to the Dáil on the day on which he was elected President of the Executive Council. As it was uncertain whether the former administration would hand over power peacefully, it was feared that Father might be assassinated. Father himself was unarmed, but a photograph of Vivion standing by his side clearly reveals Vivion's hand on the gun in his pocket. This was no mere carelessness; the message was clear for those who wished to see. In the event, the transfer of power was smooth and peaceful.

As Ireland's new head of government, Father was proud to receive a personal letter of congratulations from President Franklin D. Roosevelt whom he had met in 1919 while raising money for the Irish cause. (A practising lawyer at the time, Roosevelt had confirmed the legality of the bonds which Father raised for the Irish cause.) The letter was framed and placed in his office, but when the USA entered World War II, Father felt it would not be diplomatic to keep it there, so it was transferred to the office of his personal private secretary. Much to his consternation and anger, some quick-fingered thief removed it – notwithstanding the tight security which was in place at the time. Despite exhaustive enquiries, nothing is known of the whereabouts of this historic document.

Another major event of 1932 was the Eucharistic Congress, with even the children involved in months of preparation. At school, Miss Farrell drilled us from a special hymnal which had been brought out for the occasion. Learning the Latin words was a struggle. As the time grew near we were all issued with metal badges which we were required to wear on the lapels of our coats.

People came from all over the world to attend the Congress and Father's mother and cousin Ellen even planned to travel from America for the occasion. All was made ready to receive them as we children looked forward to meeting our only surviving grandparent. Father, however, was to receive sad news that his mother had died unexpectedly on 12 June, casting a dark shadow on the forthcoming celebrations. In spite of this, two cousins came to stay, so Emer and I spent the week of the Congress with the Coughlans who were now living in Terenure. Before this, Dr and Mrs Farnan arranged for the family to view the arrival of the Papal Legate as he drove in procession to the city centre. We had a splendid view from their front drawing room in No. 5 Merrion Square.

Dense crowds lined the streets. In the distance, I could see workmen on the scaffolding of the new part of Holles Street Hospital which was then in the course of construction. At last the procession came into sight, led by a troop of Hussars, a mounted unit which had been formed especially for the occasion. They were splendid in their blue uniforms and gold braid, their sabres flashing in the strong sunlight as they rode their magnificent, prancing horses. This was their first public appearance and I think they attracted more interest than the Papal Legate himself! The Hussars remained a ceremonial escort for years to come, although they were subsequently disbanded to the great regret of many.

The Coughlans then brought Emer and me to town for the benediction service which took place in a splendidly constructed altar on O'Connell Bridge. So great were the crowds, however, that we did not get near the bridge and were held back in College Green by soldiers who stood in semi-circles with fixed bayonets. They stood around lamp posts to which loud speakers were attached. We also accompanied Mrs Coughlan to the climax of the Congress, the open-air mass which was held in the Phoenix Park. She was driving the well-worn 1921 Citroen and had to struggle to keep it from stalling on the steep climb up Knockmaroon Hill. Blessing herself several times to assist her progress, we eventually arrived at our destination to be met by other members of the Coughlan family. We then joined the crowds as they moved to the 'Fifteen Acres' where mass was to be celebrated. Just before the ceremony commenced, Eamonn Coughlan lifted me onto his shoulders and he said 'Look at that crowd! They say that there are more than a million people here!' On this misty, overcast Sunday, the voice of John McCormack singing 'Panis Angelicus' came over the crackly loudspeaker system. During the mass, a flight of six

Avros from the Air Corps flew overhead, keeping a neat formation in the shape of a cross.

That afternoon, Mrs Coughlan brought us to tea in the popular Rosses Hotel in Dun Laoghaire. Looking out to sea, we could see that the whole of Dublin Bay was full of great ocean liners at anchor, having brought visitors from many parts of the world. They had to anchor there as the draught was too great to allow them dock in Dun Laoghaire or the port of Dublin itself.

Once the congress was over, the visitors returned home. In early July Mother again heard from Mrs Ryan who extended another invitation for us to spend our holidays at Kendleston during the August of that year. Although the weather that year was not as good as it had been in 1931, nothing could diminish our enthusiasm. In spite of the rain and even a few thunderstorms, there were several bright, sunny days when we could help on the farm and Brian could go riding; in fact even the bad weather did not deter him. Emer renewed her acquaintance with the cocker spaniel, Sal, then tried to befriend a lately arrived chow called Bruno. Although he was quite aloof and often kept to himself, he came to tolerate our presence.

Mother stayed with us more often during our second year at Kendleston and engaged a maid, Maire Dunne, to cook and look after the house. Barney was still there, as was the outside staff. Whenever it was exceptionally wet, we stayed indoors, lit a fire in the study and listened to Mother read Dickens' novels. Brian, Ruairi and Emer enjoyed them, but I often found the stories far too sad.

Brian, I am sorry to say was fond of shooting in the nearby cherry orchard. It is sad to think of the slaughter of so many birds to prevent them eating the fruit. It was a common thing to hear the sound of shotguns coming across the fields. One particularly wet and cold day we were all confined to the house, even Brian did not go out. Again a fire was lit in the study and to make things more cheerful we had pancakes for tea. In the afternoon we heard a few distant shots and thought this unusual due to the heavy rainstorm which was then taking place. That day Mother was not staying with us, there were only the four youngest, with Barney and Maire in the house. Towards evening about seven o'clock there was a knock on the hall door. We went out to see who it was as we did not expect visitors at such an hour on this wet day. It was John. He began by apologising for coming to the front door as he would ordinarily use an entrance through the yard. He then handed us the evening paper, the

*Evening Mail.* This was odd for we never received an evening paper. Following this he spoke in a low voice telling us that there had been a terrible accident in the cherry orchard that afternoon. It seems that two of the Deveraux boys, aged twelve and fourteen, had been out shooting. They had placed themselves well into the orchard. One came suddenly from behind a group of trees when his brother accidentally fired and shot him dead. It was a terrible tragedy which affected us all very much, particularly Brian who had been with these boys the day before. The gloom of that event stayed with us and remained in our minds notwithstanding many other and happy joyful events.

There was a curate in Greystones, Fr William Murphy, who became a frequent caller and we enjoyed his visits. He had only lately been ordained and could not be more than in his late twenties. Fr Murphy had a particularly fine tenor voice. He sang a lot while he accompanied himself on the piano. Mother enjoyed his songs and ballads, a lot of which were very amusing. Not alone did he sing well, he also acted the part. I still remember the title of one which my mother often asked him to repeat as she thought it so amusing; it was 'Maud, Maud the girl that has studied abroad'. Later Fr Murphy was to become a curate in Booterstown. I last spoke to him when I was patient in the Mater Private Nursing Home having had an operation for a hernia. He was there for much more serious reasons; in fact he was dying of cancer. We had however a pleasant half an hour or so together reminiscing about his visits and singing in Kendleston all those years before. He died in the early part of 1964.

We had just returned from our holidays at Kendleston when Mother asked if I would like to start taking music lessons again. When we lived in Elm Villa, I had commenced taking piano lessons with a Miss O'Connor who lived nearby in Serpentine Avenue. Through my mother's friendship with Margaret Keady, who lived at No. 15 Waltham Terrace, we were introduced to another teacher, Miss Clare Hand, who lived at number 9. From the day we met, Miss Hand and I developed a wonderful friendship, which lasted until her death at the age of ninety-nine in June 1987.

My violin and piano lessons commenced almost at once, and Mother soon purchased a better violin to replace the one which had been bought for Éamon many years before. Throughout the coming years, I not only enjoyed these lessons but also the examinations in the Royal Irish Academy of Music. Thanks to Miss Hand's excellent teaching, I achieved first class honours. Although it was always hard work, I have treasured memories of Miss Hand's drawing room with its old fashioned furnishings and the well worn Tomkins upright piano, which was succeeded by an even older Schiedmayer Grand.

Clare Hand was a member of an exceptionally gifted family. She herself had been a pupil of Esposito – the undisputed doyen of musicians in Ireland in the early twentieth century – who thought highly of her. During one of her music lessons, Clare remembered that the telephone rang and Esposito did not answer it. When she drew his attention to the fact, he displayed a fit of temper. She later learned that he was afraid of telephones, although he would not admit it.

Clare's elder sister Mary (Cissie) was an organist and a Bachelor of Music, a rare enough thing for a woman in those days. Cissie and Mother discovered that they had a common link, in that they were both born within twelve hours of each other in 1878. Mother and these two ladies became great friends and she later said of the sisters: 'They are two of the cleverest women I have ever known.'

Clare and Cissie remained unmarried and lived together all their lives. Both loved their small garden, although it cannot be said that they were great housekeepers. For them the most important things in life were music and books. They were exceptionally well read, positive fountains of knowledge on so many subjects. A bit odd in their ways, they lived a very isolated life. Clare particularly lived in the past and once remarked: 'The world really never recovered from the mental breakdown which it received in the last war,' meaning World War I. They spoke of their time before that as if it was only yesterday, and their harking back to a bygone age was quite apparent at times. Their father had been part of the British establishment and their mother, judging from the pictures in the house, was a talented artist.

Cissie and Clare had studied at the Royal Irish Academy of Music during a period when it enjoyed a considerable reputation for excellence. As part of their tuition, they were required to attend concerts so that they could experience good music excellently performed. Cissie loved to talk about these concerts, particularly one given by the famous Russian pianist and exponent of Chopin, Vladimir de Pachman. De Pachman then enjoyed an international reputation but was very eccentric – indeed in ways he was quite mad. As he performed, an attendant sat beside him at the piano with whom he often carried on a conversation, continuing meanwhile to play most beautifully. At times he even hurled abuse at the audience. Miss Cissie said that he once took exception to a lady's hat and proceeded to abuse her throughout the entire performance. I have an old 78 record in which de Pachman plays Chopin in quite an excellent way. Even while making the recording, he was unable to contain himself and constantly condemns the instrument upon which he is playing: 'Terrible piano! Terrible piano!' The recording engineer simply gave up and one can hear in a clear tired English accent, the engineer, saying: 'Try it again, will you?' To no avail, it seems, for the engineer's voice-over remains in the recording.

Miss Clare also remembered being told to attend a performance by a violinist of considerable distinction who was as yet virtually unknown locally. There were few in attendance at the theatre, so when the artist appeared, he invited the tiny gathering to join him on the stage. They did so, and Clare said she was absolutely enchanted by the performance. It was only later that she realised the soloist had been Fritz Kreisler.

Miss Cissie told another story of a concert given by the Polish pianist, composer and statesman, Ignace Paderewski. It seems that the maestro was in such good form that he gave encore after encore to the sound of ever-enthusiastic applause – but much to the consternation of the stage manager who was anxious to clear the house for another performance. The more the manager waved his arms in protest, the more Paderewski continued playing!

Both these ladies often helped Mother choose and arrange the airs to which she had written words for her plays. Like my mother, Cissie lived to a great age, dying in January, 1969 at the age of ninety-one.

In the summer of 1932, an English lady, Edith Ellis called on my mother. The sister of Lord Parmor, she was a member of the Society of Friends and had considerable sympathy with the Irish cause. Her visit came just in time for my tenth birthday and she gave me a book called *Birds and Beasts at Home*, a typical English children's book of the period with stories personifying wild creatures such as Robin Redbreast and Brer Rabbit. I enjoyed these charming tales so much, that, in later years, I read them to my own children and eventually to my grandson.

This book, however, had much more significance than a simple birthday present. Father had only been the head of government for a number of months when a heated dispute erupted between himself and the British prime minister, Ramsey McDonald. Their disagreement centred on the highly contentious land annuities which the British had been receiving from the Irish tax payers and which amounted to vast sums of money for the time. As he and his party regarded these payments as wholly unjustified, Father resolved that he would put an end to them once and for all. For their part, the British were equally determined that they should continue. This impasse led to the so called 'Economic War' which was not finally resolved until my father ultimately settled the matter as part of his famous negotiations with Prime Minister Neville Chamberlain in 1938. The sum of £10m was paid in full and final settlement. The payment was made by an ordinary cheque which Father signed personally.

From 1932 up to the settlement, however, the British tried all sorts of threats and pressure, employing various tactics when they felt they were not getting their own way. They hoped, quite wrongly, to cause trouble in Ireland and force another election. Indeed to increase the pressure further, they were secretly planning to send additional troops to the Irish ports which they still held under the terms of the treaty of 1922.

Miss Ellis knew Lord Shankey, the British Chancellor of the Exchequer, who was then acting as Dominion Secretary. With Lord Shankey's full knowledge and approval, Miss Ellis was dispatched to Dublin to make contact with my mother. Following the visit, during which she gave me the book, she had several discussions with Father at which he told her of his strongly held views on the subject of land annuities. Through Miss Ellis, Father sent a memorandum directly to Lord Shankey who in turn brought it before the British cabinet.

Edith Ellis' friendship with my parents was obviously being used by the British establishment, but it was Father who turned it to his advantage. The book in its own small way was therefore the device which Miss Ellis had used as a decoy to cover the main purpose of her visit.

# CHAPTER IV

*Father in Power* • *The Move to Bellevue*
*My Days in Blackrock College*

E ven greater changes came about in 1933. In January of that year, my father called a snap election which took place in February. Thanks to his shrewd political judgement, he succeeded in obtaining an overall majority in the Dáil, giving him the power and authority to implement many of his policies. He also turned his mind towards drafting a new constitution to replace the existing Free State one. In time, this constitution, one of Father's greatest achievements, would be recognised as one of the finest in the world.

I have recollections of him in his study as he worked on the draft, but his eyesight continued to cause him trouble. He could only write by using a pen with a very large nib, which meant that vast amounts of paper often overflowed from his desk onto the floor. One day I remember going into his study, where I was warned not to walk on the many sheets of paper which were scattered on the floor. In time I believe these drafts were destroyed, but I often think it would have been interesting to see those portions of the new constitution which were rejected or otherwise as first drafted.

Father had great trouble with what was to become the now-repealed Article 44, as it was difficult to describe the Catholic Church and yet not offend other Christian denominations. It was the Church of Ireland archbishop, Dr Gregg, who gave him the solution. 'Why not,' said Dr Gregg, 'use the words with which they describe themselves? – The "Holy, Catholic, Apostolic and Roman Church".' Solving this problem meant that Father was in buoyant humour that evening as he told Mother of his meeting with the archbishop.

He also found it hard to accept the adverse criticism which some women (including his close friend Dorothy Macardle) levelled at Article 41 and contended that their arguments were a misrepresentation of the article's true meaning and intent.

It was my father, rather than my mother who thought of moving to a larger house. Bellevue is on the northern side of Cross Avenue, then in the occupation of the Lee family. The Lees, however, were not the owners but held Bellevue on a lease and had been in the house since 1914. They had moved from a larger and more pretentious house, 'The Grange' in Stillorgan, long since demolished. Before the Lees left Bellevue my mother had several meetings with Mrs Annie Lee. Very rapidly they became good friends. Mother had a positive gift for making friends easily, and this, regardless of a person's religious or political background. She also had a capacity to size up a character quickly. The pair had long chats together and it was then that Mrs Lee told her of the sadness in her life. Mother had a great compassion for the sorrows and trials of others, having known many in her own life.

Annie Lee's husband, Edward, died in 1927 aged seventy-three. Annie had a particularly sad early married life, for no less than five children died under the age of five months. Four sons survived, however, two of whom were at that time carrying on the very successful and extensive family firm of Edward Lee & Company. My mother listened with great sympathy as Mrs Lee told her the fate of the other two. Joseph Bagnall had been a practising barrister. Like so many at the Bar at that time he joined the British Army at the outbreak in the 1914-18 war. He was commissioned in the 6th Battalion of the Royal Munster Fusiliers but was killed in action in August 1915 while leading his men during the Dardanelles campaign. Lieutenant Lee was just twenty-seven.

Annie Lee's loss did not end there; within a month and a day before the war's end, her eldest son Robert Ernest was to lose his life. He was a doctor and a captain in the Royal Army Medical Corps. He had been home on leave to Bellevue and was about to return to France. He said goodbye to his mother, to whom he was especially attached, and boarded the ill-fated 'Leinster' to sail to Holyhead. The ship was torpedoed five miles east of the Kish lighthouse on 10 October 1918, with the loss of 501 lives. As the ship went down he managed to climb aboard a lifeboat but as he did he spotted a woman and child struggling in the water. It was now dark and the sea was choppy. He jumped back into the sea and helped the woman and child aboard but, in the confusion and darkness, he drifted away and was lost. He had bravely given his life to save the woman and child. Annie Lee went on to tell Mother that this woman called to see her in Bellevue to express her gratitude for her life and that of her child. Captain Lee was thirty-five when he died. He had served through the entire war only to die so near its end.

In its earliest days Bellevue had been the home of the Countess of Brandon. She was said to have been remarkably beautiful and was greatly admired both in Ireland and England. The story goes that her beauty was so striking that all stood up to gaze at her when she entered the House of Lords. She also owned other properties including a house in Merrion Square. The countess lived to a great age and died in 1789 at the age of ninety-one. The next occupant was a Captain Tisdall whose initials are cut in stone over the hall door. The captain had a novel experience in 1789. One night he heard intruders. He leapt out of bed, seized his pistol and discharged it through the window. It would appear that the would-be intruders fled, one of them being severely wounded. They were arrested and brought to trial, coming before the greatly-feared Lord Chief Justice Bushe who remarked 'I believe that the shooting of one assailant, in valiant self-defence has more effect upon evil-doers than the capital execution of a dozen criminals!' Other residents through the years were Dr John Gilmore; William O'Connor, a barrister; and a clergyman named Denham Smith. Henry Beweley lived for a time in Bellevue.

Due to the many additions and extensions which had been added in the nineteenth century there were long rambling corridors to the bedrooms, two of which were exceptionally large with a remainder of average size as one would expect in such a house. In our time there was a spacious conservatory to the front, from which an entrance gained from the dining room. This later room was commodious with a bay window but rather on the dark side. In the oldest part of the house, in our time called the breakfast room, there was a room which had been the parlour in the eighteenth century. It contained a fine, but slightly damaged, Adams mantelpiece. This was the room where the family generally ate and where my mother did her correspondence and some of her writing. It was there too that I did my school homework.

Bellevue had a large basement which ran under the older part of the house and the drawing room. It contained many dark passages, kitchen, pantries, stores, wine cellar, even a butler's pantry and a vast back kitchen used only as a store and which we boys made a play den. There were extensive out-offices in the yard to the northern side including stables, garage, fuel houses and the like.

The house was surrounded by some five acres of land which included Edwardian rose and vegetable gardens and two somewhat dilapidated greenhouses. There was a tennis court and extensive lawns to the rear where we played 'clock golf', the course having been left behind by Mrs Lee. There were also two fields in which Mrs Lee had kept a cow to supply milk for the household.

To the north, Bellevue was bordered by Willow Park, owned by Blackrock College, to the west by the Hermitage, and to the east by Dunamace which had been the home of Kevin O'Higgins.

Shortly before we left Springville, the Hermitage had been the home of Lt Colonel Henry Lucas St George Stewart, who had lived there with his sister since 1908. He died on 3 June 1933 and was said to be 93 years of age. My memories of him are few but I do recall seeing him being brought out for a short walk helped by two servants, a little stooped man with a grey beard very slowly making his way with the aid of two walking sticks. He was a Scot and in his will he directed that he be buried in Greenock, Scotland. He had been commissioned in the Highland Light Infantry and served in what he described as 'My Old 74th'. His will also directed that he be given a military funeral with pipes. His executors were to present the regiment with his regimental 'jewellery and badges'. The will also contained the odd provision that he wished 'All family portraits, paintings and likenesses to be burnt unless given to any person who will respect and value them.'

Two of his servants lived in the gate lodge. I believe they were man and wife. They kept two goats which grazed on the grass banks skirting Cross Avenue. They tethered the goats to a lamp post – one of only three lamp posts on the entire road and which were lit by gas. When the colonel died we heard a romantic story. The information came to us, probably from the local gardaí. His wife pre-deceased him by many years. There is only one mention of her in his will. The story we heard was very touching. We were told that he had married when he was twenty-one and that his wife was only nineteen and that she died in childbirth a year after the marriage and that the child did not survive. We were further told that he directed that he be buried with her in Scotland (where his sister is also buried). The will, however, is silent on such a wish but if the story is true it proved his love for his spouse after some seventy years of widowhood.

In those days, Cross Avenue and the surrounding roads were full of old British military types. Next door to Colonel Stewart lived Lt Colonel Forest in Lymehurst, afterwards the house of my father's friend, Dan Brown, solicitor and later Land Commissioner. Col Forrest was a very dapper man, always beautifully groomed. He wore a bowler hat and carrying a rolled umbrella as he walked to SS Philip and James' church. Even as a boy, he gave me a friendly smile as he passed. If he happened to be passing my father, he tucked the umbrella under his left arm, stood to attention and gave a smart British army salute, saying 'Good morning, sir' or 'Good day, sir', as the case might be.

Another of these military personages was Lt Colonel Edgeworth who lived in Cherburry on Booterstown Avenue. He was much less friendly. Like so many of these lovely old houses, it has since been demolished to make way for modern housing developments. A writer of some note and a kinsman of the novelist Maria Edgeworth, Col Edgeworth's family was also related to my friend, the pianist Charles Lynch.

A familiar sight on Cross Avenue all those long years ago was that of a landau driven by a coachman wearing a top hat, whip in hand, trotting along in the course of the afternoon. Its occupant was a somewhat wizened old lady who was always dressed in black and who was known locally as 'The Blackbird'. I later learned that she was Lady Crosthwaite who then lived in a house in Stillorgan, later demolished to make way for a bowling alley. Locals said that she was nearly a hundred years old. She steadfastly refused to get into a motor car, saying that such things were 'abominable contraptions'. How different the road and district were then before building took place on the lands at Chesterfield and Glenvar. There were wide open fields in which cattle grazed, stands of ancient oak and other trees, and the familiar summer sound of the corncrake coming from the lands of San Souci.

In the 1930s, Cross Avenue had only one cement footpath which ran along the north-eastern side. On the other side, the path had a clay surface. Strangely, the Protestants used the clay path on their way to divine services in SS Philip and James' church, whereas the Catholics used the cement one as they proceeded in the opposite direction to mass in Booterstown. It was almost a case of 'Never the twain did meet'.

We moved to Bellevue, which we all came to love, on 1 September 1933. My parents did not purchase Bellevue but took it on the lease under which the Lees had held the property. The move itself worked out quite smoothly, although there were other events which preoccupied both my parents. That same day, news came that the opposition in the Dáil had united against my father and Fianna Fáil.

The moment we took over at Bellevue, the question of domestic help to run the place became an issue. Maire Dunne was still with us and my mother consulted Margaret Keady who once again came to our assistance. She recommended William Felton and Alice Holmes, both of whom lived in Deansgrange. Willie was then unemployed and was glad to take up the post as gardener. Maire was to be cook while Alice, a good-looking girl in her twenties, became what was known in those days as the 'parlour maid'. Both Willie's brother and Alice's father had worked for a branch of the Orpen family, as did Alice herself for a short while. Maire, Willie and Alice stayed in Mother's service for many years and showed great loyalty to the family.

Brian longed to own a horse but money was tight, so Mother, with her usual skill, found a compromise. Our milkman then was Francis Graham, a kindly old man with a large grey moustache. He was a deeply committed Presbyterian from the north and spoke with a strong northern accent. He did his rounds in a beautifully kept milk float with gleaming brass on the churns. An odd time he let me drive it. This well kept vehicle was drawn by Tony, a very intelligent and lively horse. Tony was by then coming to the end of his career and so Graham offered the animal to Mother so that the pony could enjoy his last days in a good home. Mother willingly accepted. While Brian would have preferred a more suitable animal he was nevertheless delighted. Bridle and saddle were purchased and Brian took over the care of Tony. Although Tony was old he still had a great spirit and Brian even succeeded in teaching him to jump which Tony did very well. A little later Frank Aiken gave us an indefinite loan of a hunter called Elma. Between the two animals Brian and I had many hours of pleasure with these horses. A little later the famous Cossacks came to the Horse Show in the Royal Dublin Society. Brian brought me and we saw them perform the most extraordinary and highly dangerous acts before an enthusiastic crowd. When we got home, we saddled up Tony and Elma and, very much led by Brian, tried to imitate the dangerous acts we had seen that afternoon, including trying to pick up a handkerchief on the ground whilst we passed at full gallop using a long bamboo cane as a lance. Brian succeeded, I did not.

In 1933 Father went to Rome to receive his first papal decoration, The Grand Cross of the Order of Pius IX. News reached Mother that the honour to be conferred was not that decoration but a Papal Title. This disturbed her greatly as she had no desire to become 'The Countess' although strangely after 1916 she was referred by some as 'Madame' and so appears in *Thoms Directory* of 1923. My mother, Vivion, Máirín and Ruairi were in the drawing room discussing the rumours and as to whether they were true or not. I was also present. I could see that Mother was disturbed, so to cheer her up, but perhaps a little naughtily and remembering that while Father liked music he had in fact no singing voice, and further knowing, that John McCormack had been created a Papal Count, I interjected 'Don't worry Mum, if Dad sings for the Pope 'When Through Life Unblessed We Roam. [a favourite of Father's] he won't make him just a Count but a Papal Duke!' Mother looked at me, burst out laughing saying 'Oh, you little scamp,' but somehow this seemed to ease the situation and what later turned out to be an unfounded worry.

My parents did not entertain very much, except for a close-knit circle of friends. Among the guests at one party in our early days in Bellevue were Frank Aiken, Dr Jim Ryan and Gerry Boland. Charades were very popular then, so it was decided that this game would be played. My father had charge of one team which included his three cabinet colleagues. The team disappeared from the drawing room and some time elapsed before they returned; indeed Mother wondered about the cause of the delay. At last the door was pushed open and there, to our astonishment, appeared the team, all on their hands and knees and a large pair of antlers (which had been left in a corridor upstairs by Mrs Lee) strapped to Father's head! As they came in, they made weird noises as though imitating wild animals. Despite their best efforts, however, they failed to illustrate the word and their efforts proved futile much to Mother's amusement!

In 1933 Father's eyesight began to cause great anxiety and he went to Switzerland for treatment. It was an anxious time for Mother, as it was obvious that Father's sight was deteriorating rapidly. Yet this period saw another major development in his political career. As an international statesman he became the President of the League of Nations. This was not only a great honour for him but also for the country. In gaining international recognition for Ireland, he was deeply committed to the concept of the League and hoped, vainly as it transpired, that he could help to ensure international peace. By then, Hitler had come to power in Germany while Mussolini was flexing his muscles in Italy. Fascism was truly on the march.

Father met Mussolini, whom he told me he found to be an arrogant, bumptious little man who strutted around the room. Father formed an instant dislike and disgust of him. He had a much better impression of the King of Italy, whom he also met at this time. The king entered the room in full military uniform, saluted smartly and gave Father a most welcoming handshake.

The following year was one of considerable disturbance both at home and abroad. The Blue Shirts had come into being led by General O'Duffy. I remember them distinctly as they strutted around Blackrock and Booterstown, greeting each other with Nazi-like salutes. They were obtrusive and wished to make their presence felt. I have a special memory of what came to be known as 'Blue Shirt Sunday' which in much later years I discussed with my father. He told me from intelligence he had received from Captain Sean Brennan and from other trusted sources that a *coup d'état* was expected following a march on Government Buildings.

After Father came to power in 1932 a special force was recruited as part of the Gardaí. It was known as the S Branch. This force was made up of men who had fought in the Black and Tan War and later on the anti-Treaty side in the Civil War. One, Jimmy Kenny, served under Pearse in the GPO in 1916 when he was only sixteen. Jimmy Kenny was very small, he could not have been more than five foot one or two inches. He loved telling me the story of how when Pearse saw him in the GPO, the morning the Rising commenced, Pearse said to him that despite his youth he could stay, adding with a broad smile 'You'll be safe, you're so small the bullets will pass over your head'! Jimmy lived on into old age. I attended his funeral to pay my respects to a brave man who had served his country well. The S Branch was a particularly trusted body of men. No other part of the Gardaí could be so relied upon. As part of their duties they became my father's personal bodyguards; they also guarded government ministers and certain vital institutions of state. In a short time the family came to know them well. They had the nickname 'The Broy Harriers' (a pun on the hunt, 'The Bray Harriers'), as Colonel Broy was then Commissioner of the Gardaí, replacing General O'Duffy who had been dismissed by the government.

When it became clear that a *coup d'état* was imminent the Broy Harriers were mobilised and a heavy guard was placed on Government Buildings, other vital installations and likewise on Bellevue. A theoretical line was drawn up Merrion Street and orders were given to open fire if the Blue Shirts should pass this line. At the last moment the Blue Shirts called off their march and mercifully the crisis passed. Some modern revisionists have tried to deny or at least soften down these events. This so upset me in view of what I had known, that I checked the facts again with my father when he was President and he confirmed what I had stated. It has become fashionable with some historians to try to revise episodes such as the above which occurred in Irish history in the mid-1930s.

I have personal recollections of that day. I was confined to the house and forbidden to go out into the grounds. In spite of this I ventured into the garden and was met by one of the guards, Leo McCourtney, who afterwards became one of my father's drivers. We were standing under a yew tree at the side of the drawing room. The tree is still there. Leo begged me to go inside and when I protested he said 'Please do as you are told,' to which I said, 'Why Leo?' He answered, 'Because there may be trouble' and in a quiet voice he added, 'Shooting'. I obeyed his command and remained inside for the rest of the day and did not venture out until quite later that evening when I was told I might do so.

I have equally clear recollections of another day about this time, when a group of Blue Shirts stood around at the entrance gates shouting and taunting the guards. There were about a dozen of them. I was standing in full view of the gates when one of the guards named French, whipped out a Thompson sub machine gun, pressed home a loaded magazine, drew the bolt and pointed the weapon in the direction of the gate shouting out: 'If one of those bastards put a foot inside those gates I'll let him have it full in the belly.' I was shocked, not so much by the event itself, but by the language he had used. French's stand was sufficient. The Blue Shirts fled immediately. Poor French himself did not live all that long afterwards and died from tuberculosis.

Another incident about this time caused quite a stir. Father was returning from the office late one night, and as the car was about to turn into the entrance gate, he noticed a bright red glow in the sky. It was clear there was a fire. The car had scarcely stopped when he jumped out, thinking that the house was ablaze and shouting 'Are they out? Are they out of the house?' The fire brigade was already on the scene and the officer in charge quickly reassured him that it was not the house but the guards' hut which was in flames. At the same time, he warned everyone to stand clear as ammunition was exploding. The cause of the fire was simple: coals had fallen out of the stove and the timber floor was engulfed in flames within minutes. In spite of the noise of the fire and the exploding ammunition, I slept through the whole thing. The next day, I saw the burnt-out ruins of the hut and the many scorched trees and bushes which surrounded it. I had great fun, however, collecting dozens and dozens of spent cartridge cases.

The unfortunate guard who happened to be in the hut that night was John O'Connell. He was one of the most loyal and best-liked of the men. In earlier years, when Father was on the run, O'Connell worked as a guard for Dublin South Eastern Railway. He often recognised Father and warned him of possible arrest, enabling him to escape

In a very short while, the Office of Public Works had built a new and more substantial hut to replace the one which had been burnt. Despite this, O'Connell's colleagues nicknamed him 'Hoodoo', a name which stayed with him to the end of his career.

In October 1935, Mussolini invaded Abyssinia (now Ethiopia) and began his brutal war. Father came home one day and told Mother that the emperor, Haile Selassie, had contacted him asking for arms to fight the Italians. Sadly, he had to explain that our little country was in no position to assist him.

One evening in 1936 as I was riding my bicycle around the paths at Bellevue, Ruairi called me and told me to come into the study: there was important news on the wireless. I entered the room to see Father sitting beside the wireless set. Seeing me, he put his fingers to his lips to indicate silence. I sat down and listened. Hitler had just sent troops into the demilitarised zone in Alsace Lorraine. When the broadcast ended, Father turned to Ruairi and said: 'Well, I know what I would do if I were the French Prime Minister.'

Ruairi later took me aside, got out an atlas and explained the significance of these events. It was about this time that Ruairi became my mentor. With his deep love of history and political astuteness, he took great pains to explain so many of the momentous events occurring at home and abroad.

Despite the many pressures in his life, Father decided to take me in hand and teach me mathematics. Father was so outstanding in this field that Einstein said that there were only nine people in the world who really understood his Theory of Relativity, and Eamon de Valera was one of them.

Brian had obtained full marks in his Intermediate and Leaving Certificate examinations and Vivion too was gifted in mathematics and science. Ruairi, Éamon and Emer were also very much at home with the subject. Máirín, however, although pressurised by Father to read mathematics in her first year at university, had no taste for advanced mathematics and so abandoned her studies and turned to botany in which she excelled. As the youngest I was singularly deficient and never came to grips with many aspects of mathematics.

I spent long, weary hours in my father's study as he drew beautifully formed geometrical figures. He often took me for long walks in the garden so he could get some much-needed exercise and give me a lesson at the same time. He brought a walking stick with him and as he explained a point, he drew diagrams on the surface of the path. Many are the scars which those paths bore, with countless triangles and other geometric figures. Many too were the hours when I looked on vacantly and the less I understood, the deeper the scratch in the path! Unimpressed as Father was with my poor answers (and indeed his impatience, to the point where he almost lost his temper) any gleam of comprehension did not go unnoticed or even unrewarded. In a few such cases when I answered well, he thrust his hand deep down into his trouser pocket and pressed a half crown or two-shilling coin into my hand. On such comparatively rare occasions, peace reigned. The tall, dark figure and his very thin youngest son then walked back to the house with a mutual feeling of satisfaction.

During one lesson when I was about twelve or thirteen, Father set me a problem. A man was planting cabbages. He posed the question of the number of plants required if he set them in an area of triangles, parallelograms or squares of a certain size with a given space between each plant. He launched off enthusiastically, offering several complicated propositions of how this problem could be solved. At this point, and to my great relief, we were told to come to dinner. As we ate, I told Mother of the task in hand and remarked, rather boldly, that if it took Father so long to decide how the cabbages should be planted, they would have withered by the time he had made up his mind! She smiled broadly saying, 'That must be the practical Flanagan blood in you!' Although Father laughed heartily too, this did not prevent the lesson from continuing when the meal was over.

Occasionally, and much less often than with mathematics, he gave me lessons in Latin. These were mostly prayers. I found this more agreeable and in this subject he was a more patient teacher.

Although I look back on those mathematics lessons with feelings of fear and detestation, all credit must be given to my father for his teachings. Without him, I would not have matriculated and finally emancipated myself from this dreaded subject.

My mother was a passionate believer in the proper use of time. She ardently held the view that time was something very precious to be spent on work or useful and creative pleasures or recreation, but never to be wasted. She was particularly hard on anyone who said that they were bored, unless through illness, or felt time on their hands. This question of precious time passing came to a head when she had a dream that she phoned the local grocer named Fitzell who had a well-stocked and well-kept shop in Booterstown. She said to him in the dream: 'Mr Fitzell, I want to give you a special order, please send me as much time as you can, and I mean T-I-M-E not thyme. I never have enough of it!'

In September 1934, I was sent as a day boy to Blackrock College where I remained until matriculation in 1941. My memories of these days are mixed, but my happiest years were my first and last. Some teachers were still there from my father's time; some had even taught him! One of these was Fr James Keywell, a very old man who taught me Christian Doctrine. He was still greatly feared, although not so much as when he had been a younger man. Master O'Hanlon told me that when he was in Blackrock College as a boarder in the early 1890s, Fr Keywell, then Dean of Discipline, found him with chalk and saw where young O'Hanlon had put a slight mark on a wall. Fr Keywell took the boy to his room and beat him mercilessly with the leg of a chair. O'Hanlon made no bones of describing the dean as positively sadistic. Otherwise, Master O'Hanlon spoke with great loyalty and affection for Blackrock College. By the time I knew Fr Keywell, he had greatly mellowed. He always wore his biretta in class and seldom took it off. On the rare occasions on which he did, his bald head bore a definite ring around it, a sign of the many years during which the biretta had lain there. When cross, he ground his dentures, the first sign of his anger. I was lucky, for my mother had drilled me in catechism and other religious subjects. Indeed the only prize I ever received in the college was one for Christian Doctrine, having obtained first place.

Discipline in the school was severe, but I am sure that it was no different from other boys' schools of the period. We were issued with report books in which we received our weekly marks in all subjects, including conduct and deportment. The scale of marks ran from nine to zero. Seven to nine was good to excellent. Six was fair. A mark below this meant trouble. We were then categorised as being on the 'Honours list', the 'Pass list' or the 'Black list'. Each Friday, all the day boys were assembled in the Concert Hall (known even in my time as the New Hall although it had been built in 1914). The Dean of Studies, the teachers and the Dean of Discipline took the stage and each boy's marks in each class were read out. If an unfortunate boy happened to be on the Black List, he had to report to the Dean of Discipline's office where he was severely caned. While my marks were usually in the middle, and sometimes on the Honours List, I was never on the Black List, although once or twice I was too close for comfort.

The teaching staff was exclusively male, and in addition to the priests, there were a number of lay professors at the college. They were a dedicated group of men devoted to the school and its long tradition. Among them was John J. Hughes, a tall, bald-headed, awkward sort of man with huge feet and a cast in one eye which was not obscured by his horn-rimmed glasses. His gown never hung on his shoulders as it ought to but instead fell to his waist. But if his appearance was against him, he had the most beautiful mind and was an excellent teacher. He was most learned and was recognised far beyond the school as an expert in geography. For generations, he was known to Rock boys as 'Juxter'. In many ways, he was our Mr Chips. We all loved him and had great respect for this perfect gentleman. I still can call on the fund of knowledge he imparted. One day, he brought a turnip into class to show us some aspect of physical geography; he particularly wanted to describe the inner core of the earth. He took out a tobacco-stained pen-knife (he was a dedicated pipe-smoker) and cut the turnip into segments which he left on one of the desks. When he came to look for it, the segments were missing – one of the boarders had eaten them! He protested but he continued with the lesson.

Another prominent lay teacher was Hugh Houlihan, known to us boys as 'The Houley'. He was particularly gifted in mathematics, and Brian and he became very close, despite the fact that he was violently opposed to my father's politics. When he heard of Brian's death, he wept bitterly.

While I studied very little science, I can remember the smells of chemical substances, and even loud bangs, which emanated from the science room where Michael O'Shea was the teacher.

Edward Halley was another lay teacher of note and an expert in both Latin and Greek, although I had him for history. He was considered severe and at times a little sarcastic but nevertheless a first-class and dedicated teacher. In one test, I placed historical events in the wrong order. He wrote in the margin: 'You must have your events in proper chronological order.' On that day, I learned the meaning of the word chronological, which he told me to look up in a dictionary. In time, his son, whom I number among my friends, although many years my junior, entered the Holy Ghost Order and later became president of the college.

In my last year at Blackrock, I was taught history by Fr Michael O'Carroll DD. He was an outstanding teacher with a great grasp of his subject, coupled with the gift of capturing his students' interest. We remained close friends until his death in January 2004 at the age of ninety-two.

Blackrock College had its own peculiar system of prefecting. Unlike other schools, this post was filled not by the senior boys, but by young men who were some three years short of ordination. We had to address them as 'Sir' or 'Mister'. They wore the clerical garb, but minus the cape which was reserved for the ordained. All the priests wore soutane, cape and corded cincture with tassels as well as a biretta. During winter, they wore a wonderful overcoat known as 'douillet', made of material similar to cavalry twill which stretched down almost to their ankles. We envied them in their warmth as we sat in the poorly heated classrooms. The older priests wore pale turquoise-blue stocks under their Roman collars; this was in memory of the Congregation of the Immaculate Heart which, many years before, had been incorporated with the Holy Ghost Order. Even if a prefect was refereeing a house match, he wore his soutane which he tucked up to his waist and held it there with the cincture. Priests often did likewise. I have clear recollections of Fr Finnucan, a great rugby coach, doing this.

Junior boys (mostly day students) were in a minority in the college, and we were allowed to take off the last class on Saturday to go to confession. We all freely availed of this and dashed to the chapel where we elbowed each other to be last on the bench and thus use up the time. The confessors included some very old retired priests, among them Fr Laurence Healy, and one or two retired bishops. Bishop Neville, with his neatly trimmed white beard, was a tiny little man who could not have been more than five feet tall. Bishop Shanahan was quite the opposite, a giant with a full-flowing white beard who was blind in one eye. He was famous in our day for having converted so many thousands to Christianity in Nigeria.

Despite the jostling on the bench, time came when we had to go into the confession box. There we told our sins: the usual ones, bad thoughts and disobedience. The confessor said nothing, a number of them were deaf, we got the usual Hail Mary as a penance and then left feeling mightily pleased that we had missed the last class, but even better as all would be repeated the following Saturday.

Latin was not one of my stronger subjects, although Vivion, Éamon, Ruairí and Emer were particularly well-versed in many Latin texts. Br Anthony, a young red-headed man, was in charge of the school bookshop where we could purchase all our needs: books, paper, pens and so on. He was very popular with the boys and I never saw anyone dressed in a soutane run as fast as he chased us down the corridor. It was his job to censor the books before they were sold, and I well remember that some leaves from *Horace Book 1* were neatly cut out with a pair of scissors. I am pretty sure that I remember the 'naughty' odes were 3, 13 and, if I am not mistaken, number 23. Naturally, all this censorship aroused our boyish curiosity, so much so that one of the lads who was good at Latin got hold of an uncensored version which he translated for us. We felt this was real daredevil stuff and besides, it had the advantage of providing further fodder for the weekly confessions!

Two brothers, Fr James and Dan Leen, had been contemporaries of my father. Fr Dan, my maths teacher, was severe and rather dour, with little or no sense of humour. One day, he gave us a test in algebra, and prior to this, my father had given me a brand new copy of a textbook, the famous Hall and Knight book on algebra which contained answers. The edition issued by the school did not. In the course of the test, I consulted the answers. Fr Leen saw this. He walked down the room, lifted the textbook from the desk and commenced tearing out the pages where the answers were printed, damaging the binding of the book in the process. I was taken aback, not that I would have minded anyone destroying a book on mathematics. Father saw it differently. When I got home, I told him what had happened. He was furious. He believed the text should contain answers which he considered were desirable if properly used. I must confess, however, that in an effort to solve the problem, I made certain deductions from the answers. Father took a rather dim view of this, although he did say that in one way, it was a clever thing to do. Whether he took up the matter with Fr Leen or not, I do not know.

We juniors had physical training once a week and our instructor was a man called Goddard who invariably dressed in a white polo-necked jumper and long white trousers. He certainly knocked hell out of us, but we enjoyed his class. He taught physical training in other schools and also taught Phyllis, my future wife, in her school.

Rugby was a second religion in Blackrock College. Even in my time it had built up an unrivalled tradition. Although the college had no head boy as such, the captain of the senior rugby team was *ex officio* the head, although he might well not have been the brightest in his studies. Every boy, whether he wanted to or not, was required to play the game; if he didn't turn out for a house match, he could be punished. In my day, a round ball was absolutely unknown within the precincts of Blackrock College. Apart from my slight build, I had no real talent for rugby although I took a keen interest in the school's fortunes. Here again I did not take after my father. He played an excellent game of rugby and there was talk that he might try out as an international. Ruairi also played a good game and was a particularly good place kicker. The most I ever achieved was to be first sub on an under-thirteen cup team. I remember my last match when I was fifteen, it was a house match played in one of the more remote pitches in Willow Park. I had no choice and was put playing wing forward. Towards the end of the game the ball came to me with a clear run to the line and just as I was about to touch down a class mate tackled me shouting 'Oh no you won't Dev.' That was the end of my rugby career. I had, however, some success in the sports field and won prizes for running. This came to an end when I injured the big toe on my left foot.

Sports have never greatly interested me. I cannot work up a fever of enthusiasm as so many do, nor can I understand how people risk life and limb to get a ball into the net in one game, whereas in another sport it breaks their heart if they do. Today, my attitude is very much in the minority. Sports of all kinds have become so widespread and popular and with some, the very essence of life itself. Certainly my grandson, David, would not share my view for he, like the majority of his generation, is greatly interested in most sports.

In 1934, Mr Corless, (he had not yet been ordained) was in charge of music. He was recruiting voices for the first-ever performance in the college of a Gilbert & Sullivan opera and discovered that I had a voice. When I told him of my training under Miss Farrell, he appointed me to lead the chorus. The college took these productions very seriously and spent lavishly on them. The opera was *H.M.S. Pinafore* and Éamon, by then a past pupil, played the part of Sir Joseph Porter. In the following year, I was giving lead parts as Yum Yum in *The Mikado* and as Tessa in *The Gondoliers*. As a past pupil, I played the part of Don Alhambra in *The Gondoliers* and the Mikado in *The Mikado*. Fr Egan was the producer of these operas and was an exacting task master who always demanded the highest standards.

I enjoyed this work enormously but it took a great deal of time from my lessons for which I was to suffer, for we had frequent afternoon rehearsals and sometimes well into the evenings, as late as ten o'clock at night. I had become virtually a day boarder. During this period I was however exempted from playing rugby lest I should catch a cold and thus affect my voice.

I have a particular memory of returning one winter's night in 1935 from an opera practice. It was well after ten o'clock. Almost always a priest escorted me home through Willow Park from where I would cross a low wall into Bellevue. This night I crossed the wall as usual and, as expected, was challenged by one of the guards. He quickly recognised me but I still gave him the password and then I proceeded along the path leading to the house. When I had reached a point not far from the eastern side of the house I saw a figure standing, pointing a Thompson sub-machine gun in my direction, its blue steel barrel visibly shining in the moonlight. At once I called out, much to the relief of Sergeant Casey, who had been sitting on a chair under a tree. Mercifully he recognised me instantly and of course there was then no need to give the password. He did confess, however, that he thought for an instant that I was an intruder. Of the two of us he seemed to be more shaken.

This story has been told elsewhere and while I have the greatest respect for the writer, I fear that the version given to him is to say the least highly coloured. There was never any question of me 'Sportily tying to elude an armed Sentry' or 'making my return in the dark through bushes'. Even though I was young I knew far too much about the tight security in Bellevue and would never have dreamt of or risked such foolhardy behaviour. Conduct of that kind would be folly in the extreme especially with members of the S Branch.

Two other priests took an active part in the opera productions. Fr Timon, a very large man with big brown eyes, was a beautiful pianist and always most sympathetic and encouraging. Fr Kennedy was not a Holy Ghost father but was working for his higher diploma in the college at the time. He too was an excellent pianist and a jolly, red-headed little man.

In December 1934, when *H.M.S. Pinafore* was first performed, the stage was still lit by gas which made the heat and strong odour unbearable. The following year, large sums of money were spent in installing electricity and the most up-to-date stage lighting, along with a complete refurbishment of the stage itself.

Among those with whom I sang and acted were the late Bill Foley, afterwards of Abbey Theatre fame, and the late Frank Purcell, who also went on to make a name for himself on the stage. Both were older than I, Foley being a contemporary of Ruairi's. I have special memories of duets with the late Tony Hughes who was then a past pupil. He had a lovely light tenor voice and we greatly enjoyed singing together. He died when he was quite young.

Our performances attracted considerable press coverage. Mother was thrilled at the good notices I received but Father was not so keen as he thought that so much publicity might spoil me. I often wonder would he have felt the same if my distinction had been in mathematics!

Fr McQuaid, as he was then, was president of the college. My parents attended the performances of these operas as guests of honour. Father was required to make a speech at the conclusion in which he thanked the school for the invitation and complimented them on the performance. It became a tradition that he asked the president of the college to add an extra free day to the Christmas holidays which of course was always granted. Many loud cheers came from the gallery. Other free days came when 'Rock won the rugby cups so much so that the boys translated the motto of the school *Fedes et Rober* to 'Free days and Rugby'.

One year Dr McQuaid was ill and the vice president, Fr Keywell took his place. He proudly led my father into the crowded hall to the seats at the top. Even as an old man he had a characteristic walk as he plunged along swinging the upper part of his body from side to side. Father was to make his customary speech and remembering his own school days and Fr Keywell, as his teacher, deliberately hesitated as to what he should ask by way of additional holidays, knowing full well the reply which would come from the boys in the gallery. With one voice there was a mighty roar 'four', the dreaded mark habitually given by Fr Keywell. The place was in uproar and even old Keywell himself enjoyed it, but in the event only two extra days were added.

The school's sports day in 1935 was wet as usual. As Clare Hand said: 'If you want to be sure of bad weather chose the sports day in Blackrock College or the procession in Zion Hill.' We had to turn out in our long white trousers, white cricket shirts, school ties, white socks and shoes, dark blue blazers, and of course the school caps to match. This was very much insisted upon in those days, and a boy could be punished for loosing or not wearing his cap. This applied mostly, if not exclusively, to the junior day boys. One of the priests pointed out a very old man in the crowd, quite stooped and using a walking stick. He was accompanied by two others by his side. The priest said: 'Look boys – see that gentleman? He is the seventh boy to come to Blackrock.' This was remarkable, as the school had been founded in 1860.

It was during my first year at Blackrock that I met Laurence Cassidy, known to all as Larry. We became firm friends and remained so until his untimely death at the age of fifty-three. He was redheaded and rather plump in appearance, the antithesis of me, but we found so much in common, although he was slightly my junior. We spent many happy hours together in our respective homes and Mother became very fond of him and occasionally gave him lessons in Irish. Larry's parents, Laurence and Kitty Cassidy, were in turn very kind to me. Laurence Cassidy Senior was the founder and owner of the thriving drapery firm, Cassidys. His family invited me to stay with them when they went on holidays, first to the Grand Hotel in Greystones and in later years to Parknasilla, Co. Kerry. In the mid-1930s, just as Mrs Farnan had done earlier, the Cassidys took me out shopping at Christmas and bought me expensive presents. The family always lunched in the Hibernian Hotel and I sometimes joined them there. It is regrettable that this fashionable landmark has now disappeared.

When we grew up I saw less of Larry as our lives went in different directions, he to his family business with his younger brother Vincent, while I pursued my studies in the law. After I qualified as a solicitor I acted for the firm and we renewed our friendship. I had long since become Taxing Master when I heard that Larry was ill. I was grieved but I had no idea that it would prove terminal. He died unexpectedly on 23 December 1978. With his passing, I lost someone who had been so much a part of my boyhood and all the happy memories of being in his company.

In 1934, Frank Aiken was Minister for Defence. He was largely responsible for the formation of a new reserve in the army known as the Volunteers. Among the early recruits were my eldest brother Vivion, Mat Feehan who in later years became a Lt Colonel, and Vivion's college friend, the barrister, Richard Cooke. Vivion took his soldiering seriously and his time in the army proved most beneficial to his health, as his asthma began to improve. Vivion, Mat Feehan and Dick Cooke were not long in the force before being commissioned. Although Vivion had nothing like the height or physique of his father, he looked well in his somewhat Germanic uniform. I was proud of my soldier-brother, and he bought me many of the famous W. Britain's toy soldiers and all sorts of extras such as artillery and tanks. Ruairi took an even greater interest and made some excellent model planes, sometimes from the most basic material. The Cassidys and other friends contributed to my collection and I soon had a truly splendid model army and air force which gave me many hours of pleasure in the attic, where I had made my den, or the back kitchen.

I had a tactical reason for choosing these places: to play alone in my self-inflicted exile. I knew that Father seldom, if ever, went to the attic or the back kitchen, and if Mother suspected a maths lesson was imminent, she often covered up for me with great diplomacy. Although she was a firm believer in lesson time being lesson time, she felt we should also be free to pursue our own interests. Father, on the other hand, thought that we should be available to suit his mood or limited time at home.

All this made me live in a quiet world of my own. I have always been content with my own company. Only Ruairi was privy to my many imaginings, so much so that he created an entire world with maps of imaginary countries (mine, of course, to be the most powerful). It was Ruairi who suggested that its name be Ivernia. Viv eventually discovered Ruairi at work and asked what he was doing. When Ruairi explained, Viv replied, 'What? Are you playing God?'

Safely tucked away in the attic or back kitchen or the rose garden or in some remote part of the grounds, I played my imaginary games of politics and war against a powerful enemy, basing my thoughts on the events were taking place in Europe and in Ireland, as explained to me by Ruairi. I gave funny names to my imaginary countries. Strangely, one I choose was Tito, years before the dictator came to prominence or indeed was even known. I also published my own newspaper which was circulated in the family, bad spelling and all, with my childish illustrations to act as photographs.

Certain editions amused Father greatly, and he noted my efforts to imitate happenings in the real world at the time. Ivernia, of course, had to have a head of government and ministers. As it was a republic, there had to be elections, so Ruairi helped me to devise a system of proportional representation. The candidates where Nessa, Dinny, Tony, Elma, the animals in Kendleston and neighbours' pets. Everyone in the family was entitled to vote, including Maura, Alice, Willie and even a chosen number of the guards. On my instructions, Ruairi was told to rig the election in favour of my candidates. Father was suspicious, however, and voted the other way; at his suggestion, the other 'voters', including Vivion, did likewise. The result of the election was obviously not what I had expected. I was furious and retired to the attic to decide what should be done. I declared that the election was null and void. Henceforth, Ivernia would be a monarchy with the king living in a palace at Kendleston. Father exploded with laughter when he heard my announcement, and even more so when he saw the relevant coverage in my newspaper.

Another of my favourite pastimes was 'saying mass' in the attic where I set up an altar, made paper vestments, used a wine glass for a chalice and strawberry jam to make wine. I also brought morsels of bread and used my own altar boy's vestments. When my mother discovered these rituals, she was a little apprehensive and decided to speak to Fr McQuaid. He did not disapprove but said that I should be encouraged, going so far as to send me the cape in which he had been ordained. I suppose he thought I might develop a vocation for the priesthood. Little, however, did the future archbishop know that at that time, I was learning about the Reformation during history lessons and had developed a special interest in this subject. I decided that the 'Church of Ivernia' also needed reformation, which I duly carried out with savage cuts in the liturgy and the reduction of clerical power. Not even Ruairi or my mother knew about all of this. Certainly the future archbishop would not have approved.

Many years later, Mother was speaking to Fr Dinnan, a protégé of Dr McQuaid who was then president of Blackrock College. She said to him: 'You know, Father, that Terry was born on Whit Sunday. I hoped that he might enter the Holy Ghost Fathers.' To this, Fr Dinnan replied with a broad grin: 'Mrs de Valera, we wouldn't take a present of him!' Nor did it make any difference when the Capuchin friar, Fr Aloyisus, one of the men who had administered the last rites to Pádraig Pearse and other leaders of the Rising, put his cloak around me, when he visited mother in Bellevue.

Although I had no vocation for the priesthood, I nevertheless enjoyed my time as altar boy in Booterstown Church. My special interest was funerals. I freely admit to having had a morbid streak since childhood and I loved visiting graveyards. They have a peculiar solitude and peace, and one can discover much information of historical interest. As an altar boy I volunteered for funerals and, more precisely, the receiving of the remains. I usually carried the great brass cross or acted as an acolyte, carrying the large candles which were made of brown tallow, specially used for funerals. We left the vestry in procession, the priest wearing an enormous black cope decorated in silver. If I was not on funeral duty, I waited to see the hearse and mourning coaches arrive. The hearses were magnificent black and silver vehicles pulled by four beautifully groomed black horses in gleaming harness. These animals were bred in Belgium. The driver and his colleague wore long black overcoats and top hats. The horses had high feather plumes mounted between their ears. For a married person, the plumes were black. For a single person or a child, they were a creamy white.

The churchyard in Booterstown is in front of the church and is comparatively small, so it was indeed wondrous to see the driver, high up on the box with whip in hand, drive the hearse in and turn at an angle of 360 degrees. A number of the drivers boasted of their ability to do this. I can still feel the atmosphere when the silence was broken by the crunch of the horses' hooves and the wheels of the hearse moving over the gravel as the mourners stood waiting to receive the remains of their loved one.

Canon Breen was then parish priest of Booterstown. A kindly old gentleman who hailed from Co. Tipperary, he was tall and rather heavy, with a reddish complexion. He did his parochial rounds wearing a top hat and carrying a walking stick with a silver knob. Canon Breen was very much the epitome of the old-style parish priest.

It was during my days as an altar boy that I came to know the church well. I particularly liked the music and often sang at benediction. Even now, when I hear the organ in Booterstown, it brings back many memories. In those days, it was pumped by hand, a duty which I had on occasion, as had my father when he was a boy in Blackrock College. This instrument was completely refurbished in 1978 and I attended the recital to mark the occasion. The organist was my friend, the eminent musician, Professor Gerard Gillen. It was however a sad time for me, as Ruairi had died a very short time before. One of the hymns that night was 'Then Sing my Soul' to that beautiful Swedish air. It had been one of Ruairi's favourites.

One particular benediction remains a source of embarrassment. Each acolyte, and there were four of us, carried an enormous heavy brass candlestick some five feet tall. The candle itself was held in by a spring mechanism and we had been warned that if the candlestick was put down too heavily or accidentally kicked, this could trigger the spring and send the lighted candle flying through the air. As the procession was well under way, and in full view of the congregation, my foot knocked against the candlestick. There was a sharp click and to my horror the lighted candle took off, travelling across the top of the procession and landing on the bald head of the canon, splattering the poor man with hot candle grease. He carried on bravely as though nothing had happened while I tried desperately to do likewise. He did not reproach me when the service was over, and simply complained about the vagaries of these candlesticks. I was lucky. Had benediction been taken by the then hot-tempered senior curate, things would have been very different.

Booterstown is an ancient parish. The present church is said to be on the site of a monastery and it was claimed that a few yew trees growing in the adjoining convent grounds dated back to the time of the monks. While there is now no trace of these trees, a plaque in the church shows a continuous line of parish priests back as far as the year 1616. In addition to Booterstown, the parish once covered Blackrock and Donnybrook, extending as far as Dundrum and beyond.

The Verscoyles were a powerful Protestant family in the area. Although they had split from the Catholic Church at the time of the Reformation, they never fell out with those who remained Roman Catholics. One member of the family, Barbara Verscoyle, had remained a staunch and committed Catholic. When she became concerned that she and her fellow Catholics had no proper place of worship, she appealed to her cousin, Lord Fitzwilliam, to provide a site for the church. Not alone did he provide the site; he also engaged an architect and built the church. (As well he might, for the Fitzwilliam Estate had increased rents by 89% between 1783 and 1815.) Fitzwilliam made one important proviso: the building's exterior should not look like a church, so that it would not offend the Protestant neighbours. The church was built in 1812, some seventeen years before the Act of Catholic Emancipation.

When Barbara Verscoyle died in 1837, it was her wish that she be interred in the church for which she had been responsible. This wish was carried out. The only other burial within the church was that of Monsignor Forde, one-time parish priest and a special adviser to Cardinal Cullen at the time of the First Vatican Council. The monsignor died in 1873.

When extensive renovations, including a complete new floor (the old wooden floor was replaced with poured concrete), were carried out in Booterstown church some forty or more years ago, steps were taken to locate the exact site of the burial place of Barbara Verscoyle's remains and those of Msgr Forde.

Many years previously, when I was an altar boy, I had long conversations about the history of the church with the then clerk, Tom Maguire. One Saturday in the early 1930s, he pointed out some rather rough plaster work over the arches in the main aisle, saying that the large plaque to the memory of Barbara Verscoyle (now in a side aisle) was where it had formerly been situated and then went on to point to the floor in the main aisle saying that this was where Barbara's remains lay.

During the course of work on the new floor the graves of both Barbara and Msgr Forde were duly located, but not the spot which Maguire had shown me as the site of Barbara's burial but exactly opposite in the area formerly known as the gospel side, i.e. the left-hand side facing the altar in the main aisle. The monsignor's grave was also on the gospel side, adjacent to the sanctuary.

It is rare indeed for a lay person in the Catholic Church to be buried in the actual church itself. This privilege, however, was given to Barbara Verscoyle, the foundress of this church, now approaching its bi-centenary.

When moving the altar to conform to the regulations pursuant to Vatican II, they discovered an older altar, much less ornate and rather depressing in black marble. Around it the workmen also found newspapers dating from 1858.

Throughout its long history, Booterstown Church had a number of well-known and famous parishioners. Among them were the O'Reilly family who lived in Sans Souci, once regarded as the manor house of Booterstown and long since demolished. I remember the O'Reilly family still in residence, although they sold the property to the Christian Brothers in 1937 who, in turn, sold it off for building in recent years. I last saw this once magnificent house on the evening before the North Strand bombing in 1941 when the Auxiliary Fire Service was practising with their hoses against the walls of what was then a gaunt and sad ruin.

Other famous and noteworthy Booterstown parishioners were Donal Ó Buachalla, the last Governor General, Kevin O'Higgins and his family, the poet and scholar Denis Florence-McCarthy, and the historian Dr R. R. Madden. The latter lived at number 3 Booterstown Avenue, which was the home of my wife, Phyllis, in her early childhood. Dr Madden was well-known for his afternoon dinners which went on for hours and which took place every other Tuesday. His guests included John Patten, brother-in-law of Robert Emmett, Dennis Florence-McCarthy, and the historian Sir John Gilbert (who married the writer Rosa Mulholland). At the centenary of

Dr Madden's death some years ago, I had the honour of unveiling a plaque on the refurbished Madden grave in the old graveyard in Donnybrook, preceded by a special mass in Booterstown. Madden's funeral took place from Booterstown church in 1886 and was attended by a large gathering which mourned the loss of this distinguished Irishman and scholar.

Chief Justice Conor Maguire and his family were parishioners for many years, as was Count John McCormack; his funeral service took place from this church. Judge James Greene and his family were parishioners from 1912 until his death in 1939.

Another family of note were the Brudenell-Murphys who were prominent parishioners long before we came to Booterstown. Mrs Brudenell-Murphy had endowed the parish heavily and many of her gifts adorned the church, including two stained-glass windows.

Our family's connections with Booterstown church went back some 75 years. This was by no means a record, however, for other families such as the O'Reillys were parishioners for even longer periods of time.

While no seats or pews as such were allotted, the parish families of long-standing habitually sat in their usual chosen seats. No one but a member of their family would dare take an O'Reilly seat, on the gospel side at the top of the nave. My family occupied the seat about half way down on the opposite side.

Cross Avenue had other family connections. The lands surrounding Glenvar bordered both Cross Avenue and Mount Merrion Avenue, the main entrance being on the latter road. The only access to Cross Avenue was by means of a wicket gate. My father was on the run in Glenvar in 1921. On a summer evening that year a Lancia open tender arrived at the main gate. It contained eight to ten soldiers of the Worcester Regiment. Father happened to be out in the grounds taking the air but spotted the tender. His first instinct was to make his escape. He knew of the existence of the wicket gate, ran towards it but to his dismay found it locked. His escape was cut off. He was arrested and brought to the Bridewell Prison and later transferred to Portobello (now Cathal Brugha) Barracks but after a short while he was released. His own diary entry reads 'Released… did not know what to make of it, went to Greystones.' The wicket gate remained until the late 1930s when it was demolished as the lands were developed for building and a road now runs where the gate was formally situated. When I knew it, it was obvious that it had not been opened for years as it was partly covered by ivy.

My cousin, the late Don Cotter reminded me of another story of this period when Father was on the run. We believe this incident happened in 1920. Father was in the Phibsboro district and thought that he could spend the night in my mother's old house in Munster Street. He went there but it was now in the early hours of the morning. He did not want to disturb the household so he thought that he would open a window and gain entry to the house that way. He used his penknife to open the latch of the window, climbed inside and then crept upstairs, where he knew that there was a disused bedroom. As he mounted the stairs, however, he stumbled making a noise. Dick Cotter heard this and fearing that it was an intruder, most likely politically motivated, seized a poker and lashed out at the figure on the stairs. Lucky for Father the poker came down hard on his shoulder and not on his head for had it been the latter Dick Cotter's action could have proved fatal. It certainly proved to be a painful escape for Father.

Another historical event of this period was a .45 bullet lodged on the road-side of the wall of the rose garden in Bellevue. Phyllis knew of the existence of this bullet since her early childhood and had a formula for finding it. It was lodged some half-way up the wall. Many years ago we both discovered it and I regret that I did not remove it then for later when I went to look for it, it had disappeared. I endeavoured to find out the history of this bullet and succeeded in ascertaining that an IRA party fired on a tender full of Black and Tans which was passing down Cross Avenue but with what effect I am not sure. I know that the IRA made good their escape through the grounds of Herberton and thence to Mount Merrion Avenue. Certainly one thing is clear, they would not have received any help or encouragement from the then-occupier of Herberton as Judge James Green who lived there was a committed unionist. He was then a county court judge for Armagh and remained a judge in the north up to the time of his death in 1939. His father had been a barrister who prosecuted the Fenians in the nineteenth century for high treason and whose outstanding case was that of the *Crown -v- Mackey* which was tried in Cork where he failed to secure a conviction. There is no doubt from notes in the brief that there was a blatant attempt to fix the jury. When we moved to Herberton I found the briefs and other papers relating to this trial in the coachman's house where they had lain for many years. It is from these papers that I obtained the information given above. I gave them on indefinite loan to the state papers in Dublin Castle. Judge Green's son, also named James, was a senior partner in the well-known firm of solicitors, Maxwell Weldon. I came to know him and found him a most pleasant and friendly colleague. He was born in Herberton in 1912 and grew up there. The gardener O'Grady had planted an Albertino rose that year. I took a slip of the rose and gave it to James as a memento of the place where he was born; he told me that the rose flourished. James R. C. Green died in May of 1990.

There is yet another story of how a house in Cross Avenue figured in my father's life in quite a dramatic way. This was in 1923. Blackrock College owned Clareville as part of the college complex. My father was in hiding in Mount Street, deep in the centre of Dublin city for part of the Civil War. Many attempts had been made to locate him but to no avail. At this time the Civil War had nearly run its bitter and horrific course.

The pope sent a legate, Monsignor Luzio, to Dublin in the hope of contacting both sides with a view to negotiating a settlement, or at least initiating one. Father could not have met the legate in the open, for the moment he would have tried to do so he would have been arrested. The question then arose as to how a meeting with Msgr Luzio and Eamon de Valera could be arranged. Once more his faithful friends in the Holy Ghost congregation came to his aid through the agency of Frs Joseph Byrne (afterwards provincial of the congregation and later bishop), Larry Healy and Bertie O'Farrell. Fr Byrne made contact with my father to appraise him of the latest position.

Msgr Luzio was staying at the Shelbourne Hotel. The three priests together then devised a clever plan. Fr O'Farrell collected the monsignor at the Shelbourne and drove him to Clareville using the entrance on Cross Avenue. He knew only too well that he was being shadowed by agents of the Free State side. He arrived safely at Clareville and there the monsignor was asked to give Fr Healy his overcoat and hat. The monsignor obliged. Then Fr O'Farrell and Fr Healy, duly disguised as the monsignor, set off in the car once dusk had set in, driving towards Dun Laoghaire. The agents followed them exactly as they had anticipated. When Fr O'Farrell and Fr Healy had safely departed, Fr Byrne took the monsignor by a pathway to the main part of the college where there was another car waiting. They boarded this and drove to Mount Street without further molestation. There my father met the monsignor. Further contact continued between them, but regretfully came to nothing. The Free State side did not trust Msgr Luzio, feeling his sympathies were too much with the republicans. They even made suggestions to discredit him (with appropriate prejudiced press coverage). Their attitude was sufficient to make him feel that the Free State side did not regard him as a duly accredited emissary of the Vatican. Father soon realised that the legate's mission would fail as indeed turned out to be the case. This was most certainly due to the negative activities and attitudes of those on the Free State side.

The families in Cross Avenue were to know other sad events. I recall one fine afternoon in July 1935 when news reached us that one of Canon Northridge's sons, George, had been killed in a road accident at Ballsbridge outside the RDS. He was driving a Morris Minor car, a model which long ante-dated the more famous one. It seems that he was endeavouring to pass a tram which was running southward, but did not realise that there was another tram running in the opposite direction and between the two, the car was crushed. No car could withstand the impact of such massive vehicles. He was taken to nearby Baggot Street Hospital where he was dead on arrival. He was twenty-three years of age. My parents were greatly disturbed by the news and that evening called on the canon and his wife to express their condolences.

# CHAPTER V

## *Family Tragedy*

By 1936, life was progressing smoothly for the family. In January of that year, I attended a farewell to 'Bookie' Devine on his retirement.

For a year or two previously, my brothers and I listened to Henry Hall's afternoon programme on the BBC. With so little light music being broadcast at the time, this programme became quite popular. While listening to Henry Hall, we tried to pick up the latest tunes. A few dance records and other light music were brought into the house and played on a giant RCA radiogram, a gift to my father and very high-tech at the time, probably the first in Ireland to have a facility for making home recordings on little wax discs.

Another tradition involved assembling in a room in the basement for a sing-song each Saturday night. Vivion, Ruairi, Éamon, Brian, Eamonn Coughlan, and my cousin Don Cotter joined in, and we competed to see who could remember the tunes and words which we had heard during the week. Popular music of that period which while sometimes trite, even brash, was on the whole tuneful and reasonably intelligible, performed by trained professional musicians. The singing then was so different to the 'pop' music of the present day with its vulgar incessant thump, thump, where so many of its performers claim to have 'written' so called 'numbers', although the vast majority do not know even the rudiments of music notation. To me by far the greatest output is nothing short of a prostitution of music, driven by the sole desire of making vast sums of money and regardless of the consequences. Far too much of this vulgar rubbish is directed towards young and even very young, but worse follows with highly publicised gigs, targeting the young which so often become the venues for drugs and general decadence. It is a pity that all these vast sums of money and energy are not directed towards good and wholesome music. The truth is that this is purely a business with little or no regard for any real artistic content or true merit, and essentially transient in its nature.

A year or two previously, Brian wished to take up horse riding more seriously. My mother had two first cousins on her father's side, Thomas and Laurence Flanagan, known to us as Tom and Lar. Both were dentists. Lar was also a doctor who lectured in dentistry in UCD. He was an outstanding horseman and joint master of the South Dublin Harriers with his friend Peter Dunn for the years 1936-44.

Lar occasionally visited us in Bellevue to play tennis with Éamon, Ruairi and Don Cotter. They all wore long white trousers in those days but Lar's were half-way up his calves. He had an old-fashioned but deadly way of serving, which he took from the corner of the court, much to the surprise of his fellow players. Like everything else in his life, Lar approached it as a serious business. When he was not there, I often imitated his odd movements on the court, much to the amusement of my elders.

Both Flanagan cousins had a great affection for my mother, which was warmly reciprocated. When she approached Lar to help Brian with his riding, Lar willingly agreed and took an almost fatherly interest in Brian from then on. Each Sunday, Lar drove himself and Brian to the riding school in the Phoenix Park in his beautiful Adler car, a model which had been imported from Germany since 1934. Brian was the smallest in the family, of slight build with thick, black curly hair and hazel-coloured eyes. He was passionate about horses or anything to do with them; my mother records that horse riding 'was the joy of his life'. He would have loved to become a jockey, but when he mentioned this to my parents, they laughed and would not hear of it. He confessed to Ruairi that he would give up all his talents in mathematics, and everything else in life, just to be with horses. He hoped to have a good horse in Bellevue in time and succeeded in winning my parents' approval.

Brian, however, was somewhat odd in his ways. He often cut himself off, lay on his bed and read Dickens or poetry. He could be intensely morbid and often spoke of death. A very short time before he died, he saw me playing with my soldiers and decided that one must die and be given a military funeral. He then disappeared and returned with a cleverly made cardboard coffin in perfect scale. This was used in the obsequies and the funeral was duly carried out. I still have this macabre souvenir.

Father had just got a new car, another Dodge. It was black, and when Brian saw it, he remarked: 'It would be great for a funeral.' This was within only three weeks of his death.

Brian could also be very playful and loved playing practical jokes, perhaps too much so for in that way he never really grew up. One of his pranks was to fill a large paper bag with water, sneak up to the escort's car and lob it in neatly as the unfortunate guards were about to move off to follow Father. I too took part in this prank but the guards never once spilt on us. On one occasion, they got their own back by giving us a thorough drenching with a hose. Father knew nothing of these things until long after Brian's death.

Brian's great friend, Br Sturmius in Blackrock College, was a German who had fought for his country in World War I. Together, he and Brian made explosives in the school's science laboratories. I once saw Brian blow a large branch clean off of a tree with the power of the explosion, he having invented his own detonator.

Brian had been going for his customary rides with Lar for about two years, including one or two of the hunts. His interest in riding excused him from the family drives which Father organised for almost every Sunday afternoon. We drove to Wicklow or the Dublin Mountains where Father could have a long walk which he so much enjoyed. We were divided into groups, Ruairi and I leading with my parents at the rear. If a car came along, and this was not very often, Father roared out from the back: 'Indian file' – which meant that we were to walk in single-file until the car had passed.

Brian was deeply religious and on Sunday 9 February 1936, Mother and Brian were at 8 o'clock mass. When they returned about 9 o'clock, he came into my bedroom and apologised for bursting some balloons which I had collected. He said he had been experimenting with gas and they had exploded. He then said: 'Don't worry. I will get some more,' then dashed out of the room to keep his riding appointment.

Father and Máirín had been at 12 o'clock mass, and by the time they returned, I was playing in the attic. Shortly after this, a telephone call came to say that Brian had met with an accident and had been taken to the Mater private nursing home. Later, we learned that his usual horse was not available on that particular morning, so he had been given another mount with which neither he nor the riding school were familiar. He sprang into the saddle and rode out, accompanied by Lar, and broke into his traditional full gallop across the Fifteen Acres. He had not gone all that far when his horse became completely unmanageable, bolted and veered off in the direction of a clump of trees. Brian was seen to struggle violently in an effort to control the animal, now galloping in frenzy, but the horse dashed on under some trees. Throwing himself along the neck of the horse, Brian tried in vain to protect himself but collided violently with a branch which struck the back of his head and flung him to the ground. When he was admitted to the Mater, it was obvious that the injuries were serious. Doctors and surgeons were quickly summoned, and although they made every effort to save him, he died shortly before 3 o'clock. He was twenty-one years and seven months old.

On hearing that Brian was in hospital, both Father and Éamon rushed to be with him. Mother sent Ruairi, Emer and me to the church to pray. When we returned, Brian was gone. My parents and the family were distraught. Lar Flanagan and close relatives and friends arrived. Toward evening, there were many callers including Canon and Mrs Northridge expressing their sympathy to my parents as they themselves had done on the tragic loss of the Northridge's son some seven months previously. Although Lar Flanagan survived Brian by many years, he never got over his death. Lar had a riding accident a number of years later and received a serious leg injury. He never rode again.

Among the callers that evening were Dr and Mrs Jim Ryan. Mother was quite inconsolable and remained so for a very long time to come. Máirín very bravely took over. As my parents wished that I should be spared the shock and trauma of the funeral, Mrs Ryan took me back to Kendleston. I spent a very sorrowful week there in snowy weather. Eoin Ryan did everything he could to keep me occupied amid the snow and gloom of that week.

Brian's funeral took place at Booterstown church. The crowd was so vast that the church could not contain all those who wished to express their sympathy. The seats at the top were also rearranged in 'choir form' to accommodate the large number of clergy present. It snowed heavily the day of the funeral, 11 February. At the last moment, the horse-drawn hearse could not proceed and by strange irony, a motor hearse had to be pressed into service. The funeral cortege was more than three miles long. Brian was laid to rest in a newly acquired family grave in Glasnevin Cemetery. Messages of sympathy poured in from all parts of Ireland and indeed all over the world, including personal messages from the Pope, King

Edward VIII, Mussolini and Emperor Haile Selassie of Ethiopia.

On my return to Bellevue a black diamond-shaped patch was sown on the sleeves of my jacket and coat, the usual sign of mourning in those times. It remained there for several months. Mother wore only black for a period of some two years, while Father wore a black tie for about the same time.

For several years to come, Father never missed visiting Brian's grave each Sunday morning. He had a simple granite cross placed over the grave and always stressed that he himself wished for a simple memorial. By tradition, those of the family who are buried in this plot have only their name, date of birth and their date of death. Mother did not attend Brian's funeral committal; it was not the custom for women to do so in those days. She never visited the grave, and she said that she could not bear to do so.

Somehow, life had to go on and I was soon back at school which served as a distraction. One day, however, I went to the stable and, seeing Brian's saddle and bridle, I remembered the words of the song which we had sung the night before his death, 'There's a Bridle Hanging on the Wall'. His bridle remained untouched for a very long time. I have it now, a poignant memory of sad and happy days long gone.

In spite of Brian's death, my father continued his interest in horses and regularly attended the annual Horse Show at the Royal Dublin Society. His presence at this show continued over a period of many years.

Before World War II, the coveted Aga Khan Trophy was a purely military competition. For several years, a number of countries had sent teams to compete for the much sought-after cup. There was a great spirit of rivalry between the competitors. I have vivid memories of the competition on 7 August 1936, less than six months after Brian's death. Father attended as head of the government. I was not with him on this occasion, but among the thickly packed crowd of more than 42,000 people. The ceremony began by each country's team parading in front of my father and other distinguished guests, led out by the No. 1 Army Brass & Reed Band which played each country's national anthem. When it came to the turn of the British team, a small but vociferous section of the crowd, composed of fuddy duddy ex-British army types and matronly tweeded women, long past the flower of youth, began to sing 'God save the King'.

This immediately raised a strong feeling of indignation and resentment among the vast majority of the crowd, so when it came time for the host nation's anthem, the crowd responded by singing in full voice 'The Soldiers' Song', which echoed around the grounds.

Towards the end of the competition, the atmosphere was indeed tense, when it became clear that the winning of the trophy lay between the British and Irish teams. This was a golden era for the Irish military jumping team which had been winning international prizes, although they were not fielding their best horses on this occasion. The British team was excellent, but could it be beaten? The air became electric. Ireland was last to jump, and it all depended on their last rider, Captain D. J. Corry, securing a clear round. I can still picture that final jump. The horse and rider were still airborne when the vast crowd exploded into tumultuous applause. Ireland had won but only by one point.

I took particular note as my father congratulated the Irish team. He lingered longer than usual as he had a word with each member of the team and the Irish national anthem was again played. This time, the crowd sang it louder and with even more gusto. It was a moment to savour. The demonstration by the small but conspicuous pro-British element had been given a resounding answer, sufficient to ensure that they did not repeat this ill-advised display at a future time. Father described the day's events to Mother when he came home that evening. He had told the Irish team 'We are all very proud of you. You have done the country great credit.'

This pro-British display at the RDS attracted notice throughout the country and was commented upon in the press. The *Irish Press* said: 'The playing of 'God Save the King' for the English team gave a section of the people with stand tickets an opportunity to display the usual lack of sympathy and good taste which they exhibit on such occasions. It goes without saying that they sang it with gusto as the tune was played… Apparently nettled by the display of bad taste shown by those who sang the British anthem, the people in the popularly priced enclosures sang "The Soldiers' Song"… The Tricolour seemed to flutter somewhat more proudly in the breeze when the Irish team lined up to be presented with the trophy.' The *Press* also reported: 'A tremendous cheer heralded the approach of Mr de Valera.'

From 1936 onwards, Father sometimes took me when he journeyed down the country. These were enjoyable trips and, in fairness, never once did he mention mathematics. He wanted me to enjoy these journeys and to derive benefit from them.

One such journey was to Cork for the official opening of the rebuilt city hall which had been destroyed by British troops in 1920. He was very friendly with Senator Dowdall and stayed in their delightful home in Blackrock where Mrs Dowdall, a lady of strong and forceful character, was a most welcoming and generous hostess. The senator had a chauffeur, quite an old man who drove a large ancient car, and it was the custom for the senator and his brother to meet my father some distance outside Cork city whenever he had the occasion to go there. Father never said a word about this ordeal because the chauffeur insisted on leading the way and driving at not more than 15 or 20 miles an hour. Father's driver and the escort were always annoyed by his method of driving and the speed at which he led the procession.

Father was to deliver a speech at the official opening, with Mr W. T. Cosgrave, leader of the opposition, also present. I was seated in the front row beside Mrs Dowdall. Father had scarcely commenced when a very large, fat man, a member of the Cork Harbour Commissioners, stood up in the audience. In a loud voice and strong Cork accent, he said that he thought it would be an excellent idea if Mr de Valera and Mr Cosgrave spoke at one and the same time! Heads swiftly turned in his direction but my father continued as though nothing had happened. The commissioner continued to interrupt. Some stewards moved in and forcibly removed him. Mrs Dowdall thought that I was a trifle upset. She put her hand on my knee and said in a loud stage whisper: 'Don't worry, my dear, a little too much luncheon!'

It was during this trip to Cork that I had my first trip on the River Lee and out into Cork Harbour. There I saw a great liner at anchor while the tender plied between the ship and the harbour in Cobh. There too I saw a British destroyer at anchor, as the Forts here were still in British occupation. Little did I, or anyone else present, know then that some two years later, we would be back to take over these Forts as the British departed.

Towards the end of 1936, came the crisis in Britain with the abdication of King Edward VIII. There was great fuss and excitement as the controversy dragged on with people expressing their attitudes about the question of divorce. We saw little of Father at that time for he was heavily engaged in political manoeuvring, anxious to take all possible advantage of the crisis which sorely affected the British establishment.

Mother, while in no way a monarchist, and totally opposed to the concept of divorce, could not conceal a certain sympathy for the king. I know that she was influenced by the personal telegram which he had sent on Brian's death only a few months previously. My father, along with the prime ministers of Canada, Australia and South Africa, was asked by the British Prime Minister, Stanley Baldwin, to make known his views on the crisis. Father declined to give any advice. He firmly believed that this was solely a matter for the British and not for him.

On the home front, Irish had always been a second language in the house. It was frequently used but never in an oppressive way. Sometimes someone might say something in Irish while another would answer in English, or vice versa. Neither of my parents believed in any form of compulsion and were strongly opposed to such a concept, fearing that any force would have the opposite effect to that which was intended.

Máirín and Ruairi were proficient to the point of being bilingual and had no difficulty whatsoever in using Irish in the most difficult and technical subjects – Máirín in her botany or Ruairi in history and archaeology and other subjects. Emer was also a considerable Irish scholar, and Vivion, like his knowledge of other subjects, was equally at home in the use of the language. Éamon was quite comfortable speaking Irish, nor did it cause any difficulty for Brian and me. Sometimes when we were out for family drives on a Sunday, nothing but Irish was spoken.

My Aunt Bee's only son, Don Cotter, became a regular visitor to Bellevue in those years. He had started in Blackrock College on the same day as I had in September 1934. Somewhat my senior, his great passion was sport. He always took an active interest in the fortunes of the GAA and did much to further the interests of this organisation over many years. Although he had no time for rugby, he played a good game of tennis and had an interest in cricket.

For a number of years, Don came back from school with me each Saturday and spent the remainder of the day with the family. With my brothers, we all played football in Bellevue – always Gaelic, for Don refused to have anything to do with the egg-shaped ball. We also played hurling, a sport in which Éamon took a special interest. Don was not only a good footballer but also skilful at hurling. He did not care much for riding, so this interest entered little into our pastimes. Don loved all types of sport and entered into each game with great enthusiasm, to say nothing of his bravery. If we tired of our game, he agreed to play something else, more to please me than with any deep desire on his part. Gifted with his hands, Don made cowboy outfits with which we enjoyed playing.

One summer Saturday in the mid 1930s, Don and I tired of football and thought we would look for some new adventure. There was a large loft over the stable with a room adjoining it. Strangely, this room had no window, the only entrance being a door high on the wall some twenty-five feet from the ground. We got hold of a ladder, climbed it and managed to open the rusty bolt. As we opened the creaking door, the daylight flooded in. We climbed into the room but there was little to see except a large wooden box. We opened the lid and to our great surprise, we saw portions of a skull and a goodly number of human bones. We alerted Ruairí, Éamon and Brian. Éamon took charge, and decreed that they were indeed human bones. The mystery, however, was not as great as we had hoped, for a previous resident of Bellevue, Captain Robert Ernest Lee, had been a doctor and these bones had belonged to him since his student days. They had obviously been locked away many years before and forgotten when Mrs Lee left Bellevue.

Éamon reverently took the bones, cleaned them and placed them with his own collection which he in turn had used for his medical studies. Among Éamon's collections was a particularly fine female skull which he said was anything up to a hundred years old. He thought it was the skull of a pauper, as this was the source of such bones at that period. According to Éamon, the deceased would have been about twenty or twenty-five years of age with a complete set of teeth and a beautifully shape head. I often saw Éamon deep in study with the skull placed before him on a table. At night he put the skull on top of a wardrobe. Once or twice I slept in that room with the skull gazing down at me. I never felt the slightest fear – indeed she became one of the family and I missed her when Éamon married and took her away to his own home.

There was a tremendous rapport between my mother and Don Cotter. They were devoted to each other and in many ways, she treated him very much as a son. When it came to lesson time, I found him a great help as he was gifted in mathematics and often helped me with my homework. He knew my mother as Auntie Jane and my father as Uncle Ned. Both Mother and Don enjoyed playing tricks on each other. My father had a great affection for Don, while Don absolutely revered him. Father particularly liked Don's talent for mathematics, his high standard of integrity and national spirit. Don too had a special affection for Brian and felt his loss deeply. While working on the final revision of this book news came to me of the sudden death of Don Cotter, most likely caused by a broken heart, for only days before his death, one of his daughters and a baby granddaughter were tragically killed in a road accident. Nevertheless, I look back to the happy memories of our boyhood and recall Robert Louis Stephenson's lovely lines:

If two may read aright,
These rhymes of old delight,
And house and garden play,
You two, my cousins, and you only may.

Even after we moved to Bellevue, Kendleston was far from just a wonderful memory. From 1932 for the next quarter-century or more, Mrs Ryan held a party each St Stephen's Day, inviting the de Valera family and other close friends, including Frank Aiken, in the early days his wife-to-be Maudie, and her sister Mina. Both these ladies were distinguished musicians, Maudie a violinist, Mina a cellist. Other guests were Cearbhall Ó Dálaigh, his fiancée, Máirín McDermott, and members of the O'Neill family of Uplands. These parties followed a set format. We arrived for lunch at 1.00 p.m., after which the younger generation played games around the house. If it was fine, we ventured into the grounds where I could relive so many happy memories. The grown-ups remained indoors and in later years, we joined them in their conversation.

At 7.00 p.m. we met in the dining room for an elaborate and

traditional supper at which the younger members of the family were sometimes served Mrs Ryan's special home-made elderberry wine. Supper over, we assembled in the drawing room where Mrs Ryan, in a slightly commanding way, organised charades in which all were expected to take part. She took these games quite seriously, dividing us into teams according to the numbers present. These teams included Dr Jim Ryan himself, her eldest son Eoin, her daughter Nuala and in later years her younger son Séamus and her pretty niece Noreen O'Sullivan, later to become the wife of Col Mat Feehan.

On St Stephen's Day 1946, Mrs Ryan invited the poet Patrick Kavanagh. He arrived quite late for lunch wearing a worn-out, none-too-fresh tweed jacket and very baggy trousers. Having enjoyed a good supper, he returned to the drawing room with the rest of us. Before the charades began, Ruairi tried to engage him in conversation, thinking that he might like to discuss literature or poetry. Ruairi was surprised at the poet's lack of knowledge on things which Ruairi expected him to know. It was clear that Ruairi was making little progress, so the conversation ended with a much more spirited discussion on the relative merits of Sweet Afton and Players cigarettes!

We were not long assembled in the drawing room when Mrs Ryan stood up and called the company to attention with the inimitable way of clapping her diminutive hands. Teams were chosen with Ruairi, Phyllis and me on Kavanagh's team. We were next to choose the word which we would have to act out. Surprisingly, the poet did not excel and in the end, Ruairi had to choose. Neither did Kavanagh show any skill at acting as he spoke in his thick Monaghan accent. He was gauche in his movements and efforts to illustrate the chosen word. He lacked imagination about how the task was to be tackled, yet at the same time, he was constantly trying to impress and draw attention to himself, even show off a little. When the charades were finally over, he became much more lively and talkative as Dr Ryan pressed a very large whiskey into his hand.

Eoin Ryan told another story about Kavanagh. Mrs Ryan had invited him to visit her in Kendleston, and he arrived literally hours late, saying that he had lost his way. When Mrs. Ryan came to greet him, he said 'I wouldn't have come at all if I had known it would take so long!'

# CHAPTER VI

*My Mother's Recollections • Marriage of my Parents*
*The 1916 Rising*

It was after Brian's death that my mother began to speak more about her past life, reminiscing about her family, her childhood, her days in the Gaelic League and her early married life. It was then, too, that she started writing plays and stories for children, which served as a distraction from her grief.

Although I remember well so much of what she told us, I asked her to record these memories for me. When she was in Áras an Uachtaráin, I purchased a hard-backed notebook in Helys, the stationers in Dame Street. I gave this to her, and in it she recorded in her own neat handwriting so many of her precious historical recollections using, as she stated, a pen which had belonged to Brian.

My mother was born at 10.00 a.m. on Saturday 1 June 1878, in a little house in Skerries Street, Balbriggan, Co. Dublin. The house has long since disappeared, but some years ago I had the pleasant task of unveiling a plaque commemorating her birth, and now affixed to the house built on the site of her birthplace. She made her First Communion on 8 June 1888, and at Confirmation, she was given the name Cecilia.

Mother's parents were married in 1868. My mother was the second eldest of five surviving children, the others having died in infancy – something all too common then. Her father Laurence Flanagan, one of a large family, was born on 25 November 1836 in Carbury, Co. Kildare. Laurence's father was also named Laurence, but my mother did not remember him although he lived until the age of ninety-three. All she knew of him was that he loved animals and had a faithful donkey called Hark. Her father remembered the Great Famine of the 1840s. Although it was not as severe in that part of the country as it had been in so many others, he could still recall his own mother saying: 'Now, boys, to your daily labour.' This meant that Laurence and his brothers were to try and harvest sufficient edible potatoes to make a meal.

Laurence was put to the grocery trade, but this did not suit him, and he trained as a carpenter in which he showed particular skill. Although he had little formal education, he was self-taught and an avid reader. He acquired a sound and thorough knowledge of English literature and taught himself French in which he became proficient. In later life, he learnt a little Irish and was a strong supporter of the Fenian tradition and later of Parnell. When Queen Victoria visited Ireland in 1900, he was in charge of workmen at St Peter's church in Glasnevin, Dublin. He was with his men on the scaffolding which overlooked the royal procession, and as the queen's carriage passed, he told his men to keep their hats on and to turn their backs. They did so willingly. In recent years, my friend Tony Behan, an avid collector and expert on old postcards, showed me one in which the scaffolding is clearly visible and dates from the time of this incident.

Laurence Flanagan married Margaret Byrne, a native of Balbriggan who was born in 1838. They met when he was in charge of the building of Blackhall, a house on the southern side of the town of Balbriggan. After the marriage, the couple emigrated to America where Laurence met John Mitchel. My mother records how her father 'was struck by the gentle bearing of Mitchel who wrote with such force and vigour'. Laurence was a strong supporter of Mitchel but he had little or no time for Daniel O'Connell. He often had 'great arguments' with an uncle of my mother's, Thomas Christie, an ardent admirer of O'Connell. Laurence Flanagan, however, did not yield or alter his view.

After some years in the United States, the family returned to Ireland. As times were hard, they emigrated to Glasgow for a period but, as Laurence said, in the end the easiest money was to be made in Ireland so he returned and stayed.

Laurence was a foreman, or clerk of works, with the building firm of Kiernan of Talbot Street. There he remained for some fifty years, devoting himself to the interests of the firm and helping to build up its business. His day commenced at 6.30 a.m. and he did not reach home until after six in the evening. He left the firm without being given any form of pension, not even an extra week's wages. Like his daughter, however, he had a great way of managing money and he built up a not inconsiderable saving. His brothers and sisters had the same trait. The eldest, James, became a doctor and settled in England; a sister became a governess to a wealthy English family. Another brother, Michael, was a teacher whose sons were in school in Blackrock College with my father. Bridget became a governess to Dona Maria Pia de Sabonia, Queen of Portugal. Mother told us that when a young princess died, the queen sent for Bridget Flanagan, saying: 'Ah, Miss Flanagan, tell me more about her [the Princess] as you knew her so much better than I did.' Bridget also spent some time with the Portuguese royal family in their estate in Kiev in the Ukraine. The queen gave Bridget an ornate silver rosary as a memento of her time as governess.

Mother had another cousin, Mary, whose husband was British Consul in Portugal and became, as my mother states, 'a great friend of Roger Casement'. Yet another cousin was 'Boysie' Cooper; he was related to the poet and was no mean poet himself. I met him when he visited us some forty years ago, when he had an extensive practice at the English Bar. My mother's uncle Frank became a senior traveller for Sir Maurice Dockrell, and in so doing, made a lot of money. He was the father of Thomas and Laurence who my mother describes as 'among my favourite cousins'. My mother states that they all retained a great love of Ireland.

Laurence Flanagan (my mother's father) told a story of a forebear who had been a yeoman in 1798. One day, while the yeoman was guarding the bridge at Leixlip, none other than Lord Edward Fitzgerald came along in disguise, dressed as a sheep drover and complete with a flock of sheep. When he saw the sentry, Lord Edward asked: 'Is there any depasturage on the other side?' The sentry replied: 'No, my Lord, but you may pass!' When Vivion heard this story, he quipped: 'That fellow was a rotten sentry and should have been shot!' For my part, I think it was a sure indication where the sentry's real sympathies lay.

There is a sequel to this story. More than thirty-five years ago, I was browsing in Mitchell's, an antique shop in Cuffe Street, Dublin which has been demolished in recent times. In a dark corner, I spotted a picture heavily covered with dust. I took it in my hands, and removed some dust and saw that it was an old coloured print depicting the exact scene of the sentry and Lord Edward. Beneath the picture was a caption which exactly matched the words used by my mother, but with the added advantage of revealing the name of the sentry as Dempsey. I asked at once if I could buy it, but when I told Mr Mitchell the reason for my interest, he said that there could be no question of price and generously presented it to me. I had it cleaned and re-framed and gave it to my mother, which pleased her greatly. She was thrilled to find that her memory had been so accurate.

Her father was living and working in Athlone when she first went to school at the age of five, although they returned to Balbriggan after about ten months. By then, she had been nicknamed 'Doll', a name given to her by her father; when he first saw her, with her auburn hair, he said: 'A real little doll.' Some of her older friends, including her sisters, used this name.

Mother also went to school in Balbriggan, but the family returned to Dublin when she was nearly seven. Their first home was near Clonliffe Road and she went to St Francis Xavier School where she was taught by Miss McVeigh. She was apparently quite a character, and my mother spoke of her so often, I felt I had known her myself. Miss McVeigh called her Ginny and my mother records: 'So I have been called Doll, Jane, Ginny Jenny, Janie and Sinéad.'

Miss McVeigh taught English and arithmetic very well. She loved the stage and took a great deal of interest in preparing the girls for the school play – as my mother remarks, 'something that pleased me'. Sadly this could not be said about Miss McVeigh's abilities in needlework, and her knowledge of the craft was demonstrated in one of her dressmaking classes. She began by taking a large piece of brown paper and scissors, held the paper up before the class, then held it against one of the girls, saying at the same time: 'Now dear, start by cutting a piece at random!' She called all the pupils 'Dear' and if she smacked them, she would say: 'Hold out your hand, my dear.'

As for singing lessons, I cannot do better than quote my mother's words: 'She was musical but her method of teaching singing was that she lilted the firsts [the soprano part] and the seconds [the alto part] and then started off. If she was not satisfied with our singing she shouted, "Sing up, you fools!" She accompanied us by playing on the harmonium or singing the tune and went on: "Lah, Lah, Lah... Look at the music... Lah, Lah, Lah... Mind your bass... Lah, Lah, Lah." Sometimes as a dance tune was being played, she would get a couple of girls to dance while another played the harmonium.'

Miss McVeigh did not die until the early 1930s. Earlier I accompanied Mother (although I stayed in the car) when she visited her old friend on the north side of the city. After a considerable period of time, Mother came out smiling. When Mother arrived, she brought her to her bedroom, offered her a chair, then pushed a bantam hen off her bed and sat down, saying: 'Get out of the way!' Miss McVeigh died shortly afterwards, and

Mother was sad to say goodbye to this clever, eccentric and loveable person who, in many ways, had failed her as a teacher but in other ways had shown her great kindness.

Despite much of Miss McVeigh's poor teaching, it was through her influence and that of her father that Mother became what was known in those days as a monitoress (a student teacher) and this at the age of twelve. Mother had to pass medical tests and the doctor was so surprised at her slight thin figure, that he said: 'Are you going to teach?' Nicknamed Tiny by the other girls, another doctor thought that she was so frail that she would not live very long, although in fact she lived into her ninety-seventh year. She was put to teach in the infant schools.

Mother herself considered that she was far too young to be made a monitoress, but by the age of seventeen, she was ready to enter teacher training college, although candidates were not accepted until they were eighteen. Fr Waters (a Jesuit and manager of the school) took a special interest in her and wanted to send her to university at his own expense. She would dearly have loved this, but he died shortly afterwards and the plan came to nothing.

In October 1890, her mother had a fall. She never really recovered from this back injury and lost the use of one of her hands, which meant that my mother's elder sister, Mary, had to take over the household. Mother said of this tragedy: 'The house was never quite the same.' She spoke of her mother with real affection, describing her as someone who was always cheerful and looked on the bright side, no matter what the trouble. According to Mother, she was completely unselfish and always sympathetic to the misfortunes of others.

One point which comes out so clearly and often appears in her record is her veneration of her father. She says, 'I had a sort of worship of my father and was very proud of him.' She often spoke of his high standards of integrity and his great love, almost a passion, for the truth and dedication to duty. His love of her too is obvious as, for instance, he never once missed visiting her every Sunday during her time in the training college.

Mother spent her holidays with her Aunt Kate (her mother's sister) who lived alone and ran a shop in Balbriggan. Remembering those days, she says:

Amongst the pleasant recollections of my childhood are those of the happy holidays I spent in Balbriggan. From the time I was about nine until 1905, I went every year to Aunt Kate's little house. I thought the place lovely: 'Beauty is in the eye of the beholder'. When I read Robert Louis Stevenson's poem 'Goodbye Goodbye to Everything', I remember at the close of the holiday, saying: 'Goodbye front strand, goodbye back strand...' There was very little in the way of amusement or variety, but the freedom and the bathing and games we made up gave us much pleasure and joy. Toys were few but we got great delight from making grass dolls. The roots were the hair and it was only a detail that there was no face. Bathing was a constant delight but to my shame be it said I never learned to swim.

The ballad singers were a constant source of interest. They always came into the shop and got a copper. Aunt Kate said to one of them: 'Isn't it a wonder you would not be arrested for begging?' 'They cannot arrest vocalist or street musicians,' was the reply. One set of beggars gave me anything but pleasure. These were a vagrant class who dressed as sailors and wore peaked caps, white trousers and blue jerseys. They were generally deformed, one leg or arm missing. They sang mournful songs as they moved slowly through the town, one of which was 'The Sailors Grave':

A dash, a plunge and our task was o'er
The billows roared as they roared before.

When they entered the house, they were threatening and inclined to bully. While we were still living in Balbriggan Larry [her brother] when out one evening... it was dark, I think, and he left the hall door open. We heard a crutch coming along the hall and in a moment, a tall red-haired sailor appeared at the door of the kitchen. Fortunately, my father was in and when the sailor saw him, he said, 'Excuse me!' He would probably have demanded money and bullied if Father had not been there. I remember, as a more grown up girl, when I was standing at the door of the shop, a big burly fellow dressed in the usual costume crossed the street and said words that I would not repeat! They were somewhat of a menace. My horror of them must have had a terrible effect on me for, after fifty years, I have recurring dreams about them.

I would like to spare all children the fear that I suffered in my childhood; ghost stories held terror for me. Thunder and lightning, in fact anything that could cause trouble or anxiety, was a source of misery. I have begun to think of late [this would be in the late 1960s] that fear is a source of many ills. It, in some cases, leads to deceit and dishonesty.

Perhaps one of Mothers' most precious memories was when Parnell came to Balbriggan. She said that there was great excitement in the town, and one of her cousins organised a tin whistle band to greet 'The Chief'. A great crowd assembled at the railway station. Her brother Larry was lame and could not march, but he carried a placard. Amusingly she records: 'On one side was written "CHARLES STEWART PARNELL" but on the other "COONEY'S PASTE BLACKENING" [a boot polish of the time].' Parnell noticed the lame boy, came over and shook Larry's hand. Mother stated that this was Larry's 'most proud remembrance.'

She goes on to describe the day:

> The men took the horses from the carriage and drew it along. I can still see them straining forward as they passed. I was standing at a window in Station Street holding a green branch, but my courage failed me and I did not keep my place as the procession passed.

Mother often spoke of Parnell's visit and mentioned that, although he looked pale and worn, he spoke in a clear voice with great sincerity. The only part of his speech she could recall clearly was when he concluded with the words, 'God Save Ireland'.

When Parnell died, my mother was part of the vast crowd as the funeral procession passed on its way to Glasnevin Cemetery. She had brought her sister Brigid (Bee) with her. Bee was then only six years, while Mother was thirteen. She wept bitterly as the cortege passed, but she was far from being alone among those who so clearly showed their emotion and sorrow.

Mother entered the teacher training college in Baggot Street in September 1896 where she came under the direction of Mother Gonzaga, the principal. She was a person who showed her authority and the pupils feared her, not least my mother. Another teacher whom she feared was Mother Malachy. Music was part of the curriculum, and the method used was the tonic sol-fa system. They were also taught the theory of music. Mother did well in her examinations, obtaining 80% in practice and 88% in theory.

She records that her needlework was poor but in English she excelled. From my childhood, I recall her speaking of Prof. McGuinness whom she revered as a teacher of English. She also said McHarty Flint's elocution classes were 'a source of delight'. She obtained her first teaching position in Edenderry, Co. Offaly. She was not happy there, however, mostly due to the harsh attitude of the principal, Mrs Moran. In later life, Mrs Moran expressed regrets and asked for forgiveness.

It was while she was in Edenderry that Mother took up serious reading. She read Dickens, Scott, George Eliot and a great deal of poetry, particularly Byron, Keats, Shelley and Longfellow. She had of course a deep love for, and great knowledge of, Shakespeare's works, and her love of poetry was apparent throughout her entire life. She said: 'I have always had a delight in poetry. When I saw the rain drops on the leaves in the morning, Byron's lines came into my mind:

And Ardennes waves above them her green leaves

Dewy with natures' tear-drops as they pass'

Many years later, I remember Father often asked her to find some apt quotation, and seldom, if ever, did she fail to find or provide one, often from memory alone.

Mother continues:

I did not read much as a child. There were very few children's stories to be had, at least in our house. I remember, I think I was sixteen, the first summer holidays that I gave up playing. I was sitting at the front strand, and one of the other girls remarked something about my not playing anymore. We remained children longer in those days.

Mrs Moran had a brother, William Kennedy, who took an interest in my mother; she affectionately called him Uncle Bill. He was in the National Movement and bought Arthur Griffith's paper, *The United Irishman*, which he brought to my mother's attention. When there were celebrations in Carbury to mark the centenary of the Rising of 1798, she says: 'I began to take an interest in Irish affairs… as a child, still very young, I knew Thomas Davis' poem 'Fontenoy' by heart and used to recite it with great vigour… but the national schools of that time were not at all national.'

In the summer of 1899 two men, Archer and Lloyd, started a branch of the Gaelic League in Edenderry. This was the first Mother had heard of the League. Some local people joined it. My mother returned to Dublin in September where she obtained a teaching post as a fully qualified teacher in St Francis Xavier School. While in this school, where she taught from September 1899 until December of 1910, she records: 'The atmosphere was not congenial as the three teachers in the school had all West British tendencies and my great interest was Irish. I think we grow to love what we suffer for. These teachers are all now dead. They were all considerably older than I.' She also remarked: 'I would like to say a word to parents and teachers. Never display temper as a means of enforcing discipline. Temper is a cowardly thing.'

The meeting with Archer and Lloyd ignited a spark which aroused her interest in the Irish language. On her return to Dublin she was determined to pursue this, but as she records, 'I did not know how to go about it.' Then she goes on:

> The Árd Chraobh as we know it now was when I joined the Gaelic League called the Central Branch (November 1899). I remember there was a discussion about the name. Kent said that it should be The Árd Chraobh. I think it was Eamon O'Neill said that it should be An Árd Chraobh. Eoin MacNeill settled it by saying An Árd Chraobh was the right form. Here are some notes I got from Eamon O'Neill: The Central Branch of the League. He could not say when it was organised as a separate unit, but the first report of the year ending on 30 September 1894, mentions the proceeding of the Central Branch during the year 1893/94. The Central Branch was first at 57 Dame Street. It was then moved to the Café Royal, a building since incorporated in Clerys. A further move was made to 24 Upper O'Connell Street and finally to Parnell Square. The Gaelic League was founded in 1893. Rooney wrote or said that it was the 'Re-incarnation of the Irish Nation.' I myself always held that it was largely from the Gaelic League came the spirit that brought about the Easter Rising. I was delighted to find what Pearse had said about it. Here are his words: 'The Gaelic League will be recognised in history as the most

revolutionary influence that has ever come into Ireland. The Irish Revolution really began when the seven Proto Gaelic Leaguers met in O'Connell Street. The germ of all future Irish history was in that back room!'

She goes on:

I heard that there was a branch of the Gaelic League at 24 Upper O'Connell Street. Very shyly I went to the door. A girl, Miss Gannon was her name, was in the hall and as John MacNeill came along she directed me to him to ask him where I could find a class. He brought me to a room where Eamon O'Neill was teaching. This was November 1899. The class had been working since September. Eamon O'Neill held an examination after some time. I remember I could write 'anois' and that was practically all. After some time we had another examination. I got second place. I think it may be for that exam, but I am not quite sure, I got my first prize for Irish. Indeed it was only a token, a copy of an Irish Grammar. Funds were not high in the Gaelic League. When I was in the second book of O'Growney I was asked to teach the first one. Teachers were scarce and we were all just helping each other along.

I continued learning in the Árd Craobh and taught in the Craobh Colm Cille. In that branch I taught a children's class in Irish history. Enthusiasm took the place of learning and at least we got up a great spirit. What with Irish classes, excursions, language processions and many other interests, my life was a pleasant one.'

As time progressed she won several prizes in competitions concerning the Irish language.

Mother continues:

The language processions used to go through the streets of the city on a St Patrick's Day, and a collection was made at the same time. We had tableaux on carts and some of them were picturesque. It was great fun dressing the characters. I remember I helped get up Earnán de Bládh as Raymond Le Gros. When the procession was over I asked Earnán how he got on. 'I felt very foolish,' said he. As I write now I think of all the early members of the Árd Craobh: Tadhg O'Donoghue, Pearse,

Eamon O'Neill, Michael O'Hanrahan, Eamon Kent. I always say it was the Gaelic League rather than any other organisation that brought about the Easter Rising. I remember Pádraig Mac Elling saying: 'This movement can end only in one way and I wonder how many of us will be ready.' Instead of feeling sad and lonely as I write I have a feeling of peace and joy to think that so many of these brave souls are safe with God. I would like to linger on naming more of these noble men. One, Ernest Joynt, I think of with gratitude and respect. He was a Protestant, a gentle soul and true to language and country. He wrote a long article on Irish history and mentioned me in it.

Mother's reminiscences continue:

We had an excursion to Tara one time, possibly from the Colm Cille branch. I don't remember the details perfectly but I was reminded of it some time ago by Gilchrist O'Brion who was present with his mother. We were drinking water from a well, possibly a wishing well, and someone said: 'Here's that we may soon have a King in Ireland.' 'Oh, no,' said I, 'a Republic.' Then Gilchrist's mother added: 'May you be the president's wife.' I do not well remember all the circumstances but I remember the words.

Even from tender years, my mother's great love of the stage was apparent. She records:

I always approached this subject with a little regret and longing. My visits to the theatre bring something of the same emotions. It was years after my first visit to a theatre that I read Lamb's essay *My First Play*. He was only six when he went to a play; I was twelve, and my feelings must have been something like his. My heart beat to suffocation as I waited for the curtain to rise. The production in the old Queens, was only a stupid pantomime, *The Fair One with the Golden Locks*, but it was a scene of enchantment for me. My joy was such as to pass the limits of 'aesthetic pleasure'. After this, my father took me to the theatre now and then – we did not spend much money on amusements then.

As a child, I made up plays and when I was about twelve, I wrote and composed *True Hearts*. The kitchen table was the stage and the hero, Myra Jones, a young Protestant friend of mine, was dressed in a man's suit which was about three times too large. The idea of make-up was to wear a mask. Poor Myra got too warm and in the middle of the performance took off the mask.

Mother was wonderful in the many ways she allowed us to possess the house. I learnt numbers and poems by heart and recited them for Father when he came home in the evening. I could learn poetry with great ease, and my recitations became widely known among our friends. Miss McVeigh gave me great praise for reading poetry. In some cases, though she did not know it, I was not really reading, for I had the poems off by heart. One day I read Mackey's poem 'Daily Work', and when I had finished, her remarks were something in this strain: 'Bravo, Ginny! That's none of your Maggie Doyle's muttering or Katie English's stuttering.' Maggie and Kate were class mates of mine.

One evening, Father saw a poem in the evening newspaper which afterwards became a very popular recitation. It was known as 'Dawn on the Irish Coast' or 'The Exiles Return'. A note with the poem told of its origins. It appears that the poet Loche was standing on the deck of a homeward-bound ship when an old man, an exile returning to Ireland, called out, 'Ireland Alanna, I bid you the top of the morning.' I learned the poem at my father's suggestion. One day when there were priests and other visitors in the school, Fr Waters got me to recite it. I had no shyness or self-consciousness when anything in the way of acting was concerned. I understood the poem and delivered it as the words suggested. One well-known Jesuit, Fr Barron, gave me great praise, but said he hoped that I would never go on the stage. All the audience made a fuss of me and dear Fr Waters was delighted. My wish was for the stage but I know all that now.

I always had a part in the school plays. In one, *The Little Old Woman Who Lived in the Shoe*, I was the Old Woman. I adapted this play into Irish and it won prizes at the Feiseanna.

At two dramatic entertainments in the training college, I had important parts. McHardy Flint singled me out and brought his wife to the hall to listen to me. During an elocution lesson, he asked me to read a passage from Shakespeare's *Warrick on the Death of Gloucester*. He gave me great praise, and one of the girls said afterwards: 'Did young Flanagan curdle the blood in your veins when she read that?' The other monitoress and I sometimes stayed in school after hours to act plays. Miss McVeigh did not approve and sometimes caught us in the act. I can still see her head popping in at the door as she said: 'Go home, you fools!'

There were about five or six monitoresses and some of them acted men's parts. The plays were home-made, founded on stories we had read in novelettes, and Maggie Claire and I were the principle composers. Some of the monitoresses had failed their exams (poor Miss McVeigh's teaching) and the story went around that the girls had wasted their time reading novelettes. Miss Doyle, the principal, and Miss McVeigh called me one day and would not let me go until I promised that I would not read such stories until I was twenty-one. I struggled against giving the promise, but yielded at last.

I read a lot of light rubbish after that, but looking back on the periodicals that came my way, the worst of them were nothing more than that they were silly and impossible. I would be glad to see young people use even paltry books rather than read nothing. If the habit of reading is not acquired early in life, it will never come later on. Our childhood plays were very often tragedies; our idea of tragedy was that everyone should die. The characters died in various ways. Some fell from cliffs (the desks), while others perished in different ways. On one occasion, a character was left unaccounted for. 'Oh,' said Katie Scully, 'let Mary die of the fright!'

Father took me to the theatre now and then. The first play I saw was *The Shaughran* in the Queens. In those days they did burlesques and others dealing with Irish life. No matter what may be said to the contrary, I think that these plays were ever so much better than the modern ones. The enthusiasm of the audience added much to the enjoyment. I saw Frank Dalton and his sister in *Cailín Báin* and the acting was really good. *The Lily of Killarney* is based on the play, which in turn is an adaptation of Gerald Griffin's novel *The Collegians*. I was sixteen before I saw a play by Shakespeare in which Frank Benson and his wife took the leading parts. Mercutio was magnificent. There was an account of the play in the paper of which the writer said 'The audience had a grudge against Tibalt for putting Mercutio off the stage so soon.' Mrs Benson was fine in the soliloquy: 'Farewell – God knows when we shall meet again.' I used to declaim these passages, and when Larry [her brother], threw cinders at me, I bowed and thanked him for the bouquets!

Father took me to see *She Stoops to Conquer* before I went to the training college, and all this helped me to enjoy McGuinness' lectures.

In the Gaelic League I had many parts in the plays. I think the first Irish play produced in Dublin was the one written by Eamon O'Neill, . It was staged in the Rotunda and I took the part of the Spanish ambassador. I had a lovely costume (hired). I really did not quite know what I was saying, but I had to bow and move about – I was in my element. There was another play, *Seán na Scuabh*, and the author told me he had intended me for the girl's part but it was given to someone else.

Mary Butler and her sister Belinda asked me to take the part in the play written by Dr Hyde, *The Tinker and the Fairy*. It was acted in the garden of George Moore's house in Ely Place and Dr Hyde and I were the principals. Moore directed the staging of the play but he left it to ourselves to interpret the parts. As the rehearsals went on, he said: 'I say! I say! You are doing this awfully well! I'll give you something.' He wrote a very eulogistic article about me and sent me a lovely umbrella, 'In remembrance of your escape from the rain': the day had been a bit threatening. Some time after the performance, I was introduced to Yeats. His remark to me was: 'I believe you and the wind were the success of the day.' Edward Martyn came to me and said: 'Your vocation is to be an actress.' There were a great many people present at the performance for which Esposito composed the music; Kuno Myer was the prompter. I shall never forget the gentle smile as he shook hands with me and offered his congratulations. Michael Davit was very complimentary. He spoke Irish to me and remarked about my Irish that women could achieve what men could not.

I know this all seems very self-laudatory but I live that happy day over again as I write. My hair was loose about me and Edward Martyn asked: 'Is that a wig?' I remember the kind voice of Dr Hyde as he said, 'Sí sin a gruag féin' (that is her own hair). My joy was complete when Peader Macken (killed during the Easter Rising) called out at the close: 'Maith an cailín' (Good girl). Oh, these were the days in this life worth remembering. None of my own people were present; we did not move in high society. I went home and had a quiet tea with father and mother. Moore said that he could get me an engagement on the stage and Willie Fay (I think it was sometime after when I acted in another play) asked me to join the Abbey. He said that I was the best actor on the Irish stage. Moore asked me to join the dinner party that night but I didn't for I would not feel at home in such high society.

I took part in other Irish plays. Dr Hyde and I again acted together in *An Pósadh* (The Marriage). It was a great joy to me to see Éamon and Terry on the stage at Blackrock College. Éamon's acting in the some of the plays, especially *The Bishop's Candlesticks* was very fine. Terry's 'Yum Yum' in *The Mikado* was acknowledged by everyone to be a wonderful performance for a child of thirteen.

Before I leave the stage, I would like to talk about some tableaux which Miss Milligan and Anna Johnston (Eithna Carbery) staged, in what was then the Antient Concert Rooms in Pearse Street. I took the part of one of St Bridget's maidens. Eithna Carbery helped me to prepare for the tableau. I admired her greatly and kept near her, handing her the pins. I remember sensing that she was in love with Seamus MacManus from the way she seemed to linger a little in pinning on his bandoleer. They were married sometime after the autumn of 1901; she died on 2 April 1902. At the time that the tableaux were shown, Miss Milligan's play *Red Hugh* was performed. These tableaux were not held under the auspices of the Gaelic League. There was a society, Cumann na nGaedhal, conducted by Arthur Griffith, William Rooney and others. I saw Rooney and heard him speak but I never met him. Father was much impressed by his speech. Maud Gonne and a number of other women organised a children's treat to counteract the influence of the gatherings arranged in honour of Queen Victoria. Maud Gonne and others founded a society called Ingheana na hÉireann which I joined, along with Mrs Bradley, Máire Ní Chinnéidí and Mrs Dudley Diggis. We each took a name of an Irish saint or heroine. Mrs Bradley took Bridget, Maud Gonne was Maeve and I was Fidelma. We read papers in turn. Mine was written on Inghean Dubh, the mother of Hugh O'Donnell. I stayed in the society for some time but considered it was doing no real work, so, I then gave all my energies to the Gaelic League.'

Mention of Maud Gonne reminds me of what my mother said of her. Mother paid tribute to her undoubted beauty; she said that 'she had large proportions', by which she meant a rather full figure. Mother considered her somewhat condescending, self-opinionated and all too conscious of her beauty, although she spoke of her attractive, rather full speaking voice.

There is no doubt that Maud Gonne was conscious of her exceptionally good looks, for she said to Mother, half jokingly, yet half seriously, that 'beautiful women over forty should be shot!' Mother also told the story of hearing of Yeats reclining on a couch gazing up adoringly while Maud Gonne gently dropped chocolates into his open mouth.

My father said that as a young man, while he was a student in Blackrock College, he was travelling in a tram when a singularly beautiful woman got in and sat opposite him. He could not take his eyes off her stunning beauty but did not know who the lady was. On reflection, he was quite sure that it could only have been Maud Gonne. I only saw her in her last years during the general election of 1948 wearing a black coat and a widow's veil. By then she was old and wrinkled and had a rather haggard look, certainly revealing nothing of her former beauty, save for her wonderful dark eyes and winning smile.

Mother continues in her reminisces:

> Among my pupils were some boys and girls who formed a little private society which we called the Raparees. We were just a few friends who came together on Sunday nights, with each one reading a paper on some phase of Irish history followed by a discussion afterwards. We met in Fitzgibbon Street and now and again the boys engaged a room and a pianist for an evening of dancing. I remember the heated arguments we had about what a non-Irish thing it was to waltz. Arthur Griffith settled the question by writing that he could not see the national harm in waltzing, as this country was at peace with Bohemia! One of my duties was to write a song or poem for the dances. I am sorry I have lost some of these, because one of them was written to the air of 'Clare's Dragoons' had a verse for each member. I remember the look on the faces as the verse for each was sung.'

Mother's record goes on to say how she met Father:

> We met at the classes [of the Gaelic League] and at Christmas 1908, I

was sent a nice plant with a card on which was inscribed 'Ó chara' (from a friend). I thought it must be Dev who sent it, but as I was not sure, I was afraid to thank him. He continued his lessons and was an exacting pupil, fond of giving posers. We met in class and at a couple of céilís and by June had decided to get married. There is a saying: 'Happy is the wooing that is not long a-doing.' Our engagement was short and indeed we hardly knew each other until we were engaged. I first wore my engagement ring on the feast of the Sacred Heart, although I did not wear it in public until a short time before I was married. Dev wanted us to get married in August, and it is here that I have noted something in Dev's character, in which respect Ruairi most closely resembles him. In small things, Dev is very much given to weighing up things; he sees all the difficulties and takes all the precautions. On the other hand, when a big matter is at stake, he will go boldly forward. His prudent friend, Jack Barrett, warned him about rushing into marriage. Of course, we did marry on a slender means but we came through in the end.

During their engagement, my parents went for walks at Howth and occasionally to the theatre. The pair were married at 9.00 a.m. in Arran Quay church on Saturday 8 January 1910. According to my mother, Fr Martin was very nervous as he had to learn the Irish for the ceremony. She said: 'He married us two or three times before he got the words right.' Her sister Bee was the bridesmaid and father's old friend, Frank Hughes, was best man. It was altogether a quiet affair with only the family and close friends present. The wedding breakfast took place at the Four Courts Hotel (long since demolished) and they had a short honeymoon in Co. Wicklow at Woodenbridge near Avoca. For a brief period, they lived at Vernon Terrace in Booterstown and soon after they moved into their first house, at 33 Morehampton Road, Donnybrook.

One thing is sure: the young, purely academic-minded Eamon de Valera appears to have known little about setting up a new home. My mother often described, laughing as she told the story, how she sent him out to buy some basic and essential fittings after they moved into their new house. He went to an auction and arrived home with a huge brass chandelier, which, when presented to the ceiling almost touched the floor! Even stranger, he bought a quite worthless cello with a large patch in its belly. He also purchased two copper plates with rural scenes painted on them and paid four old pence for each. He thought he had got marvellous bargains. In later years, he himself had many a laugh about these purchases but he loved the two copper plates and had them in his study up to his last days in Herberton.

Mother had a great love of cats and shortly after her marriage, she acquired one which she called Punguar. Her faithful pet for twelve years, she was so heartbroken when the cat died that she had it stuffed, something that she regretted later: 'I would never do that with an animal again.' I remember Punguar, but only as a stuffed object. Eventually she had the remains interred in Bellevue but this was not until well into the 1930s.

The couple's first child, Vivion, (called after his paternal grandfather) was born on 13 December 1910. Mother spoke of the help she received from her old friend, Lill Saurin, and from her sister Mary. Shortly afterwards, my mother engaged her first maid, Mary Coffey.

At this time, Father owned a motor cycle with sidecar. He and my grandfather, Laurence Flanagan, got on very well and had great mutual respect for each other. With my grandfather in the sidecar, Father brought him to Carbury, Co. Kildare, so that Laurence Flanagan could visit the scenes of his childhood, as well as the graveyard where his ancestors were buried. This was a great joy for the old man and Mother said that he spoke of that day with pleasure for a long time afterwards. Laurence Flanagan stayed with my parents for some time in 1913, the year the Volunteers were formed. Laurence remarked of the formation of the Volunteers that he was sure that 'the spirit of our dead patriots, including Davis, was present at the meeting'. From the beginning of the Volunteers, my father spent much less time at home, and Mother's records tell of the Howth gun-running on 26 July 1914:

> Dev was out all day. In the evening, a girl whom I did not know, came to the house to enquire if Dev had returned home. When I told her he had not, she told me that everyone from the Donnybrook district had come home except her brother and Dev and that someone had been shot. Needless to say, I was very anxious. Father came over and I was delighted to see him. Dev arrived later on with the motorcycle. He had helped that night to store some of the guns. From that time

on, there was something of a tense atmosphere in the house. Seoirse Irvine was with us on New Year's Day 1916 (I am not absolutely certain if it was 1916 or 1915). When speaking to Dev, he said something like this: 'If something doesn't happen this year, it never will.' Brian was born about one o'clock on Sunday morning 26 July 1915. We used to call him the 'gun-runner' because he was born so near the time of the Howth gun-running anniversary.'

By now, there were four children in the family – Vivion, Máirín, Éamon and Brian. At this time, Mother had regular visits from both her father and her mother.

In January 1916 she visited Thomas MacDonagh and poignantly remarked that within less than a year, both he and his wife Muriel were dead, leaving the three children orphans. Father told her little or nothing of the intended rising, as no doubt he did not want to worry her. But soon she became suspicious that something serious was afoot although she did not contemplate an actual armed rising.

She records:

On Holy Thursday, 20 April 1916, Dev did not undress that night but lay down with a revolver [in fact not a revolver but his Mauser] by his side. On Good Friday, we knelt down in the little kitchen at three o'clock and prayed that we would be all left together. I remember saying to Dev: 'Do you know what they are calling the Volunteers? They are calling them Sinn Féiners.' 'We are not Sinn Féiners,' said Dev. Father had been a great admirer of Arthur Griffith but Dev never belonged to the Sinn Féin organisation. Sinn Féin was really a misnomer for the Volunteers. In the early days of the Gaelic League, the motto Sinn Féin or Sinn Féin Amháin had been used as a slogan. Cumann na nGael was the name of the organisation to which Griffith and Rooney belonged, and their national policy was a very advanced one. People blame Griffith for not taking part in the 1916 Rising, but it is hard to justly assign praise or blame. I remember Miss Milligan who was anti-Treaty saying to me: 'Rooney would have been a Republican.' *The United Irishman* was the name of a paper Griffith edited and Rooney was its best contributor both in prose and verse.

The paper was suppressed by the British government and reappeared under the name *Sinn Féin*. Hence Sinn Féiners was the name giving to those taking part in the 1916 Rising. In 1916, the term was used by some, more or less. in derision. The Volunteers were a more powerful and numerous organisation than Sinn Féin.

Dev did not sleep at home on the Friday or Saturday night [21 and 22 April] and instead stayed with Michael Malone. Michael Malone was a splendid soldier, always cheerful and reassuring. One could not but feel that there was something coming, but I never realised that a rising was contemplated. Michael said to me: 'We will have a bloodless victory.' How blind I was. God knows what we can dare and what we can endure, some of the women were wonderful.

She makes a further reference to Malone which confirms what is known from other sources: 'The English officer in charge paid a high tribute to the valour and great bravery of Michael.'

Mother continues her recollections of the Rising:

On Easter Sunday morning [23 April 1916], Paídín O'Keefe called to our house with a copy of the morning paper. He seemed greatly agitated. MacNeill had called off the Rising. Even then I did not see the full significance of it all. That night, I had a headache and was in bed when Dev came home to say goodbye. I had no idea that it might be his last goodbye. He then went to the room where the children slept. Viv says he always remembers that goodbye.

On Monday morning, the twenty-fourth, a messenger came from Dev, telling me to send him his kit and to cover it in brown paper. The O'Rahilly was in the house while the messenger was there and they spoke some words to each other. The O'Rahilly himself was killed in the Rising. I must have been very dull and wanting in understanding, for even then I did not sense what was going on. In the afternoon, Bridget, the maid, went out to a matinee in the theatre. She returned soon and I remarked that she was back very early. I shall never forget her reply: 'The Volunteers are digging trenches in Stephen's Green.' Then I understood all.

Bridget came in on 4 May and said: 'Rebel leaders suffer the extreme penalty... What does that mean Ma'am?' Thank God Bee was there. Poor Bridget was very good but had not too much imagination. Máirín, who was barely four at the time, said: 'Bridget don't bring in any more bad news to Mummy.' In the evening I went into the house next door and the bad news was confirmed.

The following days were anxious ones. Every morning brought bad news of another execution. The military raided our house and no one – none of our friends – was allowed to come near the house. A kind little neighbour, Mrs Cockrane, an Englishwoman and an admirer of Lloyd George, minded the children while the military raided. I have often thought of her since and remember her with gratitude and affection. The soldiers made a thorough search, and after them the G-men came. Sometime before the Rising, I gave Dev's birth certificate to my people in Munster Street. When the G-men were searching through Dev's papers, I got frightened and forgot I had given the certificate to my people. One of the G-men asked: 'What nationality is Mr de Valera?' 'He is an American citizen,' Bee replied. It may have been that remark that reminded me of the birth certificate, and I asked them what papers they were taking or some such question. Bee said to me 'Sílim go bhfuil siad agamsa' (I think I have them). 'No more of that now,' said one of them, but it was enough to ease my mind.

Bee was very much more courageous than I, and she said to the G-men: 'At least you might have behaved better.' One of them asked: 'How did I not behave like a gentleman?' 'Well, you didn't remove your hat when you came in,' said she. When they were going out, they saluted and said: 'Good day, Mrs de Valera. Good day, Mrs Cotter.' Although Bee and I were brave enough during the raid, I think we cried when the G-men left.

Dev does not believe that it was the American influence that saved his life. His name was just the first of those who were spared. Perhaps the growing feeling in the country had something to do with the ending of the executions. But when we said this to Fr MacCarthy, who came to tell us of the reprieve and that the executions were over, he said: 'No, I have to see a fine fellow die in the morning.' I think it was Seán Mac Diarmada, which would mean that it was the morning of 12 May.

There seemed to have been little hope for Dev, but Bee went to

Munster Street and got the birth certificate which she brought it to Fr Flanagan in Marlborough Street. Fr Flanagan said it should be brought to the American Consul. Molly Cotter and Marie Dixon brought it to the Consul. I went then to the Consulate myself and the Consul and Vice-Consul were very kind to me. I went to them several times and when I apologised for my importunity, the elder man said: 'You are as welcome as the flowers in May'.

Travelling through the city was difficult. Things were dislocated after the Rising. The trams did not run as usual, though they were still in action. Most people, I think, had now given up hope that Dev's life would be spared. Mrs Cornwall, my neighbour, continued to reassure me and her faith in prayer as well as that of her husband helped me very much. I remember poor Mary [her sister] saying: 'You would bear it wouldn't you?' I could not be brave about it, but one day I said: 'Thy will be done.' Looking back, I doubt I had the strength to say it sincerely, for I fear I never really bowed my head for that cross.

That night [the Wednesday after the Rising] I was putting Éamon to bed, I looked out the window and saw a cab stopping at the door. A priest got out, Fr McCarthy from James' Street. Bee opened the door and said: 'We can bear any news, Father, if it is not death.' 'It is not death,' was the reply.

At this point in her writing, a poignant marginal note reads:

Here I would like to say that Éamon, though only two-and-a-half, said 'Tá Daidí imithe, ach tiocfaidh sé ar ais arís' (Daddy is gone but he will return). When she heard him say this, Josephine O'Sullivan said: 'Out of the mouths of babes and sucklings.'

A short time after the news of the reprieve, I got a letter from Dev from prison. He told me I could visit and bring two others with me. I think he mentioned Bee, but she said it would be better to take the children, Viv, aged five and Máirín, four. When we arrived at the prison gate, another women was there with her children. She looked poor and may have been of the vagrant class. When she was asked by the man at the gate what was the sentence, 'A fortnight,' was the reply. Then it was my turn. 'What sentence?' 'Penal servitude for life.' I remember the look on the man's face. We were brought in and poor Dev appeared at the grating wearing prison dress. There was a warder present, and when we began the conversation in Irish, the warder said that he could not allow us to continue in that language.

About a month before Máirín's fourth birthday, Dev had bought her a doll's pram. At the same time, he bought a toy pistol for Viv. While Dev and I were talking in the prison, he said: 'I'm sorry I could not keep my pistol for Viv.' Immediately, Viv took the toy pistol from his pocket. 'Right,' said Dev, 'keep it and use it when the time comes.'

I promised Dev to be a mother and father to the children until his return. I had the opportunity of fulfilling this promise for many a day, although the children were too young to understand the significance of the parting. When I look back over my long life, I marvel at the wonderful disinterested kindness I have received. I could write volumes on the neighbourly, friendly attitude of many, many people, even those of different religious and political creeds.

I think it was Msgr Dunne who told me I would find many friends. When Dev was in Mountjoy, he was anxious to recover some pen he had lost or mislaid, or which had been taken from him. Msgr Dunne told me to ask Canon Waters, then chaplain to Mountjoy, about the pen. When I was speaking to Canon Waters, I told him I had a letter from Fr Byrne in Rockwell in which he, Fr J. Byrne, said he was proud of Dev. 'It's a shame for him,' said the canon. Still, he was kind to me and gave Dev a copy of *The Imitation of Christ*. I got into the tram one day while the executions were going on. Mrs Wyse Power was in the tram and shouted when she saw me: 'The world is praying for him.'

The next step was to leave the house in Donnybrook and go back to father and mother in Munster Street. My friends and neighbours were extremely kind, and different people stored my furniture. I had practically no money except thirty pounds which I got when I sold Dev's motorcycle. There were generous donations sent from America and Australia, but it was later on that I received money. Mr Dix [a Protestant solicitor and an eminent member of the profession who practised under the style of H. T. Dix & Sons] asked me did I want money. He was a kind, kind friend. Tom Flanagan too, as always, was generous and likewise Mother Malachy.

Many years ago, the late Jack Bolton, solicitor, having completed some legal business with me in his office, handed me letters which my mother had written to E. R. McClintock Dix in the autumn of 1916. Dix would have been in the unionist tradition. He was a great enthusiast about the Irish language and knew my mother from their days together in the Gaelic League. He had a great affection and respect for her.

These letters are not without interest, concerning a life insurance matter and my father's will. The Mr Hughes to whom my mother refers is Frank Hughes, one of my father's closest friends since their youth, and the best man at his wedding. These letters were written only some six months after the Rising and very shortly before Ruairi's birth. They read:

> 34, Munster Street,
> Phibsoro,
> 14th Oct. 1916.

A chara dhílis, (My dear friend)

I beg you will forgive me for troubling you and not consider this letter an impertinence. I cannot call to you as it is impossible for me to get away from home at present.

Eamon had his life insured with Scottish Amicable Society and the time for paying the premium is the 13th Oct. each year. I wrote to the Gentlemen with whom he insured and who is a great friend of his asking would I send on the money. He replied and said that he was not quite sure, till he made enquiries whether Eamon's connection with the Rising would affect his policy. The Secretary wrote to him, as you will see by the enclosed letters and said as far as the Society was concerned the Policy was alright. But Mr. Hughes, Eamon's friend, wants to be clear on another point. If Eamon died before his release from prison would the Government have any claim on the money coming under the Policy? Would you be able to answer this question for me? I hope it is a very remote possibility that Eamon should not live to be free again but Mr. Hughes is a very careful, far-seeing man and wants to be clear on every point.

I hope you will forgive me for writing to your office.

Things are a bit strained here as the baby wants so much looking after and I cannot go out for any length of time.

You have always been so kind to me that I venture to trouble you again. I don't know if you heard my sister died on the 30th August. I hope le congnamh Dé, the Trials will soon be all over. Tá súil agam go bhuil tú féin agus do bhan go han-maith. (I hope you and your wife are very well).

Le meas an-mhór (With great esteem),

Sinéad de Valera

(P.S.): I hope it will not be too much trouble for you to reply to me and return enclosed letters, please forgive me for being such a nuisance. I feel ashamed to worry you so often.

34, Munster Street,
Phibsoro,
15th Oct. 1916.

A chara dhílis, (my dear friend)

I am very grateful indeed for your prompt reply to my letter and for all the trouble you are taking on my bchalf. I shall send on the money to Mr. Hughes. Eamon made a sort of Will but I don't know if it would be sufficient. He simply wrote that he bequeath all he possessed including the Policy of his Life Insurance to me and he got two friends to put their signatures to it.

I shall not attempt to thank you for your kindness. All I can do is to ask the kind God to specially bless all the kindly Gaels who have been so kind to me.

Thanks so much for thinking of sending the machine[1]. Do not trouble for the present please I cannot do anything for a few weeks.

Le Míle Buidheachas agus mór-mheas. (A thousand thanks and great esteem)

Sinéad de Valera

---

1. It is not now known to what she is referring when she mentions 'the machine'.

34, Munster Street,
Phibsoro,
27th Oct. 1916.

A chara dhílis, (my dear friend)

The address of the Insurance Agent is Mr. Hughes, Kiltimagh, Co. Mayo.

He is an old friend of Eamon's. They were at Blackrock together and have been close friends ever since.

When the time came for paying the premium this year I wrote to Mr. Hughes and received in reply the letter which you have seen. After hearing from you I sent on the amount of the Premium £18 and this morning I received the official receipt.

In the meantime I wrote to Eamon in Dartmoor and asked him about the Will. I hope I have not made a mistake in bringing the Insurance business before the Prison Authorities. I thought Eamon might get permission to write a special letter to me but I have not heard from him since. I hope it will be alright.

I shall not attempt to thank you – all I hope is that your goodness is rewarded in itself.

Le meas an-mhór (With great esteem).

Sinéad de Valera.

(P.S.): I shall not write to Kiltimagh acknowledging receipt till I know if you wish to communicate to Mr. Hughes.

A perusal of these letters demonstrates Mother's attention to detail and her decided business acumen, notwithstanding the traumas and worries of the time. It is also refreshing to note how quickly and so willingly Dix complied with her requests and furnished the advice she needed. He proved himself a true friend.

Mother's record continues:

Bee was terribly good to me all this time. As soon as we could set things up, I went back to Munster Street. Dev and Thomas Ashe were together on the boat going over to England, and I think it was Ashe who said: 'I wonder why you and I were spared.' Ashe's later tragic death evoked much sympathy and indignation. Here let me remark that at the time of the Rising, there did not seem to be many in sympathy with 'The Rebels'. Too many were regarded with hostility and some had for them a contemptuous pity.

In May, I left Donnybrook. Bee had Brian in her arms and poor Punguar sat quietly on my lap as the tram moved along. Kitty took the three children to Balbriggan where Aunt Kate welcomed them and gave them a place in her little home. She and Kitty kept them until Dev's return in June of 1917.

The year 1916 was a hard one for the Flanagan family. Mary [my mother's sister], after a very long and painful illness, died of cancer on 30 August. It was my first experience of the death of a loved one. She had always been like a mother to me, though only eight years my senior. Father's fine mind had been failing from the time he suffered a stroke. Sometimes he got the strangest ideas. It was sad to see his clear judgement and huge memory becoming dull and clouded. I worshipped him as a child. I fear poor mother did not get all the devotion she merited. For Father, it might be said, that 'Blessed are they that hunger and thirst after justice for they shall have their fill', and of Mary 'Blessed are they who mourn for they shall be comforted.' For Mother, 'Blessed are the meek for they shall possess the land.

Poor Ruairi came into the world at a hard time. He was born in Munster Street on 3 November 1916 about 7.30 a.m. Mother and Miss Mooney were the godparents.

Dr Tuohy [father of the greatly gifted and tragic artist Patrick Tuohy RHA] and Nurse Mooney were very kind. When I asked Dr Tuohy for his fee, he danced around the room and said: 'My fee, my fee! And these poor fellows dying for us!' How kind everyone was. Jack Barrett, Dev's friend, sent toys from England at Christmas, and I could have set up a shop with the matinee coats that came for Ruairi. Ruairi was named after Roger Casement who was executed before his birth on 3 August.

Here is something for which I will always thank Dev. He used to give my mother the Christmas turkey. From prison, he said that a fee which he was to receive for setting an examination paper was to be spent on Mother's turkey. Poor little soul, she was very near death at the time. She died on 11 January 1917, just four months after Mary's death. Poor Brian and Ruairi were hard to rear under the circumstances. Father's mind was now much impaired, and he did not seem to fully realise what was happening.

In June, we got word that prisoners were coming home. I must digress here to tell of the release of the prisoners from Frongoch, those who had been sentenced for their part in the Rising. Shortly before Christmas, I was upstairs in Munster Street when I saw Dick Cotter passing the window. Dick told me afterwards that when in prison, he asked the English soldiers what was de Valera's fate, but they would not tell him. Almost everyone thought that he must have been executed. Seoirse Irvine wrote home from prison that he was sorry for all, but most of all for Sinéad and the little children.

The release of the men from Frongoch put new spirit into the people. The executions had evoked sympathy, and by the time the Frongoch prisoners arrived, this feeling had grown. The morning they returned, I was waiting at home with the two babies, Brian and Ruairi. Poor father hardly knew what was going on. A short time before Dev arrived, a young man who lived opposite knocked at the door and said: 'Mr de Valera is coming over the bridge!' Fr Tom Roche had taken Dev away from the crowd and brought him home in a cab. The prisoners received a tumultuous welcome. How easily crowds are swayed. Not more that a year before, the crowds had jeered and mocked as the prisoners were being led into captivity. Dev looked odd in the prison clothes. There were marks of bug bites on his hands.

Father often spoke to us of the momentous week during which the fighting had taken place. His battalion, the third, was like the others in the Republican Army, grossly under-strength, chiefly because MacNeill had called off the Rising and in so doing caused confusion regarding mobilisation. Father told us of the Volunteer's poor and inadequate equipment, depending for the most part on obsolete German Mausers (the Howth Guns) which dated back to the Franco-Prussian War of 1870. I remember him laughing as he described the kick when one of these weapons was fired. He said it was like the kick of a mule. Some of the Volunteers had even less effective weapons, including pikes. To add to their difficulties, they were woefully short of ammunition and explosives. A further difficulty was the shortage of officers due to the confusion caused by MacNeill's orders; Father had to make field promotions.

At his headquarters in Bolands Bakery, Father became aware of the danger posed by the nearby distillery buildings which overlooked his position. The distillery's tower could command a field of fire over his positions and therefore could be used by the enemy with devastating effects. As he did not have enough men to take it, he devised a clever rouse to fool the British forces. He and a small group of his men climbed the distillery tower and hoisted a pike bearing the green flag with a harp at its centre. As he climbed the metal ladder on the outside of the tower, he exposed himself in clear silhouette to continuous fire, both sniper and otherwise. Strangely, when he told us this story, he always emphasised that his greatest fear was not of the bullets which whizzed past him but of height, for he suffered from vertigo. He also remarked that he found some difficulty in stepping on the rungs of the ladder due to his eyesight, which even then was by no means perfect. His task accomplished, he and his companions descended and retreated to the comparative safety of the bakery.

The British gunboat *Helga* (afterwards the first ship in the Irish naval service, re-named *Muirchú*) was on the Liffey. It immediately opened fire on the distillery, particularly the tower. Father always paid warm tribute to the accuracy of the gunners on *Helga*, describing graphically how the shells burst down the face of the tower. When telling this story, he held up the index finger of his right hand, imitating how the shells struck and exploded in regular pattern down the length of the tower. He diversionary trick had worked without suffering a single casualty.

Apart from the epic battle in Mount Street, my father still awaited the main assault, notwithstanding that his battalion's position was under constant sniper and other fire. Yet he was consolidating his position and the ground held in his battalion's hands.

Michael Malone was a lieutenant in my father's battalion. Father told me that he gave Malone his prized gun, a Mauser pistol, a very powerful and accurate weapon and the only truly effective one his battalion possessed. His reason for this was that he had given Malone orders to set up an outpost guarding the route which the British forces were expected to take when coming from Dun Laoghaire. Outposts were set up at the junction of Haddington Road and Northumberland Road, with another in Clanwilliam House guarding the bridge across the canal. In all, there were only a total of fourteen men in these outposts, with Lieutenant Malone and his colleague, James Grace, occupying 25 Northumberland Road.

On Wednesday 26 April, a large column of British soldiers, two battalions of the Sherwood Foresters, some 2,000 men, approached. Almost half this number came into sight along Northumberland Road. As they came forward, furious fighting broke out. For hours the battle raged until Malone fell dead, although his colleagues managed to escape. The casualties inflicted on the British were truly horrific especially from such a tiny, poorly equipped Irish contingent. The British suffered four officers killed and fourteen wounded, and in other ranks some 216 killed or wounded. There can be little doubt that, in the hands of Lieutenant Malone, my father's gun had been responsible for the greater number of casualties. Father told me that when he himself was captured, the British officers simply would not believe him that they had no machine guns, so effective was the fire. The truth is that the entire Republican forces had not a single machine gun among them. The casualties inflicted at Mount Street amounted to approximately half the total of British casualties in the Rising.

Lieutenant Michael Malone's tremendous courage and devotion to duty goes down as one of the greatest individual acts of bravery ever displayed in Irish arms. Had he been a British soldier, he would have been posthumously awarded the Victoria Cross, in the German Army the Iron Cross with diamonds, in France the Croix de Guerre or the Medal of Honour in the USA.

In 1966, during celebrations marking the fiftieth anniversary of the Rising, I regret that I did not appeal to Father to have a special medal struck for extreme bravery in battle. The first of these would have been awarded posthumously to Lieutenant Michael Malone, 3rd Battalion, Irish Volunteers.

In later years, the Mauser was returned to Father. Still more recently, I had the honour of presenting it to the National Museum, together with Cathal Bruagha's .45 Smith & Wesson and Christy Cruise's .45 Webley. There these weapons remain as a testament to glorious days in the fight for Irish freedom.

Notwithstanding the epic battle which was taking place at Mount Street, my father awaited the main assault and his position was under continuous fire. He continued to consolidate his position, and by the Friday, he had had no proper sleep for five days. (During the emergency 1939-1945 when on duty on the border at a time of 'stand to' at Christmas 1940, Ruairi had not slept for sixty-two hours.) When telling us this story, he stressed that he had to will himself to remain alert. He knew too well so much depended on him and him alone.

When Father and his battalion first occupied Bolands Bakery, much had to be done to make it a suitably defendable position. He, like my mother, was extremely fond of animals. If he heard of an animal being cruelly treated, he showed emotion to a point of near anger. Upon occupying their position, they found many horses there belonging to the bakery. Horse transport was then the main mode of transport, as it was in my boyhood and later, for almost all bakery vans were then horse-drawn vehicles. These animals were one of his main concerns, and he managed to have them fed and watered. Later, when the supply of fodder ran out, he gave orders that the horses be set free. But his concern did not end there. The dogs and cats home was nearby, and these animals were also released when it was discovered that there was no one to feed them.

Father was deeply surprised when he received orders to surrender from his commanding officers, Commandant General Pearse and Commandant General McDonagh. As communications were poor and disjointed, he had no real idea of what was happening beyond his own particular command, although he often emphasised that he was satisfied that positions were holding, indeed he claimed that it was expanding. Thus his great surprise that he was ordered to surrender. Indeed he thought it was a trick and insisted on further confirmation of the orders. He often described how his men were so disgusted that they threw their arms on the ground in protest. In compliance with his orders, he surrendered to

Captain Hitzen and marched at the head of his men as he led them away to incarceration in the RDS show grounds. He himself was brought to the Pembroke fire station where a British corporal suggested that he might escape. But Father was well aware of this old ruse: a bullet in the back as the prisoner 'tried to escape'.

The surrender to Captain Hitzen had its sequel. Father was President when the fiftieth anniversary of the Rising was celebrated in 1966. He arranged personally that Captain Hitzen, by then an old man, should be among the specially invited guests of honour. As part of the celebration, there was a remembrance at Bolands Mill, but the weather (so unlike the weather during the Rising) had turned nasty and there was very heavy rain. It had been planned that the function should take place in the open, but when the rain came down so heavily, Father called out to his former comrades in arms and the assembled company: 'Take cover' (by which he meant all were to move indoors). He added: 'That's an order... and it also applies to you Captain Hitzen.' The captain smiled broadly and obeyed immediately. The two men spent a pleasant time together reminiscing about the battle and the Rising then so long ago.

Captain Hitzen told Vivion that his colonel was, as he described him, 'a mad man'. He failed utterly to appreciate the determination and resolution of those who opposed him, thinking that his enemy was a mere bunch of untrained peasants, amateurs who could be quickly overcome. He ordered wave after wave of his soldiers forward, only to be mown down by the resolute and accurate fire of the Volunteers. The captain paid the warmest tribute to the valour of the Volunteers against such tremendous odds.

Towards the end of 1947, in my early days as a solicitor, I acted for two separate clients, each of whom had served in my father's battalion in Bolands Mill. The first was a cheery little man with a smiling face and strong Dublin accent. He told me that he arrived at Bolands Mill 'with his Howth gun and his horse and cart to fight the British Empire!' When he said this, he did so with a chuckle of satisfaction. He spoke of the great respect the men had for my father as their commanding officer, of his concern for each of them and of his constant vigilance throughout the fighting.

The other client, an engine driver on the Dublin South-Eastern Railway, although less jovial, was equally talkative. He expressed similar views and stressed my father's constant attention to all that was happening during those fateful days. He said that the men held my father somewhat in awe but that all had complete confidence in his leadership. He also said that he and his companions were greatly surprised when they were ordered to surrender.

Although I saw these men on separate occasions, it is interesting to note that both commented upon seeing Father leading the party which climbed the distillery tower and hoist the flag. It was obvious that they both enjoyed speaking of this incident and how this trick had fooled the British.

# CHAPTER VII

*Triumph and Sorrows*
*The Tragedy of the Civil War*

In continuing her reminiscences, Mother states: 'Dev was hardly home when he was selected as an MP for Clare. The Sinn Féin party, as they were now called, had already won an election in Longford.'

The contest was between the old Parliamentary Party and Sinn Féin. The vacancy in Clare was caused by the death of Willie Redmond who was killed in the war. Before this, Willie and his brother John had been Parnellites, but most of the Parliamentary Party, who still sat in Westminster, were against the Rising. Dev got a wonderful reception in Clare. I remember the look of him coming home with a bouquet, so young and buoyant. Patrick Lynch was his opponent and the election was held on 10 July 1917. Dev won by a great majority.

I remember the nuns in Greystones voted. Poor old Sr Rose was rather pro-British in sentiment and I believe she said to some of the nuns: 'I think you voted for Sinn Féin,' but her own sympathies were all with what she called 'the poor policemen'.

Bee and Dick came back to Munster Street and as there were too many of us in the house, Dev began searching for a home for us. In September 1917 we went to live at Kinlin Road, Greystones. Dev put 'Cragh Liath' as the name on the house. [Cragh Liath — grey rock, situated about two miles north of Killaloe, was the home of the fairy Aibell.] The children came home and we were all together again, but not for long. In the autumn of 1918, the terrible flu spread through the country while Dev was in prison in England. It struck so suddenly and was a terrible scourge. Bee had been down in Greystones with us and we went to see her off at the railway station. When we came home, I noticed Viv looking pale. One by one, the children took the sickness. I think Molly, the maid, was the last to get it. Emer was only something over two months old. If I had got it, I think some of us would have died. Thank God everyone recovered, though I had no doctor or help of any kind. Doctors and nurses were themselves overworked. The danger was from the patient getting up too soon.

I recall Uncle Larry telling us that during the height of the flu, he counted no less than eighteen funerals in the space of about twenty minutes making their way towards Glasnevin Cemetery.

To return to my mother's memories, she says:

> The Sinn Féin movement was gaining strength at the time. One fact that largely contributed to this was the threat of conscription. There were people who had nothing to do with the Sinn Féin movement and yet did not want to fight in the war. A remarkable meeting took place in Maynooth at this time where the bishops were in session. Dev, Tim Healy and John Dillon met the bishops and got them to make a pronouncement against conscription.

Although the British establishment realised that it would be utter folly to proceed with conscription, it obviously feared the growing strength and influence of the Sinn Féin movement and so concocted a mythical 'German plot' which had no foundation in fact. This deceitful move also gave them the excuse to make more arrests. Mother takes this up in her account when she says:

> One night in May 1918, I was waiting for Dev to come home on the last train. Some time about 11:30, I heard footsteps coming up the path to the hall door. I knew they were too heavy to be Dev's. When I opened the door, a party of policemen was outside. They came in to search through Dev's papers, and when I asked whether he had been arrested, the reply was: 'Yes, he is in military custody now.' The next morning, I was terribly frightened when I saw the newspaper heading: 'Drastic Measures and a German Plot'.

In Greystones there was no one to whom I could go for advice or consolation. I will always be grateful to Mary Sullivan for calling in that evening and saying that, in her opinion, there would be no executions. It appears that Dev, Griffith, Darrell, Figgis and others were all arrested on the way home and placed on board a ship for England. Another friend, Mrs Figgis, called a short time after the arrest and said the prisoners were in the Tower of London. Although this was not the case, it was not consoling news to me. Dev had been on his way home when John O'Connell, the guard on the train, came to him and said: 'They're after you.'

Sergeant Turnbull (the local RIC sergeant) was among the policemen who came to the house that night. He asked me to show him Dev's bedroom, which I think was an excuse to get a private word with me. He said he was very sorry for what he had to do. I believe he was. Mary Cooper, my cousin from England, was staying with me at the time, and the policemen thought that the Countess Markievicz was in the house, hence the raid.

Aunt Kate, my helper of helpers, died on 22 June 1918. Emer was born on 15 August 1918, a Tuesday morning, at about seven o'clock. Two of our children were born while their father was in prison. May Stewart and Dick Cotter were the godparents. I remember Dev's letter from prison: 'I am glad Máirín has a sister. My wishes have prevailed this time.' Dev escaped from Lincoln Prison on 3 February 1919.

Father's escape from Lincoln Prison is truly of epic proportions, worthy of some great fictional adventure, but the story is factual. Only the main facets of this intriguing tale need be told here. For a more detailed chronicle, the reader is referred to the official biography of my father by Thomas P. O'Neill and the Earl of Longford.

Father wanted to escape to cause the greatest possible embarrassment to the British government, knowing this would attract world-wide attention. He could not organise such an escape without planning and co-operation from persons outside the prison, nor was he in any way wanting in this regard, for he had the dedicated, loyal and expert services of Michael Collins, Harry Boland and others. Michael Collins used the code name 'Field' for these operations.

Father's plan was to get his hands on a master key. He regularly served mass in the prison chapel and knew that the chaplain left a number of keys in the sacristy while saying mass. His plan involved using candle-wax from the butts of used candles in a tobacco tin, provided by one of his fellow prisoners. (I often pulled his leg by remarking that it was just as well that all the prisoners were not as opposed to smoking as he was, otherwise there would have been no tobacco box!) During mass one day, he deliberately omitted to carry out the cruets for the wine and water and made an excuse to return to the sacristy. He then returned to the chapel, with the keys concealed.

The only way of making the wax malleable was to either hold it against his body or create friction with his hands. When he told this story, he often stressed that it was very difficult, but it worked. When he pressed the key into the wax, an impression was made. The next step was to make a carefully measured drawing on a piece of paper which he cut out to the exact measurements.

The question now arose as how he would transmit this impression to the outside world. This too was accomplished, and a key was made and sent into the prison inside a cake. (In the meantime, Collins and Boland were in regular touch by various clever means.) He found the key in the cake, which had successfully passed security. But when tried, to his horror, it broke. The operation was repeated as before, and again the cake passed through security. (Incidentally, he said the cake contained plaster of Paris which he thought was icing and being so hungry he took a mouthful and quickly realised his mistake.)

The second key was also a failure: it was too small and not a master key as planned. This was a tremendous set-back but, undaunted, the formula was repeated, with coded contacts passing to Collins and Boland. The third key arrived by similar means and again passed security. This time, it worked like a dream. The escape was on.

Further coded messages passed, and the time and date were fixed, with Collins and Boland travelling to England to make the necessary arrangements. Just before my father was to make his move, signals were passed by Boland flashing an electric torch. Father answered from the prison by putting a number of matches together and lighting them to make a small flash. He and two companions made off, opening the doors one by one until they reached the outside gate. Here Boland put a key in from the other side. It broke, but Father did not panic and succeeded in pushing it out from the other side. Father used his own key, the gate opened and they were free.

In his usual expert fashion, Collins had arranged the line of escape and the hiding places. Along the escape route, Boland was wearing a fur-lined coat and pretended to be my father's 'girl'. They travelled past a number of soldiers who were courting some girls, and therefore too engrossed to take much notice.

Eventually, Father made his way back to Ireland to stay with Dr Farnan. The Irish people were ecstatic at the news of the escape and he became a national hero. The news spread far and wide.

Before leaving the story of the escape from Lincoln Prison, I have one great regret. When my father was President, it became a tradition for the entire family, all three generations, to spend Christmas day in Áras an Uachtaráin. One year after dinner, we all assembled in the drawing room. I had bought a new tape-recorder and asked Father to relate the story of his escape for the benefit of the third generation and to his own children who had heard it several times before. He said that he would be glad to do so and gathered the family around him in a semi-circle, the third generation sitting around him on the floor. A nephew had expressed interest in tape-recorders and said he would take charge of the recording. I don't think Father knew that he was being recorded at that time, but he would not have minded as the recording was purely for family purposes. He was in great form and told the story well, even acting his part when he pretended to be a somewhat tipsy Australian soldier linking arms with his girl and imitating the Australian accent. When he finished, he returned to his study. I dashed to the recorder, excited that I had recorded a real gem. To my utter consternation and disgust, the record button had not been pressed and thus was lost a precious piece of history.

After his escape, Father had to remain in hiding for some time and was unable to attend Laurence Flanagan's funeral. Laurence Flanagan died in Balbriggan on 12 March 1919. He was eighty-three. My mother makes the following reference in her reminiscences: 'I remember I was speaking to Mick Collins the day after Father died, and he said he was sorry he could not go to the funeral.'

There is another story which I heard Father tell concerning his time in Lincoln jail. He was there at the time of the armistice on 11 November 1918. The prison chaplain, an Anglican clergyman, had become friendly with Father and often visited him in his cell. He came as usual on 11

November. Father had already heard the church bells ringing to mark the occasion. As Father and the chaplain were discussing the armistice and what the end of the war would mean, the chaplain suddenly burst into tears. He said that he had lost a son in the war. Father was moved by his grief and put his arms around the sobbing chaplain in an effort to console him. In a strange way, the relationship of prisoner and chaplain had interchanged.

In Mother's record, she makes a further reference to Father's escape from Lincoln.

> There was great excitement at the time of Dev's escape. It was reported that I had got a letter from him which, of course, was not true. A film man called at the house to ask me to pose for a picture reading this letter, with the children around me. Of course, I refused... While Dev was still in hiding, Mick Collins and Harry Boland brought him down to Greystones one night. The children did not know Dev was in the house. He was shut up in the dining room. I remember little Brian and Ruairi asking me: 'Are you bringing coffee to the gentlemen in the dining room?'

It was at this time that Mother's friend, Alice Milligan, wrote a poem commemorating Father's escape from Lincoln Prison. In this work, she is remembering the part which my mother took in the play *Red Hugh*, comparing Father's escape with Red Hugh's escape from Dublin Castle on Christmas Eve 1592, to hide amid deep snow in the Wicklow Mountains.

Merely Players
To S... a memory of a tableaux and a play by Alice Milligan

Memory holds a girlish picture of you,
Kneeling with a Celtic Cross above you,
Under the saintly Brigid's cloak of blue,
Innocent and fair to all beholders,
With your rippling hair about your shoulders,
When we staged the drama of Red Hugh.

So when came your hour of heaviest sorrow,
Words of mine your prayerful lips could borrow,

Prayer for such deliverance as he knew,
Who from Dublin on a night of snowing,
Fled with his companion onward going,
Over hills and vales of Wicklow through.

And of late St Brigid's Feast Day found you,
With your little children clustering 'round you,
Nigh those hills that sheltered our Red Hugh,
Did you dream then, err a day departed,
You would smile exultant, happy, hearted,
And the whole sad land rejoice with you?

Mother has added a footnote stating: 'This poem which appeared in *New Ireland*, 8 March 1919, was dedicated to Sinéad Bean de Valera. St Brigid's Day occurs on 1 February. De Valera escaped from Lincoln Prison on 3 February 1919.'

She continues:

In May 1919, there was a big reception in the Mansion House. The word went out that it was to be banned, but Dev hurried up affairs and got three American visitors to go to the place of meeting. They were Messrs F. P. Walsh, Dunne and Ryan. Their presence evidently prevented any interference. I enjoyed the reception very much. I had gone out very little since my marriage and was delighted to meet old friends and to get such a welcome from them. Dr Fogarty, the bishop from Clare, was especially nice to me. On 1 June 1919 – my birthday – Dev left Greystones for America. Of course, he had to travel secretly. We got word that he had landed safely. I was very happy to know all was well, but poor little Máirín said: 'Oh but he is so far away'. Dev was away for a great part of the time we were in Greystones. We were there for five years. He was arrested in May 1918 and was not long home in 1919 when he went to America. When he returned from America, he was in hiding for some time. Then the Civil War broke out before we left Greystones.'

In May 1920, Harry Boland came to visit Mother in Greystones. He was anxious that she should travel to America to see Father and further thought that such a visit would help serve the national cause. My mother's immediate reaction was one of great reluctance, but as she records:

> He [Boland] said that Dev was very tired and worn out in America and that I should go to see him. The visit to America was one of the biggest mistakes I ever made. Dev himself had nothing to do with my going. He did not know until I arrived... I went to America in 1920 and travelled on a false passport [provided by Michael Collins].

In much later years, she laughed about this passport for, despite Collins' meticulous care for detail, her height was recorded as 5'10", whereas, she was about 5'4".

The record of her visit continues:

> The passport was in the name of Margaret Williams. My dear dear friend, Maire O'Connor came with me. Mick Collins carried my trunk out to the car... The outward journey was slow and I was sick for part of the time [She thought the name of the ship was the New York]. I felt lonely and sad thinking of the children at home. I was nervous and uneasy during the outward voyage. When we arrived at New York, there was a bad thunderstorm.

Mother had never considered herself a good traveller, and apart from her worries at leaving the children at home, she told us that she was in constant fear, travelling on the false passport. Harry Boland met her on her arrival in New York. She continues: 'It was a huge blunder for me to go to America. I derived neither profit nor pleasure from my visit. I am not one who is easily bored, but I had nothing really profitable to do and spent a good deal of time in the hotel.' Notwithstanding her boredom and loneliness, she goes on: 'The people in America were very kind; their generosity is great.'

Father was greatly surprised to learn of Mother's arrival and the pair saw little of each other. Father was heavily engaged in serious strife with John Devoy and Judge Daniel Cohalan (both active in the Irish cause) and had to attend a multitude of meetings. One writer has stated that Father told Mother that 'her place was at home with the children'. This statement is absurd, wantonly malicious and without a scintilla of truth.

Mother stayed in America for some six weeks and frequently remarked that this time was 'the longest and least profitable part of her life'. Following, what seemed to her, to be an interminable length of time, the thorny problem arose as to how she would get home. Her notes continue:

> Now how was I to get home? We went to stay with Dev's mother in Rochester for a short time, and with Dev's cousin Lib and her husband. It was arranged that we should go home by Canada, but when we arrived at Montreal, we could not get accommodation at a hotel. We stayed at a house where the woman spoke French only. I look back on that night with a sort of weird feeling. I had a horrible nightmare. After all the planning it was decided that I should return on the passport on which I came. We left Quebec in early October.'

Mother told us that as the ship set sail for Europe, the unfriendly ocean contained many icebergs which seemed, not the glistening ice she had expected, but a menacing bluish hue. She and her generation had vivid memories of the loss of the Titanic only a few years before and all the horrors of that tragedy. Although she was filled with joy at coming home, the return journey was almost as unpleasant as the outward voyage and was full of anxieties.

Mother's record on her return to Ireland states: 'When we arrived at Dun Laoghaire, there were a number of cab-men there. The morning was wet and the men were wearing sou'westers. My nerves were in such a state that I thought the men were policemen (ready to arrest me, I suppose). We went to Mrs Barry's house in Dun Laoghaire.' She then travelled on to Greystones.

While Mother was in the USA, Dick and Bee Cotter stayed in Greystones. They were looking after the family when the sack of Balbriggan took place.

The sack of Balbriggan, although only one of many outrages perpetrated by the crown forces in 1920, attracted widespread indignation, not only in Ireland but also in America. My mother's brother Larry, her sister Kitty and husband Andy were involved.

A number of Black and Tans had been drinking in a public house when a quarrel broke out. Shots were fired, and one Black and Tan was shot dead and another wounded. There was no evidence as to who had fired the shots. Later that night, a large party of British forces called Auxiliaries, based at Gormanstown Camp about three miles away, came into the town and carried out merciless beatings and attacks on the civilian population.

John Derham, a member of Balbriggan Town Council, saw two young men lying dead in the street having been bayoneted to death by the British troops. Another lay dying in the local barracks. The British forces then proceeded to put the torch to the houses and shops. Twenty-five houses were destroyed, and the smaller of the hosiery factories was likewise burnt out. As a child, I remember seeing the ruins of this factory with some of the rusty machinery lying open to the sky.

The townspeople fled in terror, hiding in ditches and barns. My two uncles and Aunt Kitty had to flee for their lives as their premises too were sacked. Larry was very lame, with one leg considerably shorter than the other following a fall from a bridge as a boy. This leg never developed properly and he had to walk with the aid of a crutch. He was saved by being hidden behind a wall. He said himself that he was thrown over the wall, landing heavily on the other side, but this action saved his life; otherwise he too would have been the victim of the British forces' bayonets.

I heard Larry tell another story of this period. One day he was sitting in a tram, the Black and Tans stopped the vehicle and made all passengers stand while they searched them. When it came to his turn, a Black and Tan, seeing the crutch, put his hand on his shoulder and in a raw English accent said: 'Sit down, chum'. He thought that Larry had been a soldier in the war. At that point, the man sitting beside Larry slipped a revolver under Larry's bottom. The Black and Tans did not notice this. Little did the Black and Tans know Larry's real sympathy for the Irish cause and how he had served it so faithfully, despite his disability.

My cousin, Don Cotter, told me another story about Larry. Passing a group of British soldiers one day, he saw one of them kick a dog viciously. Larry could not contain his indignation and lashed out with his crutch, knocking the soldier to the ground. The soldier got the message and no further action was taken, nor did the military attempt any retaliation.

The sack of Balbriggan was discussed in the House of Commons where Sir Hamar Greenwood said: 'I myself have had the fullest investigation in this case. I will tell the House what I found. I found that 100 to 150 men went to Balbriggan and were determined to avenge the death of their popular comrade, shot and murdered in cold blood. I find it is impossible, out of that 150, to find the man who did the burning. I have yet to find one authenticated case of a member of the Auxiliary Division being accused of anything but the highest conduct, so characteristic of them.'

So much for Sir Hamar's 'investigation', so reminiscent of similar 'investigations' and 'inquiries' which had taken place in more modern times in the North of Ireland, showing that in Ireland so far as the British establishment is concerned history and methods do indeed repeat themselves.

Mother recalled Father's return from America:

> Dev came home at Christmas time 1920 and was in hiding at Dr Farnans, then at Mrs McGarry's house in Sandymount. I think it was Christmas Eve 1920 that Sinead Mason [Mrs Derrig] came to Greystones to tell me that Dev was home and that she was taking me back to see him at Dr Farnans.

She continues:

> In July 1921, the truce was proclaimed. Dev met me in Dublin one day to come home with me to Greystones. 'I have a letter from Lloyd George in my pocket,' said he. The months of the truce were happy ones, but I think that the truce broke the fighting spirit. The negotiations between our people and England began. Griffith, Collins, Duggan, Barton and Gavin Duffy were the plenipotentiaries. Dev was in Limerick early in December 1921 and was presented with a facsimile of the monument to the Treaty of Limerick. He was present at a concert or assembly of some kind on the evening of 6 December and did not know the Treaty was about to be signed. When I read the paper next day and saw the oath, I was very sad. It seemed to me as if the Wicklow hills had a reproachful look. I prayed that the Treaty

would not remain in the form which it was.

I was speaking to Fr Rafter that day and he said afterwards that I did not seem to be elated. Most people were highly pleased, although Greystones was not, of course, a strong national place. Viv came home from school one day shortly before his eleventh birthday and read the paper. 'Mammy,' said he, 'is this good? Surely Mick [Michael Collins] wouldn't take anything that wasn't good.' Even to his young mind, the terms did not seem right. Bee was more astute than I. 'It is partition' was her verdict. When Dev came home that night, he asked me what I thought of the Treaty. 'Everyone else seems pleased but I don't like it' was my reply.

Christmas 1921 was not a happy one. Dev was very anxious and tense. Molly Brien, the maid, went to England to visit her sister in the beginning of the New Year and it was almost impossible to get another maid. Perhaps the fact that I had to look after the house and the family kept me from worrying too much about the Treaty. The months that followed were not pleasant. The people were anxious for peace, but there were many who did not regard the Treaty as peace. I remember when Dev first made a protest, Seoirse Irvine wrote to me and said: 'Thank God for Dev and the words he said.' The feelings were growing on both sides and there were bitter speeches in the Dáil. It was like the Parnellites and the Anti-Parnellites time… Here I will give it as my personal opinion that the latter spirit may be healed more quickly than the earlier one, I think in years to come, people will be glad to say they were anti-Treaty.

The days that followed the fighting in the Four Courts were the saddest of all. After this, fighting between the two parties became general throughout the country. The bitterness increased. I could scarcely believe the news when I heard that three young men had been executed. On 2 December 1922, Erskine Childers was executed. It was terrible to think that men who had worked so well together should now be enemies. Later, Seán Hales and Padraig O'Malley were shot by the anti-Treaty forces, that is the Republican side. The next day 8 December 1922, Ruairi O'Connor, Dick McKelvey and Joe Barrett were executed as reprisals.

Shortly after the Four Courts, Dev went away. Agnes Culhane brought me a letter from him saying he knew I would be brave. I don't know so much about the bravery — it was a compulsory thing. Those were the terrible days. The feelings between the two parties amounted to hatred. 'Galloper' Smith, Lord Berkinhead, is purported to have said 'Let the Irish fight it out among themselves.' I shall never forget my feelings when, after the Treaty, the Free State soldiers (the name for the country was the Free State – now it was gone!) raided the house in Greystones. I think it was the one who was in charge who said to me: 'I still hold that I am following Pearse.' 'I don't know how you can think that,' said I, 'and be here tonight.'

Harry Boland was killed in July 1922. His death increased the bitterness between the parties. One evening of 12 August 1922, Viv went to the village for a message, and when he came home, he said: 'Mummy, there is someone dead.' 'Wait, don't tell me,' said I. He showed great tact and quickly he said: 'It is Griffith.' A week or so afterwards on the 22nd, the butcher's boy came to the door and said 'Collins is gone."

Griffith died very suddenly. He had just said 'Good morning' to someone nearby when he dropped dead. Collins was killed in an ambush. Brian was very fond of Mick Collins and Mick was very good to me. A short time after his death, Brian asked: 'Did Mick know I wasn't a Free Stater?' The poor little lad (seven years old at the time) did not want anyone to know that there was any difference between them. As a girl, I had a great admiration for Griffith. Mick, too, was a friend of mine. All war is bad but civil war is dreadful.

Mother's account of these harrowing times continues:

From the Four Courts' time – the summer of 1922 on – the war continued. Noel Lemass was found dead on Featherbed Mountain. Towards the end of its time, Dev was staying at 11 Mount Street and I visited him there.

Nellie Oates, the maid, came to me one day and said: 'Here comes an ambulance with a priest and a doctor. Don't be frightened.' The priest was poor Fr Albert and the doctor was Lar Flanagan. I cannot think what brought them to us in an ambulance but I suppose it was a sure way of travelling. At the time I was anxious to return to Dublin, but it was impossible to get a house. Fr Albert, who was such a wonderful friend all the time, came to see me in Greystones. It was through his influence that Francis O'Sullivan came to see me and her sister, Miss Finnegan, settled our great difficulty by buying a house in Claremount Road, Sandymount, and taking us as tenants. We, the seven children and I, came back to Dublin in November 1922. While I was changing house, my friends came to my aid. During the morning, the O'Donnells took Viv and Éamon; Agnes Culhane took Máirín and Emer; and Bee took Brian. But Ruairi said: 'I have no taste for visiting.' Myself and Terry, who was only four months old, arrived at Claremount Road on the morning of 2 November. Ruairi had his sixth birthday next day. What wonderful friends we had!

One evening while I was upstairs, a raiding party rushed in. One of them came up and asked: 'How many men do you have in the house?' 'Na buachaillí,' [the boys] said I. He looked very angry but evidently understood what I had said. He then said in English (the Irish had knocked him out a bit) 'How many?' 'Cuigear acha,' [five of them] said I, refusing to speak English. He looked through the books and it seemed as if he would take some. 'Ní bhaineann sé sin leis an lá innu,' [They don't apply to today] said I. He did not take any books but as he was going away, he said: 'Tell Eamon to beware!' I continued in Irish until they left. I made it a rule then with the children that they were to speak only in Irish when the raiders came. I was terribly indignant another time to see a young and seemingly untrained soldier laughing when I spoke Irish as if it were a joke. This was the saddest time of all, being raided by our own people.

Another night in Claremount Road, we were awakened by a loud knocking at the door. The raiders were very discourteous at first, but when they were going, one said 'Is mór an trua é.' [It is a great pity.] 'Sea,' arsa mise, [Yes, said I] 'agus is mór an naíre é' [and great is the shame].

The house was raided one night while Dev and one or two others were there but they were not found. I visited Dev when he was staying in Mount Street. Miss McKeown stayed in the house with the maid and the children while I was away. After some time, Dev sent out a cease-fire order to have the fighting ended. He was still in Mount Street and wore a beard during this time.

In the summer of 1923 (August, I think) he managed, undisguised, to leave Mount Street. As Gertie Culhane said: 'He parted with his beloved beard and succeeded in evading detection or arrest until he reached Ennis.' There was a meeting there and he, of course, was

arrested. I was in the chapel at Sandymount when I heard the shout of
'Stop Press'. A postman who met me outside said: 'Where did they get
him?' I could get no information about his whereabouts but followed
up the matter until I got a telegram from Gearoid Sullivan which said
'Eamon de Valera detained in Arbour Hill.' He was in Kilmainham for
some time and again in Arbour Hill. I hate to think of the bad feeling
there were between the two sides. At last I was allowed to see Dev: he
had not seen Terry from the time he was about three weeks old until
he was two years. In 1924, I took the seven children to Roundstone,
hoping we would hear Irish there. We heard little but the children had
two delightful months.

I heard her tell the story about an event which took place shortly before
Michael Collin's death. She had received a message from him which said:
'Send my love to Mrs Dev.' When Mother spoke of Michael Collins, which
she often did, she did so with a feeling of real gratitude and affection and
always acknowledged his daring and supreme courage. I distinctly
remember, however, her remarks when she talked of his signing the Treaty.
As always she was a shrewd judge of character, she said that the British had
found a weakness, his Achilles heel: Collins was too prone to be duped by
flattery and that the British had skilfully seized on this. She added: 'They
never succeeded in doing this with Dev or Parnell.' The latter pair had the
full measure of this cunning device. The more it was attempted, the more
they were on their guard, sensing malignant intentions.

In much later years John (Johnny) Collins, brother of Michael, came
to live in Booterstown with his family. They too became parishioners of
Booterstown church. One Sunday morning, my parents were walking to
mass, as were Johnny and his family. He crossed the road and they shook
hands, then they proceeded to church together. Johnny often called for my
mother and drove her to mass. His sons, Liam and Michael, were in
Blackrock College with me and came to play with me when we lived in
Bellevue. Liam recalled with affection coming to Bellevue when my
mother gave him lessons in oral Irish. My mother was very fond of both
Liam and Michael and said that Michael so much reminded her of his
uncle. In later years, when Michael was president of the Blackrock College
Union, he invited me to be guest of honour which I was so pleased to
receive and accept, nor has this friendship waned in the next generation.
My eldest daughter, Síle, became friends with Liam and kept in touch until

his death. Michael too is now alas dead.

Ruairi too had special memories of the time of both Collins and Boland. He recalled going with Father, Harry Boland and Michael Collins to a steep wooded place which he thought was either the Glen of the Downs or Glencullen. The three men disappeared into the wood leaving Ruairi in the car. When they returned, one of them was holding what seemed to Ruairi like a Bovril tin. He heard Boland and Collins discuss how well Father had shot the target (the box). As Ruairi records, Father was an excellent shot, whether with a shot-gun, rifle, pistol or revolver.

That night, Ruairi was allowed to stay up late. Although Father was anxious that he should go to bed, Collins protested saying: 'Only bad boys go to bed early.' When Ruairi told me this story, he said that Collins had taken him on his knee.

An instance worth recording happened during one of the raids by the Free State army. Father had a large travelling trunk which he took with him on his visits to America. It was one of those trunks with brass hinges and elaborate brass locks, which he always referred to as 'the big trunk'. In the course of the raid, the soldiers demanded that the trunk be opened. Mother looked for the keys but could not immediately put her hands on them. The soldiers would not wait and bayoneted the lock open. (Ruairi and the elder members of the family have distinct memories of raids as they lay in bed while the soldiers thrust bayonets into the mattress as they lay there.) Notwithstanding this action, my father continued to use the trunk for many years to come. As I knew it, it bore the gashes and marks on the surface when the lock was prised open. In later years, it was used to store trinkets and items of historical interest. As children, we thought it contained the treasures of the world.

Mother's references to P. H. Pearse are few but no less interesting. She described him as being shy and very conscious of what she called 'a slight cast in one eye' and of his 'somewhat lumbering gait'. She always added in a most persuasive tone of voice: 'He had a beautiful mind.'

Father seldom mentioned the Civil War, but if he did, it was with a great feeling of sorrow. He spoke to me of Liam Lynch, 'the Lionheart', of his extraordinary bravery and of his absolute commitment to the concept of the Republic. He said that Lynch 'was totally uncompromising as far as the Republic was concerned'. I remember telling him that I considered his speech on the death of Liam Lynch to be one of his finest and most deeply felt. Very quietly, he replied, with a note of sadness in his voice: 'Yes, others have said that too.' To me, it will remain one of his most eloquent. I believe that my father's words were ones of prophecy when he said of Lynch and his commitment and ideals: 'They who in ignorance calumniate you today, will tomorrow be forced to do you honour.' It was so obvious that when Father mentioned Erskine Childers, he did so with particular sorrow and the deepest sense of loss. As likewise Harry Boland.

On another occasion, I heard him remark that of all those who had taken the pro-Treaty side, he was hardest on, (and found it most difficult to forgive) were Richard Mulcahy and Ernest Blythe. Mother felt likewise, not withstanding her friendship with Blythe, which stemmed from a period many years before the Civil War.

# CHAPTER VIII

*The Spanish Connection*

As was the case with my mother, my father often spoke of his ancestors and of his days in boyhood. He reminisced fondly of his early times with his uncle and other relations in Bruree, Co. Limerick and spoke with affection of the little house which had tender memories for him.

It was at the end of 1935 and very early in 1936 that he actively pursued again his Spanish connection and took further steps to investigate this side of the family. He invoked the services of L. H. Kerney, the Irish Minister to Spain at that time. The rank of minister was in later years raised to ambassador. Minister Kerney was a close friend of my father and he remained the Irish diplomatic representative to Spain until after World War II. By his skill and devotion to duty as a diplomat, he had considerable influence in maintaining Ireland's neutrality in World War II, and this despite the odds and enormous pressure to break Irish neutrality by US or allied forces.

Kerney willingly undertook the task my father had given him and commenced investigations and in due course furnished long reports to my father concerning the progress he had made. As a major part of the enquiries Kerney was in fairly regular contact with Enrique Valera, Y Ramirez de Saavedra, the Marques de Aunon (who also had the title of the Marques Villasinda which he inherited from his mother's side on her death in 1945). The marques, whose family name is Valera, explained to Kerney that his branch of the family and some others had dropped the particle 'de' and merely used the surname Valera. The information supplied by the marques was most useful in establishing beyond doubt my father's Spanish connection. The marques himself claimed and stated that he 'had no doubt' that both he, and indeed his mother, were close relations of my father. It is of special interest to note that he was able to confirm information concerning the Spanish connection which my father had found at a much earlier date but the additional information supplied by the marques filled in some important gaps.

Originally the de Valera family were Galician, but settled in Andalucia in the early part of the twelfth century on territory re-conquered from the Moors. In the fourteenth century one Knight D. Juan Balera (old spelling for Valera) joined an expedition to fight the Moors and left Leon in the north of Spain to follow King Alfonso XI in his warfare in the south. Some people of authority in Spain claim that the (de) Valera family are descended from a Roman nobleman, Valerius, who campaigned in Spain.

The family coat of arms, which is of ancient origin, contains, *inter alia*, eight crosses. When Father was President, the Council of Nobility of Spain presented him with this coat of arms. The presentation was made by the then Spanish ambassador, Señor Juan Jose Pradera. Father was very interested in this coat of arms, adopted it and had it duly registered.

Kerney, in one of his quite lengthy reports, stated that Enrique had a discussion with Ibanez, a member of the Valera family and close relative, who at one time had been a high ranking naval officer. Ibanez had become deeply interested in the fact that one of the family had married an Irish girl in domestic service in New York and the child of that marriage, an infant boy had been sent to Ireland. He made it his business to carry out an investigation in both New York and Cuba and the marques went on to say that he had spoken to Ibanez on this subject as far back as the year 1911. Ibanez carried out investigations in New York and Cuba long before 1911. This is of particular note as these investigations and information were known to the Valera family many years before my father entered public life and thus could not have been influenced by subsequent historic events. According to the marques as reported by Minister Kerney, Ibanez died 'a number of years before the year 1936'.

The reader will have seen that contact with Enrique happened at the end of 1935 and the early part of 1936. This contact continued into February of the latter year. This was at the time of my brother Brian's sudden death and due, no doubt to this tragic event, contact with Enrique ceased and for a long period further investigation of the Spanish connection lapsed, save for one more contact in 1938 as evidenced in my father's personal pocket diary which I now possess. This loss of communication was further affected by the Spanish Civil War to be followed by World War II. With these latter events my father had many matters of vastly greater importance to which he had to attend rather than tracing his Spanish ancestors. It was to be years before he took up again the threads of his enquiries.

Enrique had hoped to meet my father in Geneva, where Father often attended as President of the League of Nations. Enrique, too, was frequently in Geneva as a Spanish diplomat. In the event, however, no such meeting ever took place. Enrique died in 1947.

In recent years I have vigorously pursued the Spanish connection and I have had the good fortune of making contact with Luis E. Valera, son of Enrique who is the present Marques de Aunon and the Marques Villasinda. We have entered into prolonged and very cordial correspondence to further establish and finally confirm the Spanish connection. The present marques, like his father and grandfather, (Luis Valera Delavat 1870-1926) is a prominent member of the Spanish diplomatic corps. He was able, not alone to confirm so much of the information given by his father to Minister Kerney, but was further in a position to provide me with a great deal of additional data, including a most important and definitive, detailed family tree going back as far as the early part of the nineteenth century, and indeed sections going back as far as the sixteenth century. He demonstrated, as the family tree shows, that both he and I had a common great-great-grandfather. This great-great-grandfather was Juan José Valera y Alcala-Gallano. He married Maria Josefa Viana and had a very large family, eleven in all. His sister, Sofia, was a very good friend of Eugenie de Montijo who married Napoleon III. Sofia joined the empress in Paris and married Aimable Pelissier, Marechal de France, who later was created Duke of Malkof. One of Juan José's children, a son, Juan Valera became one of the greatest Spanish writers of the nineteenth century and is, the marques tells me, the Charles Dickens of Spanish literature, thereby enjoying great fame in Spain and much further afield. The citizens of Dona Mencia, in the province of Cordoba, where the family established itself around the year 1520, are very proud of their connection with the Valera family. The Marques branch of the family came from the son José Valera y Viana. Another member of the family was Lorenzo Coullaut Valera (1876-1932) who was a most distinguished sculptor. My father and brother Éamon saw one of his works in Loyla and were very impressed with its excellence. He too has become famous. Minister Kerney interviewed his son, likewise a sculptor, but he seemed to have no interest in family history and was of little or no help to Kerney.

Another prominent member of the Valera family was Fernando, who was descended from the second son of José Valera and Maria Viano. Fernando was a republican and Minister for Foreign Affairs in the republican government in exile in Mexico.

My father is descended from the eighth son of Juan José and Maria J. Josefa. His name was Antonio, born in Mercia and he married Mercedes Armenteros. The couple established their residence in Seville. They had only one son, Antonio Valera y Armenteros. He was educated in Seville and for some time this son was a high ranking naval officer. The Valera family had, it seems, strong connections with the Spanish navy. Later Antonio emigrated to Cuba where he engaged himself in a lucrative business trading in sugar between the United States, Cuba and Spain, Cuba then being a Spanish possession.

Among the personal papers left by my father I found the following note:

> Don Juan de Valera – a Spanish gentleman of rank (very aristocratic in manner and distinguished in appearance – about five foot seven or eight inches and solidly built) and seems in 1880 to be between 50 and 60 years, had become associated with Cuba years before. Before the latest uprising of Cuban patriots he and his family enjoyed a large revenue from the sugar plantations (destroyed in the insurrection).

It will at once be noted that the Christian or first name of my father's grandfather is given as Juan but we now know and, as my father learned very much later, (although confirmation did not come until after his death) his first name was Antonio. Juan is of course a very common Spanish Christian name and it appears widely in use in the de Valera family often coupled with several other Christian names. We will see this in the case of his son whom he called Vivion Juan. The name Vivion, however, does not appear to have been used by any previous generations of de Valeras. The Spanish are very fond of having a string of names and so Juan almost certainly was one of Antonio's Christian names. Another of Antonio's Christian names is believed to be Ricardo.

While in Cuba, Antonio met a Spanish lady and married her. Her Christian name was Amelia and it is thought that her surname was Acosta but this was strongly denied by an aunt of Enrique Valera, the Marques de Aunon. The name Armenteros has also been said to have been her surname, but this has been confused with Armenteros Senior, wife of Antonio Senior. It could be, of course, that the lady married in Cuba, happened to have the same surname, for this is not at all that uncommon where for instance, here in Ireland you can find, say, a Kelly marrying a Kelly, although the parties are not related. There seems, however, to be the greatest doubt that her name was Acosta for the reasons stated above. While the couple had three children, the marriage was not a happy one and in time they parted. The Valera family in Spain strongly disapproved of this marriage for while the lady was very wealthy she did not belong to the nobility. There was an obvious coldness, to put it mildly, between Amelia and other members of the Valera family. She was particularly disliked by an aunt of Enrique (daughter of Juan José y Alcala-Gallano). When Kerney was speaking to this aunt, she spoke somewhat sneeringly, mentioned her maiden name which, Kerney unfortunately could not remember when he came to write his report, but he was quite certain that she stated that this was *not* Acosta. Interestingly this aunt, too, was able to confirm to Kerney the information which Ibanez had obtained years before and with which I have already dealt. Antonio and his wife had three children, Leon, Vivion Juan and a daughter Charlotte, known as Lotte. Both Leon and Charlotte died young and before my grandfather (Vivion Juan) married Kate Coll. As already stated, Antonio's marriage was not a happy one, there was a bitter quarrel, and the couple parted; Antonio leaving Cuba, taking his son with him and abandoning all his interests in Cuba, and severing all connections with the country. He then moved to the USA.

Vivion was born in Spain in 1853 and was educated on the continent. He was a gifted linguist, fluent in Spanish, French, German and English and indeed had a grasp of other languages. He was decidedly artistic and trained to be a sculptor, but when working on a piece he suffered a misfortune when a chip of marble entered an eye and from then on he abandoned sculpture and devoted himself to music. Only quite recently, additional information has come to hand. This information came directly from Kate de Valera (my father's mother). She confirms the reason why Vivion abandoned his pursuit of sculpture and turned to music. She says: 'He played a number of musical instruments with equal skill.' My father thought that he played the violin. It seems too that Vivion gave music lessons, of which I have no details. I will have much more to say of this new and additional information shortly. Vivion had a sensitive disposition. He was of slim build, not of great height and certainly he must have had small feet, for my father's mother, Kate Coll, joked that he could put on her shoes.

Antonio and his son Vivion settled in the USA. While in New York, Vivion Juan, then aged twenty-five made friends with a Dr Hogan of Henry Street and a Dr Dawson of Fifth Avenue. The former doctor must have been of Irish stock. Through his father, Vivion became friendly with a wealthy French family named Giraud who had their home in Myrtle Avenue and later in Gold Street. It was there that he met my grandmother, Catherine (Kate) Coll, who had come from Bruree, Co. Limerick. Like so many Irish people of the period she was forced to emigrate. She found employment with the Giraud family as a domestic but later as a housekeeper. The pair met in 1880 but shortly afterwards Vivion, on the advice of his father, went to Denver, Colorado for health reasons. He had never enjoyed good health. Later he returned to New York where his friendship with Kate continued. The couple continued to see each other even after Kate ceased to work for the Girauds. Kate was then working in New Jersey. The pair were married on 19 September 1881, but not in Greenville, New Jersey, as had been thought, but rather – according to recently discovered information supplied by Kate de Valera herself – in New York city 'several years after his [Vivion's] arrival in this country [the USA].' At the wedding, the best man and bridesmaid were Frederick Hamilton (a close friend of Antonio's) and Kitty Brady. Vivion was then aged twenty-eight. The officiating priest was a Fr Patrick Hennessy, who had been a native of Co. Limerick.

Sometimes the young couple called themselves by the affectionate names of Jack and Kitty. After their marriage they moved to an apartment in 61 East 41st Street, near the present site of the Chrysler Building, Manhattan, where Antonio was a regular visitor. When in New York, Antonio stayed at an apartment on 26th or 27th Street between 5th Avenue and Broadway. My father was born on 14 October 1882 at the New York and Childrens' Hospital in Lexington Avenue, situated between 51st and 52nd Street. His name was registered as George but he was baptised as Edward, which in later years he changed to the Irish form of Eamon. The name on the birth certificate was changed to Edward in 1916 at the behest of his mother when she was endeavouring to have him released from Dartmoor Prison. My father was baptised in St Agnes' church (now a place of pilgrimage for those devoted to his memory) on 3 December 1882. The godparents were Mary Shine and John Hennessy, both friends of Kate Coll, as indeed was Fr Hennessy.

As has been previously stated Vivion Juan never enjoyed good health which was apparent even before his marriage. Not long after he married Kate Coll his health deteriorated and became progressively worse. His father was greatly concerned, so much so, that he advised him to return to Colorado, where it seems, the climate suited him better. Reluctantly, Vivion took the advice and said goodbye to his wife on 30 June 1884. He did not last long, for he died in the spring of 1885. The cause of his death was a lingering lung infection, most probably tuberculosis. He wife Kate did not receive the news of his death until some six months or so later, when Frederick Hamilton, the friend of Antonio called on her to break the tragic news. Antonio had sent Hamilton as his special messenger.

Colorado at that time was still very much an outpost for the settlers and for those who had travelled to the territory. It had only become the thirty-eighth state of the union on 1 August 1876. From enquiries which I have made with the appropriate Department of the State of Colorado, I was informed that few, if any, proper records are extant or were kept of births and deaths before the year 1910. I was further informed that there is no official record of the death of Vivion Juan de Valera. This search covered the entire of the state of Colorado. Vivion Juan may well have been buried in the Catholic cemetery in Denver, later to become the botanical gardens, but this is only conjecture. While the Pacific railroad had reached Denver in 1870, communication still remained slow and cumbersome, and even at times unreliable. Furthermore, Antonio himself may well have been away from New York when the news of the death eventually arrived, hence the delay in Antonio learning of the death of his son, and in turn Hamilton passing on the information to Vivion's wife Kate.

It is perhaps appropriate at this point to introduce new important information which has only quite recently come to hand, and which was supplied to me though the kindness and generosity of Mr Joseph M. Silinonte of New York, a professional genealogist and researcher, who has researched the de Valera connections in New York for years.

When my father was in America endeavouring to raise funds by way of bonds for the Irish cause, he unfortunately encountered difficulties from certain Irish Americans, particularly John Devoy. Things became heated, so much so, that it angered Kate de Valera as she regarded certain remarks as black propaganda against my father, so that she gave a special interview to the *New York Evening Journal*. It published it fully on 1 August 1924. This newspaper is now defunct, but the following is a full quotation from this interview:

De Valera's Ancestry – Spanish, Not Jewish or Portuguese
on His Father's Side, Says His Mother
– Copyright, 1924, by Star Company –

The name of Eamon De Valera, fighter for the Irish Republic, is as everybody knows, not an ordinary Irish name. A reader asks, 'Is not Eamon De Valera, who fought so long and desperately in Ireland, of Jewish blood, on his father's side? The name, if I am not mistaken, is that of a Portuguese Jew, who was De Valera's father.'

This newspaper is able to give the answer to this question on the best authority, that of Mrs. Charles Wheelwright, De Valera's mother. She is now living in Rochester, N.Y. Her name until she married her second husband was De Valera. She says, supplying definite information:

'My first husband, the father of Eamon, was Juan Vivian De Valera [sic], the only son of parents of pure Spanish blood. The town of Valera, Spain, derived its name from that of the family. My marriage to Mr. De Valera took place in New York City several years after his arrival in this country. He was a sculptor of much ability and an accomplished musician. Because of poor eyesight he was compelled to discontinue his work as a sculptor, finally devoting all his time to music. He played a number of instruments with equal skill. Two years after the birth of Eamon, his father died. During recent years the story has been circulated that my first husband was a Jew. That is entirely erroneous. Neither was he Portuguese. I have tried to trace the origin of the story. So far as I have been able to learn, it was first published in the *Gaelic World* by John De Voy [sic]. He was something of a student of genealogy who sometimes got things wrong, and this was one of the occasions that he did. It was at the time Irish bonds were being sold in this country, and certain interests were trying to discredit my son.'

This newspaper publishes, for the general information and in reply to our reader, the statement by De Valera's mother as she gives it. The facts, of course, are in her possession, not in ours. After all, what MATTERS is not a man's ancestry, not what happens before he is born, but what HE HAS DONE SINCE HE WAS BORN.

Where reference has been made for some time past claiming that Eamon de Valera's origins, antecedents and background were Cuban, or other than pure Spanish, all that need be said is that this claim should be dismissed out of hand as groundless as is demonstrated above.

Kate de Valera was distraught at hearing of the death of her husband. She now found herself alone, with little means of support, to keep herself and her infant son. Life indeed looked bleak. She was forced to go out to seek work, leaving her infant son in the charge of Mrs Doyle of Brooklyn, whose maiden name is believed to have been Hennessy. Catherine de Valera was now faced with a momentous decision as to whether to try and keep the child or to arrange to have him sent to Ireland to be brought up by his uncle and other relations. The heartbreaking decision was made; the latter seemed the best course to be taken. It so happened that her brother Edward (Ned) was in the USA and about to return to Ireland. He had an address in New Jersey, but it seems that he was staying with his sister at 61 East 41st Street around the time of my father's birth. Ned agreed to take the infant in charge and they set out for the old country.

The ship upon which they travelled was the *City of Chicago*. Father remembered looking over the teak rails and seeing the green ocean go by. He also remembered when the ship reached Cobh, in those days known as Queenstown. The ship was a steamer of 3,364 tons and had been built in 1883. Some nine years later on 22 January 1892, it struck under the cliffs at Ringcurren off the old head of Kinsale. The passengers, their baggage and crew were saved. There is a photograph of the ship wedged against the rocks and although the vessel was a powerful steamship it had a provision on the foremast for sails! Portions of the wreck remained visible for years but finally broke up and disappeared beneath the waves.

Eventually (for as we have seen he travelled much) Antonio learned that his grandson had been sent to Ireland. He was furious when he heard the news, but there was little he could do. Further contact with him from then on appears to have been lost. In many ways, however, he is to be pitied. He had now lost his three children, his estranged wife had died prior to the year 1880, he was now alone in the world, an old man, in poor health and within a short space of time he too was dead.

In time Catherine de Valera married again on 7 May 1888, her second husband was Charles Wheelwright, an Englishman and Protestant, who later converted to Catholicism, and who, like Kate, had been an emigrant. In the course of time he prospered and made a comfortable living for himself, his wife and family. My mother met him when she was in America and spoke highly of him. The couple had a son, Thomas, who in later life became a distinguished member of the Redemptorist order. Their daughter Annie died young, on 9 July 1897, six days short of her eighth birthday. When my father was faced with a life sentence (commuted from the death sentence) following the Rising in 1916 Fr Wheelwright, together with other priests, kept constant pressure on several US congressmen and senators in an effort to have the prison sentence reduced. They even appealed to President Wilson who showed no sympathy, in fact the President and State Department refused any help. Throughout the years Thomas Wheelwright kept in close contact with Father and the family and, not infrequently, he sent us most acceptable and useful presents.

One writer in particular has taken it upon himself to direct adverse criticism towards Catherine Wheelwright for allowing her son to be sent to Ireland. In this criticism this writer is seriously mistaken. The truth as to Catherine's (Kate) attitude is quite different. After a time, following her marriage to Charles Wheelwright, when life had become much more comfortable, if not quite prosperous, and when my father had reached adolescence, she invited him on no less than two occasions to return to the USA and live in her new home.

When she returned to Ireland in 1907 she repeated the suggestion that he return with her to live in America. Father gave considerable thought to this suggestion, but as I often heard him say, he was happy in Ireland, had settled in fully and that above all else he felt that his roots were in Ireland and it was there that his future lay. The decision to stay in the old country had not alone tremendous repercussions for his own life, but as events unfolded, it likewise had a profound affect on twentieth-century Irish history and upon major political events of world-wide proportions.

When World War II had just ended, Thomas Wheelwright came on a protracted visit and stayed with us in Herberton. In all, he spent two months, from the end of 1945 to the middle of January 1946. We all took to him greatly. He was, however, a strict disciplinarian. He got on marvellously well with my father, but at times it was amusing to see him in friendly argument with his half-brother, but Tom held his view for truly he had a mind of his own. In appearance he was tall, good-looking and well-built and like my father he wore glasses. He had quite a good sense of humour but at times could be serious. He obtained permission from Dr McQuaid to say mass in the house, which he did each morning. Once or twice this got me into trouble if I were late, but much more so, if I had been out to a late hour and missed mass; his expression at the breakfast table was enough to convey his displeasure. I had by then been qualified as a solicitor for only a short time.

Mother and Tom got on particularly well. She greatly admired his very practical and business-like approach to life. He was known to us as Uncle Tom. In turn he responded warmly towards my mother for whom he had an obvious deep respect and affection.

The following July Father was to receive tragic news. Thomas Wheelwright had been killed in a car crash in the USA. Father received word on 22 July that Tom had died on the twenty-first. He had been driving two nuns to hospital when another car, driven by an Italian, eight lines of traffic away, but approaching him at speed, careered across the lanes of traffic and crashed headlong into the car which Tom was driving. He and the nuns were removed to hospital. At first he appeared to be the least injured and was very much concerned with the injuries received by the nuns, but shortly afterwards he collapsed and died. It was indeed a tragedy, for the over-excited Italian had driven across the lanes of traffic in a fit of terror because he thought that a bee which had entered his car, was about to sting him. Father, Mother and the entire family were deeply grieved at the loss of one we had come to know, respect and to love. Mother refers to Thomas Wheelwright in her records as 'We lost in him the friend who loved us most'.

The remainder of Father's childhood and his boyhood days are sufficiently documented, particularly in the definitive biography by the late Lord Longford and the late Professor Thomas P. O'Neill, leaving no need for further detail in this book.

Over recent years, a number of commentators in various fields (including the BBC) have continued to publish considerable misinformation concerning my father, so that it has now become necessary to refute a number of such inaccurate statements, which I will show have no foundation in fact.

One writer in particular has circulated a theory that my father's parents were not married at the time of his birth. To support his theory, he relies on gossip, rumour, hearsay and wild speculation. It should be noted that some of the rumours stem from black propaganda circulated by my father's opponents following the Rising, the War of Independence, the Civil War and in later periods of his political career.

The writer makes the suggestion that my father was illegitimate. As part of his argument, he relies on the birth of my father in the Nursing and Child's Hospital, Lexington Avenue, New York. It is of course true that my father was born in this hospital on 14 October 1882. The writer goes on to say: 'It [the hospital] was for destitute, abandoned children, children whose parents were away or orphans.' The writer continues, 'hardly the sort of place in which a mother would have wished to leave a child if she had a home, even that of a relation in another country.'

Before proceeding further it must be pointed out that the writer does not quote from the charter under which the institution was founded, but takes it upon himself to paraphrase and isolate some of the objectives of this institution, as for instance, by his use of the word 'destitute', but in so doing he shows his failure to understand the full provisions of the charter itself. I have before me as I write, a photocopy of the provisions of the charter as set out in the *New York Dictionary* for 1897. This hospital was founded in 1854, the charter being amended in 1866.

This photocopy does not contain the words used by the aforementioned writer, namely 'abandoned', 'orphan', or the phrase 'children whose parents were away'. What the writer has omitted to do is to refer accurately to very pertinent provisions of the charter itself (if in fact he ever had it before him) and in particular its first stated and principal objective, namely, 'for the maintenance and care of women and children and for the care of lying in women and their infants'. Where the writer does use the word 'destitute', this word in the charter belongs to other and *secondary* provisions which stand quite apart and independent of the first and primary objectives for which the institution was founded. Essentially this hospital was a maternity hospital, albeit a charitable one, but certainly, and by no means *solely*, for the purposes which the writer states or implies. His statements, therefore, regarding the hospital are incomplete, for he deals only on his limited and selected paraphrase from the secondary objectives and thus leaves the impression that the institution was solely for the purposes which he states and omits to set out the primary objectives as above. The secondary objectives did not apply to Kate de Valera. Further, the writer's contention that Kate de Valera was admitted to this hospital because she was 'destitute' or 'abandoned' is further shown to be incorrect when its charter itself states 'on payment of a sum within their (parents) means'. There would have been sufficient funds from Kate herself; or Antonio, Kate's father-in-law, if needs be.

The suggestion that Kate de Valera was admitted to the hospital because she was about to give birth to a child conceived out of wedlock is simply groundless, as the records of the hospital *itself* show her to have been admitted on 13 October 1882, accepted and registered as Mrs Kate de Valero. The misspelling of the surname is purely a typographical error and therefore of no significance. I have had personal experience throughout my life of many misspellings such as de Velera, de Valara, de Volera and even de Valero.

The records of admission to the hospital contain the following information: Kate de Valera is shown as age 23, place of birth Ireland and religion Roman Catholic. It is of particular note that this name of Mrs Kate de Valero appears twice on the particulars of admission, leaving no room for mistaken identity or her married status. Kate's brother Edward (Ned) was staying with his sister at 61 41st Street, New York immediately before and after the birth of my father, although at this time he had an address at Rahinay, New Jersey. I am again indebted to Mr Joseph. M. Silinonte, the professional genealogist, for the information concerning the hospital.

Father told me that his mother told him that his father (Vivion Juan) was ill (as alas was so often the case) about the time of Father's birth and away from home. This explains why his name does not appear on the particular of admission to the hospital. It appears from the entry that Ned accompanied Kate when she was admitted on the introduction of a Mrs Abraham.

In further pursuance of his incorrect theory, the same writer points to the fact that no official certificate of marriage has yet come to hand, and he relies heavily on the two certificates of my father's birth, in an effort to sustain his argument and upon some easily-explained errors in these certificates, which were later corrected.

Here his contentions must also fail. As to the fact that neither of the birth certificates state or show that the parents are married, I have checked carefully with the Department of Heath Vital Records in New York and have been advised in detailed correspondence with the Assistant Director of that office to the effect that, at the time of my father's birth (and which still applies today) a certificate of birth did not, does not, and need not contain an entry showing the parents to be married. There is therefore a *prima facie* presumption in law that the parents are lawfully married where the surname is that of the father, in this case Vivion Juan de Valera. This I am further advised remains the position unless the office has information or otherwise obtains information that the parents are not married. In that case this office requires considerable further detailed information before the issue of a certificate of birth. No such requirements were sought or applied to Kate de Valera. Both certificates show Kate's husband Vivion as the father and his occupation is that of artist, birth place Spain, and aged 28.

In another of the same writer's suggestions, he seems to infer that my father's father could well have been a local landowner in Bruree, Co. Limerick, called Atkinson. The writer says 'further plausibility is given to the illegitimacy theory by local gossip'. It is a matter of simple fact that Kate had left Ireland reaching New York on 2 October 1879, and that my father was born on 14 October 1882. Were, therefore Atkinson to be the father, that would make Eamon de Valera unique in the entire history of mankind having been *en ventre sa mere* for a period of over three years! His unfortunate mother would likewise be unique! How utterly ridiculous is such a contention.

The same writer also suggests that my father was discouraged and refused entrance for ordination for the priesthood in the Roman Catholic church, because those who would have been responsible for such entrance were influenced by 'rumours of his illegitimacy'. There is no evidence whatsoever to support this allegation. It is true that my father, while still a young man, but for a brief period only, considered entering the priesthood, but following much reflection was convinced that he had no such calling. In later years I heard him confirm this conviction. It was very common in those days for young men to consider ordination, especially from rural parts of the country; my father was therefore no exception. Even in my youth, many young men of my generation had such thoughts which came to nothing.

From the purely historical point of view alone, there can be no doubt that a basic and fundamental requirement for any worthwhile biography is that the work is founded upon proven facts, reliable sources and reasoned deduction. Therefore, the use of, or reliance upon, gossip, rumour, or innuendo must *per se* detract from the value of any such work and its dependability as history.

Commentators have also stated that Kate de Valera 'abandoned' her child, especially after her second marriage to Charles Wheelwright. One journalist went so far as to state that my father had an 'abominable childhood' and 'there is no known record of his alleged father Vivian' (note the incorrect spelling) and 'he like so much of Eamon de Valera was probably invented'. This suggestion is without foundation, and obviously not based upon any reliable historical source, especially when quite the contrary can, and is here, shown to be the case.

The truth is quite simple. There is ample evidence to show that a truly loving and lasting relationship existed between Kate de Valera and her son.

Right up to the end of her life in June 1932, there were no less than five protracted visits by my father to see his mother dating from her first visit home to Ireland in 1887. These visits included staying with his mother in Rochester, New York and after her marriage to Charles Wheelwright. Many letters exist such as those at the time of my father's marriage in January 1910, on the occasion of the ordination of my father's half-brother Thomas Wheelwright, and further ones through the anxious and eventful years 1916-24. More than a score are extant, quite apart from other correspondence passing between my father and the extended Coll family. All their letters are warm, loving and caring and written with an obvious degree of sincerity. Add to all this my personal knowledge of how my father treasured photographs of his mother and other Coll relations, including a picture of his maternal grandmother. He equally treasured the only known photograph of his father.

Even in old age my father never missed an opportunity to visit the old home in Bruree. In my childhood his cousin Liz came to stay with us in Bellevue and remained for a considerable time.

There is so much evidence to show the love which Kate de Valera had for her son and her pride in his many great achievements, and for his part, the deeply felt love he had for his mother.

# CHAPTER IX

*Portraits of my Father  •  Early Days in Bellevue*
*The Move to Herberton  •  The Crisis of Christmas 1940*

John Leo Burke, a friend of my parents and the family solicitor, was quite a colourful and very well-known character, handsome in appearance with beautiful, well-groomed grey hair. Sporting a colourful bow tie, he was a gifted cartoonist and possessed an exceptionally fine collection of pictures and *objet d'art*. John Burke was a true Dubliner and spoke with a slight drawl and Dublin accent.

Burke was a patron of a number of artists then working and living in Dublin, among whom was Seán O'Sullivan RHA, perhaps the finest and certainly one of the best portrait artists of that era. Burke commissioned O'Sullivan to execute portraits of my parents and each member of the family. Mother commissioned him to do a posthumous drawing of Brian. In 1933, Burke also commissioned a truly splendid oil painting of my father.

O'Sullivan also did some excellent drawings of Father; his preference was for pencil, the medium in which he excelled. While O'Sullivan was still a very young man, he studied art in Paris and was soon holding his own with many of the most distinguished artists then working in the French capital. It has been said that he became a little spoiled there, with too much adulation, but at heart he was not conceited. Certainly he was a harsh critic and could not tolerate what he regarded as poor art.

O'Sullivan tried several portraits of my mother in various media but was never entirely satisfied. He thought her features were too mobile and almost impossible to capture, to say nothing of her lively personality. In fairness, she herself confessed she was never at ease when sitting for her portrait and she positively disliked being photographed. In my view, the best portrait of my mother is an oil painting by Lily Williams RHA, painted circa 1922.

Mother was particularly fond of O'Sullivan, an affection which he warmly reciprocated; she was inclined to mother him somewhat. Father too had a high regard for both O'Sullivan's work and the man. Certainly O'Sullivan had a great respect and admiration for my father.

I had qualified as a solicitor for only a matter of months when I asked Seán O'Sullivan if he would draw a portrait of my future wife, Phyllis. I was then earning a meagre salary, but could afford to commission him. By then, O'Sullivan knew Phyllis and me very well and he generously insisted on charging a fee which was considerably less than his usual one. He took great pains with the drawing and was so pleased with the results that he asked Phyllis if he could exhibit it in the annual exhibition in the Royal Hibernian Academy in the year 1951, and in this event it was duly exhibited.

I came to know Seán O'Sullivan well from as far back as the early 1940s and had a great respect for his extraordinary talent. Unfortunately he had a weakness for alcohol, and once he had drink taken, it belied the gentle and humble personality which lay beneath his massive frame. Then he could become quite aggressive, which he deeply regretted when sober. A fine linguist who spoke Irish and French fluently, he was well read and knowledgeable on many subjects.

O'Sullivan's studio was just around the corner from Grafton Street in Stephen's Green, the same studio which had been used by Walter Osborne at the end of the nineteenth and the very beginning of the twentieth century.

Among Seán O'Sullivan's numerous portraits were those of the signatories of the proclamation of 1916, all of whom were executed in the cause of Irish freedom. O'Sullivan was commissioned to carry out the work and told me that he laboured with a particular devotion. Not that many years ago, these drawing went on permanent display in the National Gallery. Alas, for some unfathomable reason, this is not now the case, despite their national importance. Apart from this, these pictures posses considerable artistic merit in their own right. It is high-time that they are publicly displayed again.

There are numerous portraits of my father, including one by an eminent South American artist, Carlos Baca Flor, who lived for the most part in

New York. The Countess Genevieve Brady Macauley, a lady of great wealth and an admirer of Father, sought his permission to have his portrait painted by Baca Flor. In this she sought the help of my mother in April 1938. Father agreed and the countess commissioned the work. She had been greatly impressed by Baca Flor's talent after seeing a portrait he had painted of her friend, Cardinal Pacelli, later Pope Pius XII.

Accompanied by his secretary and a lady interpreter, Baca Flor arrived in Dublin in August 1938 and stayed at Power's Hotel in Molesworth Street. This hotel was chosen because it was so near Government Buildings, where the sittings took place in a room specially allocated for the purpose. The sittings, which took place almost daily and often lasted over two hours, commenced on 2 August and continued until 25 November. In addition, the artist required several specially commissioned photographs to be taken of my father.

Accompanied by the Tánaiste, Father first saw the completed work in Buswell's Hotel on 31 January 1939. The painting was then removed to Bellevue when I first saw it in the middle of February. Father gave a luncheon for Baca Flor in Leinster House on 26 February; the artist left for Paris the next day.

It may have been intended to show this portrait in the Irish pavilion at the World's Fair in New York in 1939, but this did not happen. Certainly the portrait is admirably executed with the highest degree of skill and exceptional care. In the end, however, it is a little contrived and stiff, notwithstanding the enormous effort and time spent. In my view, it does not possess the force, strength and vigour of the O'Sullivan painting.

Once when I was discussing portraits with Father, he said that he had declined a sitting with Augustus John, although he did not give the reason. This, I told him, was a great pity and loss. I have, however, an even greater regret: that he was never painted by William Orpen, the greatest Irish portrait painter of the twentieth century and truly of world stature. Although Father never met Orpen, certainly Orpen knew of him. John Burke gave my parents a present of Orpen's book, *The Onlooker in France*, in the early 1930s. I was then, and am still, fascinated with his work. When Father still had fairly reasonable eyesight, he enjoyed looking through this book and admiring the portraits, for he had met and known a number of those famous sitters.

Orpen came from a greatly respected family with legal connections going back generations. During the 1914-18 war, he became a senior war artist in the British army with the rank of major and was subsequently knighted. Deep down, he was a highly sensitive person and, as his nephew told me, he never really recovered from the horrors he experienced in the war. Even from childhood, his work attracted me, so much so that in later years I contacted the family firm of solicitors and was introduced to his former batman, Greene, then a bookkeeper in that office. He told me many interesting things about the great and obviously loveable artist. When Greene spoke of Orpen, he never referred to him as 'Sir William' but invariably as 'The Major'. I came to know the artist's nephew and grand-nephews, as they were colleagues of mine in the law and whom I number among my friends. Although part of the British establishment and having spent the most part of his life in England, Orpen was truly Irish at heart. He never forgot the land of his birth, as revealed in his writings, *Tales of Old Ireland and Myself*. In the *Onlooker in France*, he refers to my father which, due to his background, patronage and connections is, to say the least, interesting.

Orpen had been commissioned to paint the most prominent men on the Allied side during the World War I, including Lloyd George, Woodrow Wilson, Marshal Foche, General Smuts and a host of field marshals and generals in the British army. His official work was not, however, confined to such subjects, and he relates that he was once commissioned to paint the portrait of a Polish emigrant whom he called 'A Polish Messenger'. He had considerable doubt about the sitter's true identity and said that the messenger 'spoke with a strong Irish accent and, when questioned, said he had learned his English in America.' Orpen continued: 'I began to think that he must be de Valera or some other Irish hero in disguise.' At this time, circa 1918 his use of the word 'hero' is indeed remarkable, revealing at least some sympathy towards my father and his politics. I am sure that he would have found the real de Valera a fascinating subject but this was not to be.

Greene told me the following story which has not been published to date. Orpen and some fellow war artists were based behind the lines in the ruins of a French village where there were also the remains of a farm. They were making the best of their time and had been drinking heavily. Quite isolated and free from all interference, they were generally enjoying themselves. Among the artist's companions were a number of other distinguished French war artists. Orpen himself was lolling about, tieless, capless and with his tunic undone and, as Green said, 'well oiled'. Suddenly a staff car appeared. Upon seeing this, they tried to pull themselves together but it was too late. Out of the car, complete with his ADC, stepped none other than Field Marshall Sir Henry Wilson. Orpen dived into a haystack in the hope that he would be concealed but he was unaware that his posterior was sticking out. The next thing he knew, there was a sting of pain on his bottom as Wilson lashed him with a cane, at the same time shouting at him to come out. Orpen jumped down and stood stiffly to attention. With a cutting voice, Wilson said: 'Who the devil are you?' Orpen bowed his head and in a coy way replied: 'When we were in Blackrock, sir, you used to be called me "Orps".'

Both the Orpen and Wilson families had strong connections with the Blackrock district and were on friendly terms. While it appears that this was the case, Orpen himself feared Wilson and was not always at ease in his company.

Sufficient to say here that Wilson was no friend of national independence and indeed by his words and actions can be justly described as the terrorist supreme.

I have referred to what might have been if Orpen had had the opportunity to paint Father. However, there is another Irishman's work, which, in my opinion, is by far the finest portrait. It is a bust by Albert Power RHA, executed in 1945. Again, this work was commissioned by John Burke. It possesses an inner strength and sensitivity, never rivalled by any other artist for whom my father sat, bringing out the true character of the subject. I met Power when I accompanied Father to see his studio and yard in Berkeley Street on the north side of the city. He had just completed his statue of Pádraic Ó Conaire which my father later unveiled in Galway city. Ó Conaire and my father had been in school together in Blackrock College. I remember Power as a little stout man, smoking a cigarette and speaking with a distinctly Dublin accent. He seemed very humble and shy, but a first class artist.

It was through the influence of John Burke that Oliver Sheppard's beautiful 'Cúchulainn', now in the General Post Office, was chosen as a memorial to the Rising of 1916. Sheppard's work is truly admirable but perhaps a little effeminate, compared to the work of Albert Power.

Another artist of note and international fame was the Irish-American sculptor Jerome Connor. He is perhaps best-known in Ireland for his statue

1. Father and Mother on their wedding day on 8 January 1910

2. (*opposite top*) Vivion Juan de Valera in 1879–80, paternal grandfather.

3. (*opposite bottom*) Laurence Flanagan c.1870, maternal grandfather.

4. (*right*) Father with his mother Katherine.

5. (*bottom*) Me with Mother, taken in Greystones in 1922.

6. The only entire family group photograph taken.
Back: Ruairí, Vivion, Éamon, Brian; Middle: Máirín, Mother, Father,
Emer; and Front: Me. Taken in Bellevue, Cross Avenue, Blackrock, July
1935.

7. Brian on Elma in summer 1935 at Bellevue

8. Brian's burial in Glasnevin Cemetry on 11 February 1936. He was 21
years old when he was killed in a horse riding accident in the
Phoenix Park.

9. My sketch (purely from memory) of the 'ghost house',
Elm Villa, Sandymount, which was demolished in 1938.

10. Kendleston House, Delgany, Co. Wicklow from a watercolour by
Tom Nisbit RHA, specially painted for me February 1967.

11. Easter Sunday 1941, the twenty-fifth anniversary of the Rising.
We persuaded Father to put on his 1916 uniform and
Máirín took this photograph with her Brownie box camera.
Standing with Father are Vivion (*left*) and Ruairi (*right*), while I am
seated.

12. (*top*) With a 'Swallow' aircraft E1 ABX at Weston Aerodrome, summer 1948.

13. (*centre*) The Lockheed 'Hudson' in which I risked my neck by climbing into the dorsal turret and getting stuck there for our landing.

14. (*bottom*) L–R: Colm Trainor, me, Dr Jim Ryan, Father, Capt. Walsh, Frank Aiken, 2nd pilot, Lt Eoin Ryan, aircorp officer.

15. (*left*) My wife Phyllis when she was 22.

16. (*right*) In my LDF uniform, 1944

17. (*below*) On our wedding day, 1 September 1951,
at Booterstown church, Dublin.

18. The family at Áras an Uachtaráin, 1961–2.
The photo includes all of my parents' children: Vivion, Máirín, Éamon,
Ruairi, Emer and myself (Brian died in 1936).
The grandchildren are those of Vivion, Éamon, Ruairi, Emer and myself.
Father has his hands around Jane, while Síle is at the extreme right,
bottom row.

19. Síle, Mother, Jane and Phyllis.

20. Síle, Mother, Father, Jane and Phyllis.
Unfortunately, the head-dress is not the Chippewa gift
from my childhood.

21. (*top*) John F. Kennedy and Father at a reception at Áras an Uachtaráin.

22. (*centre*) 'If you don't take your time, you'll make a mess of it!'

23. (*bottom*) 'Artist and object': Jimmy O'Dea and Seán O'Sullivan RHA at the Áras.

24. Bust of Father by
Albert Power RHA,
executed 1945.
In private collection.

25. A portrait of Mother
by Seán O'Sullivan RHA
using charcoal and pastel
on grey paper, presented
by my sister Máirín to the
National Gallery in 1968.

26. (*facing page top*)
With pianist Charles Lynch
DMus, c.1978

27. (*facing page centre*)
With Yann Renard–Goulet
RHA, looking at my bust of
his eldest daughter, Armelle,
which was exhibited in the
RHA, 1951.

28. (*facing page bottom*)
Frank McKelvey RHA and
his wife Elizabeth at their
home in Holywood, Co.
Down.

29. (*top*) Leslie Mellon,
solicitor, who introduced me
to Phyllis.

30. (*bottom*) Presenting Cathal
Brugha's .45 Smith & Wesson
to the National Museum,
together with Christy
Cruise's .45 Webley.

31. With my beloved Phyllis.

of Robert Emmet in Dublin and the *Lusitania* Memorial in Cork. There is also a bust of my father which he executed when Father was in New York in 1920. A photograph of this bust certainly displays the workmanship, style and skill of this distinguished artist and is one of two studies of Eamon de Valera he carried out at that time.

Another artist of distinction who painted Father was Sir John Lavery, then an artist at the zenith of his long and successful career. An interesting work which captures much of the younger Eamon de Valera, but it would not be fair to judge the painting too harshly as the artist had only one sitting of just a couple of hours. Had there been more time, Lavery would have come to know his subject better and so penetrate to the deeper facets of his character. Although the work cannot be rated as one of Lavery's best, it remains interesting in its own right, considering the limitations which surrounded its painting.

An artist of the present time who painted Father's portrait is my friend, Thomas Ryan PPRHA. He undertook this major work in 1958 when he was only twenty-nine. It shows Father wearing the ornate robes of chancellor of the National University. His friend and mine, the late James Kenneth Kennedy, the art material supplier, took special care when supplying the canvas for this work, an ambitious undertaking, executed with skill and expertise. It is a painstaking and competent painting.

I was present when the finished work was presented to the National University around the time of the first referendum on proportional representation. Father, of course, was present, but by then, his eyesight had deteriorated. He explained to the audience that he could not see very well and therefore could not appreciate the work as he would have liked. Nevertheless, he was sure that it was an excellent 'proportional representation!' This good-humoured remark was greeted with laughter by all present.

This is a story about Burke which Father delighted in telling although it was against himself. Deep down, my parents were fond of him, despite his many odd ways; they certainly appreciated his great generosity.

Burke had a habit of calling at noon almost every Sunday to have a chat with my parents; but he was gone within the hour. He had come from his fine house in Rathgar on his bicycle and never drove a car, although his wife had a beautiful Reilly. These visits became somewhat tiresome, yet my parents did not wish to offend him. One Sunday morning, Burke arrived as usual and placed his bicycle beside two stone lions near the hall door. Father greeted him as usual, then added: 'Come, John, I need some exercise,' taking Burke for a brisk walk around the paths in Bellevue. Father deliberately increased his pace, and Burke left in a much shorter time than usual. Father was chuckling when he returned to the house. When he sat down to dinner, he said with a smile: 'Well, Sinéad, I don't think we will see Burke for a while.'

But Burke would not be outpaced. He arrived as usual the following Sunday, so Father thought that he would apply the same prescription. 'Come,' he said, 'this exercise is doing us both good.' At that point, Burke asked to be excused. He dashed around to the front of the house where he had left his bicycle, then reappeared, and mounted the machine. As Father walked, Burke cycled beside him! Burke had won and the visits continued.

Over the years, a lot has been written or said claiming that my father had little or no sense of humour; indeed one writer has gone so far as to accuse him of having 'no humanity'. There is one short answer. Those who make these accusations simply did not know the man. Those who so accuse him, display an ignorance of his true nature, or else they have been duped by unreasoning hate or prejudice. Father had an excellent sense of humour, certainly much better than average. It is true that he disliked bawdy jokes or those that were profane. One very simple example of how he found it difficult to conceal his laughter is illustrated by the following story, an example of many I could cite.

Canon Breen called occasionally to see my parents in Bellevue. The old man had a characteristic way of commencing almost every sentence by saying 'I have noticed...'. Both my parents had observed this, so much so, that my mother made quite a cant of this phrase; I often heard her using it in an amusing way. One day when the canon called, he had scarcely sat down when he commenced 'I have noticed...'. Mother told us that Father could not contain the splutter of laughter. In an effort to conceal this, he bent down, pretending to tie his shoe lace.

Throughout the years, there had been much good-humoured banter between my parents. She was so proud of being a Dubliner, whereas he was very conscious of his country roots and maintained a strong loyalty to Munster and to Co. Limerick in particular. They often 'fenced' each other with this rivalry, especially when Mother claimed that 'the Dublin Mountains were the nicest in the world'.

One morning in the 1940s, Father was shaving in his bedroom, the windows of which looked out on the Dublin Mountains so that he could see their outline in the distance. He came down to breakfast wreathed in smiles, for he had composed a rhyme specially for my mother:

I've seen the Rockies and the Alps
The Appalachians and the Urals.
That they are singular, all agree
But the Dublin hills are plural!

I remember Mother burst out laughing and with mock seriousness, congratulated him on his splendid 'poetic inspiration'. Mother, Máirín, Éamon, Ruairi, Don Cotter, myself and others actually saved up jokes to tell Father simply for the joy of seeing him laugh so heartily.

Mother also had a splendid sense of humour and could always see the funny side of a situation. Sometimes, however, like her sister Bee, she showed a slight 'barb' in a remark, a characteristic of her Fingallian blood, as shown in the following example. In her late eighties, Mother was attending a reception and met an old friend from her days in the Gaelic League who was about her own age. He greeted her enthusiastically and then remarked: 'Ah, Sinéad, isn't it extraordinary how few of us are left?' She replied: 'Wouldn't it be much more extraordinary if it were otherwise?' Father too could be quick with his tongue when the occasion required it. It is well-known that the wily Lloyd George remarked when he failed to get the better of him: 'Dealing with de Valera is like trying to pick up a piece of mercury with a fork.' My father's rejoinder is less well-known and I often heard him repeat it with a broad chuckle: 'Why doesn't he try a spoon?'

On an occasion in the Dáil, Father was attacked by Patrick McGilligan (by no means an infrequent happening), and McGilligan accused him of trying to bamboozle the opposition by using words in Latin, to which my father called across the floor of the House: 'No, those words are Greek!'

As to Father's humanity, he was very compassionate and highly sensitive, greatly concerned with the welfare of others, especially when there was a sickness in the family, to the point of showing real anxiety. Countless times, he demonstrated his love of nature and his love of animals. Quietly, he subscribed generously to charities, at times giving more than he could afford. Understandably, he had a special sympathy for those who had poor eyesight or were blind. He was very unselfish, caring little for material things. His main indulgence was his love of books. Despite his eyesight, he also continued to love and collect pens.

Of one thing I am certain. Mother, the family and I noted that if he was mistaken, he was quick to apologise. He was singularly forgiving of those who had opposed or offended him, perhaps one of the greatest attributes of his personality. This was particularly remarked upon by the British Dominion Secretary, Malcolm MacDonald. Are these the traits and actions of someone who 'has no real humanity'? I, of course, have the advantage. I knew the man in a way his critics and detractors never could. In recent times a sort of cult has grown up among some anti–de Valera commentators. In more than one instance, they wrongly accuse my father of losing his nerve, going so far as to claim that he had a near nervous breakdown in times of crisis. The truth is quite the opposite. I have a clear personal knowledge and as I was physically present, I can testify in a number of serious and major incidents in his life and career. These are: the threatened invasion at Christmas time 1940; the delivery of the so called 'now or never' note from Churchill; the bombing of Belfast; and the delivery of the American note in 1944. There were few, if any, crises in his life which were more critical than these. The outcome of each could have had such disastrous effects upon the country and its entire population.

I can confirm, and I now place on record, that in all these situations (and indeed many others in which I had personal knowledge and again was present) he displayed a unique calm and self-control which was so clearly evident from his speech, his manner and his actions. Mother noted and often remarked upon his attitude and demeanour at such times. Many of his closest colleagues and friends made similar observations. Often, my brothers and sisters and I envied his calm and self-control in moments of danger.

It is true that in minor and purely domestic things, he could occasionally become somewhat agitated but never ever, when major issues were concerned. Most certainly, he did not loose control of his astute and highly analytical mind. Fundamentally, he was far too brave, both morally and physically, to allow himself to become overcome or lose control, most particularly in a grave situation. This gift was in fact one of the greatest and most outstanding aspects of his complex character.

How often I observed, at times of great stress or crisis, how he sat or stood in silence, joining his hands together, holding his extended index fingers pressed to his lips, deep in thought and displaying an enviable concentration. Eamon de Valera was anything but impetuous in his nature. He had, as my mother states in her records, a great capacity for making a grave decision with astonishing speed if he thought that this was vital. He had the courage to 'grasp the nettle' when required, possessing an extraordinary talent to absorb the essence of a problem in the shortest space of time. He could also seize upon the details, but even more important, he had the marvellous skill of being able to measure up the possible repercussions of his decisions and actions. This was particularly so in the four instances I have mentioned above. These attributes were among the most notable and outstanding in his great leadership.

Those who make these false claims simply did not know the real Eamon de Valera; they are founded on ignorance of the man and his true nature.

Another cult which has grown up among some commentators is their attempt to lay the blame for the economic, social and moral standards and conditions of the 1930s and 1940s solely on Eamon de Valera. This charge too is without foundation. Any worthwhile commentary must deal in the context of the time covered by such writing.

In reference to the economic situation, they conveniently fail to recognise or appreciate, that this was a period of Great Depression, not alone in Ireland but even more so in Britain, the USA and even further afield. Were it not for de Valera and his party's policy of self-sufficiency, circumstances would have been much worse, especially during World War II with all its restrictions and limitations. These were days of great hardship and far outside the control of any government. Many of these writers are unable to appreciate the prevailing conditions, as they were not then born. It is so easy to be critical from afar without actually experiencing the events. Regarding social conditions, de Valera's governments strove hard to improve the living standards of the time. They implemented many practical, imaginative and compassionate provisions and programmes to achieve this, albeit with the limited resources and fiscal parameters of the time.

On moral issues such as censorship or divorce, it must be stressed that Eamon de Valera was far from being alone in his attitude and views.

Essentially, he was reflecting the spirit and ethos held by the vast majority of the Irish people. Other leading politicians of the day, such as the leader of the opposition, William T. Cosgrave, and prominent members of his party held equally strong views and were *ad idem* with de Valera and his party on such matters. It would indeed have been a rash politician of the period who would openly and publicly oppose such views on moral issues. In short, the politicians of the time were giving voice to the convictions of the vast majority of the people. Had it been otherwise, some leading and influential politicians would have expressed contrary attitudes and views.

It is true that the Catholic Church (then so deeply conservative) held a much greater influence, but again it was only reflecting the perceived views and attitudes of the greater part of the Irish population. This must have been so considering the radical changes in their attitudes in modern times. In addition the general ethos was shared by most Protestants, who in the main, shared views on moral issues with the majority.

It is difficult therefore to understand why latter-day glib-penned commentators are so quick to describe this period as the de Valera era in such a derogatory manner. If they were to compare truthfully that time against the present, they would have far less reason to be adversely critical. Much of the modern so-called liberalism and freedom which they flaunt, encourage and advance leads to ever-increasing crime, promiscuity, break-down in marriages, falling standards of integrity and an increasingly drug-ridden society. Regrettably, a great deal of this pernicious influence comes from the worse traits of American culture and outlook which the young often imitate.

These writers would serve their readers and the public better by exposing the evils which permeate modern Irish society rather than giving a totally false impression of what they so cynically call the de Valera era.

I knew the period of the so-called de Valera era through my boyhood and as an adult. I am convinced that the generation which preceded mine, and indeed mine as well, while they no doubt had faults, had in the main a far greater standard of integrity and higher moral codes than those of today. These higher standards were apparent across the whole spectrum of society, whether in a political or religious vein.

There is no doubt that common manners and the courtesies of everyday living of the time, especially among the young, were better than they are today, particularly a respect of the elderly in society and their views.

The Pembroke Estate was the ground landlord of Bellevue; my parents were not the owners of this property but held it under a lease, as did the Lees. The lease required the lessee to maintain the premises and carry out any necessary repairs, even structural ones. Bellevue was not in the best state of repair and it became apparent that major structural work would have to be undertaken. This provision came as a great shock to my parents, especially my mother, who had always assumed responsibility in such things. John Burke, it seems, had not advised my parents as he ought to have done when my parents took over the lease in 1933 and had not explained adequately, if at all, the requirement for repair and maintenance. At this point he seemed to have panicked somewhat and said that he would like to speak to his old friend, Master O'Hanlon, and another friend, the eminent architect John J. Robinson. Within a matter of days, Master O'Hanlon and Robinson called to see my mother. Robinson was then at the top of his profession, his designs including Galway Cathedral, the Church of Corpus Christi and the parish church in Foxrock.

Master O'Hanlon was then the Senior Taxing Master in the superior courts. He had been appointed by the government in 1930 on the recommendation of his old friend, John A. Costello, who was then Attorney General. Henry B. O'Hanlon led a colourful life. His mother had died at his birth and he grew up scarcely knowing his father. When he was still quite young, he went to sea and in time obtained his master mariner's certificates. He then returned home and qualified as a solicitor in 1914, remaining in practice until his appointment as Taxing Master. He built up a fine and extensive practice. Perhaps one of his most famous clients was the wife of 'Boss' Croker for whom he acted in a mammoth litigation in the USA. She was a famous and beautiful Native American princess and, it seems a person of great determination, refusing to accept settlement of her claim despite O'Hanlon's best advice. Although she was offered many millions of dollars, O'Hanlon told me that he literally went on his knees, begging her to accept the offer, but she steadfastly refused.

Master O'Hanlon had a great interest in the stage and was closely associated with the Abbey Theatre from its earliest years. A particular friend of Edward Martyn, his play *The All Alone*, was staged in the Abbey. The advertising posters for the performance were made by the artist Patrick

Tuohy RHA. Ulick O'Connor told me that he considered this play to be one of excellence and thinks that the Abbey should revive it. The Master told my parents how deeply he regretted not having purchased the beautiful little theatre in Grafton Street (the Grafton Cinema), so sadly refurbished into shops and boutiques a good number of years ago. In 1923, he could have purchased it for £1300!

O'Hanlon told a delightful story of the Olympia Theatre, Dublin. It seems that the theatre came on hard times in the late 1920s and early 1930s, when its only real source of income was its very popular bar. One evening, the bar was full, overflowing into the auditorium, although the rest of the house was virtually empty. On the stage was a broken-down, late-middle-aged English soprano, trying desperately to sing her heart out. At the edge of the crowd was a little Dubliner wearing his cap and firmly grasping his pint. He put his hand to his mouth and in a loud broad Dublin accent, shouted at the unfortunate singer: 'For jaysus sake, shut up! Someone is trying to sing a song in the bar!'.

John J. Robinson carried out an extensive survey of Bellevue but his report was not good; indeed it was most depressing. While Bellevue looked superficially sound, extensive work would have to be carried out on the roof and other vital structures. O'Hanlon then had to advise that considerable money would have to be expended to comply with the terms of the lease. Typical of him, he set to work, and despite his undoubted skill at negotiation, it was still a considerable cost for my parents. Privately, he told me that he was furious that Burke had failed to advise my parents as to their liability and so truly sorry for them, especially for Mother. Burke ran a thriving business but depended entirely on his assistant, the late Ben McGarry. In fairness, it must be said that McGarry had no direct contact with my parents and left all advice to Burke.

In the end, both O'Hanlon and Robinson advised that it would be best to leave Bellevue. The hunt for a new house commenced, but it took some time to find a suitable one. Herberton came on the market after the death of its tenant, Judge James Greene, who had lived there since 1912. Again Master O'Hanlon stepped into the breach and personally negotiated its purchase. From then on, a great trust and rapport grew between my parents, Master O'Hanlon, and his life-long friend, John J. Robinson. Both my parents had considerable faith in their business acumen and judgement. I will always remember the day I met the master. Not alone was it the day that the contract for the purchase of Herberton was signed, but the day on which Germany invaded Belgium and Holland. That morning in school, I heard of the devastating air raids, especially on Amsterdam.

Herberton itself was not in the best of condition and required very extensive renovation, including the installation of electricity. The house and lands were much more compact than Bellevue. It was built in 1866 by a man called Nolan, who did not live long to enjoy his new property. John J. Robinson said the design of the house was well ahead of its time. Nolan had planted many ornamental trees, the majority of which survived to our time there, including two very beautiful Californian Redwoods which stand to this day. My sister Máirín, an expert botanist, remarked that these two trees were of special interest as this species had only arrived in Ireland around 1866.

Our days in Bellevue were numbered. None of us wanted to leave but wiser counsels prevailed. The house held so many memories of when the whole family was together. It was the place of my boyhood and all it meant to me, even the accursed mathematics; of Brian, Ruairi and Don Cotter and my friends. My last vivid memory of the place was listening to the wireless and hearing how the German army was smashing its way through Holland, Belgium, and France.

Before we left, however, Bellevue, it seems, had a message for us. One sun-lit Sunday evening in June 1940, about a month before we left, my mother and I were sitting in the breakfast room while Máirín and Father were in his study. It was nearly 10 p.m., following a beautiful, warm sunny day and there was still light in the clear skies. Suddenly both my mother and I heard loud noises coming from the basement, as if bins, pots, pans and such were being violently thrown about. Father and Máirín also heard the din, although they were a considerable distance away in the study. A few minutes later, Máirín came into the breakfast room and asked if Maire Dunne was back. Maire had been on her day off, and when Mother said that she thought Maire had returned, Máirín called loudly down to the basement. She received no answer. Maire Dunne could be very noisy at times. She seldom walked but positively ran about the place and tended to make quite a racket as she worked.

I accompanied Máirín downstairs but there was no sign of Maire nor did anything seem disturbed. We were puzzled. Maire arrived about half an hour later, and when Máirín questioned her, she said she was getting off a tram at the end of Booterstown Avenue at about the time we heard the noises. She became somewhat annoyed because she thought Máirín was accusing her of being late, perhaps chatting to the guards. I was more concerned from a security point of view, so I brought in the sergeant of the guard. Together we conducted a thorough search of the entire basement but found nothing which could explain the noises.

Within perhaps a fortnight of the event, I went over to Herberton to see how the work was progressing. On my way, I passed the gate lodge where Judge Greene's gardener, O'Grady, lived. He was not due to move out until we took over Herberton, so I stopped to have a word with him. He wished me and the family luck in our new home, saying that he had been in the service of the Greene family since 1912. He then looked at me rather awkwardly and said that he was glad that we were leaving Bellevue as it was haunted, or as he said 'hanted'. I asked him why he thought this was so and he told me the following story. He and his contemporaries believed that Bellevue was haunted by huge, fierce, black dogs with fiery eyes. The house had been exorcised in the previous century when Monsignor Forde was parish priest (the monsignor died in 1873). O'Grady said that the young priest who carried out the exorcism had a nervous breakdown on the first anniversary of the ceremony and that he consulted his doctor. The doctor advised him to take his holiday when the next anniversary came around. He did so, but dropped dead on that day!

Years later, I was talking to Clare Hand and her sister, Cissie. They too had heard the story and elaborated on what O'Grady had told me. The Hands had a nurse, Margaret Murphy, whom I remember when I first had lessons with Miss Clare in 1932. Margaret was then very old – well over eighty – and still wore a quaint Victorian cap. At the end of the nineteenth century, Margaret took the Hand girls for walks when they were young, and their route often took them along Cross Avenue. Clare was much younger than her sister and was a little unruly at times. If so, Margaret threatened her by saying: 'I'll put the black dogs of Bellevue on you'. As children, the Hands always hurried past Bellevue for fear the black dogs would jump out on them. They confessed that they were relieved when we left Bellevue because they were convinced it was haunted. This, however, was certainly not our experience. Apart from the mysterious noise, a few weeks before, we never felt any unpleasantness in the old house, indeed quite the opposite. Although the house and the garden were full of atmosphere of times long since past, it was always friendly, and for me a reminder of the sad story of the two Lee men who had been killed in World War I.

Chapter IX

With the fall of France and the British retreat from Dunkirk, the German forces seemed invincible. It was obvious that Father could take little or no interest in the move to Herberton. As usual, all this was left in the capable but anxious hands of Mother, and it was she who decided that the name of the house be changed to 'Teach Cuilinn'. Somehow, the name did not stick and in time it reverted to the one by which it had always been known.

It was during this time that Father made his famous speech and the call to arms in Blackrock College. Thousands upon thousands joined the defence forces, including men who had been on opposite sides in the Civil War. They now stood side by side, rank by rank; a wonderful spirit of unity and patriotism prevailed. Prominent among those who joined up were the sons and close relatives of those who had fought in the Rising of 1916, the Black and Tans War and the Civil War, and those who had been involved with the movement towards independence. They included Kevin Boland, Eoin Ryan, Liam Cosgrave and Thomas F. O'Higgins. Relations of Michael Collins were already serving in the army. Garret FitzGerald managed to join the LDF in January 1942, although he was only 15. His brother Fergus was already a serving army officer.

Ruairi left his studies and joined up and was soon commissioned a second lieutenant in the 2nd infantry battalion. With the best physique of the family and, like his father, over six feet tall, he looked splendid in his uniform. Although initially he had no desire to leave his beloved studies, Ruairi turned out to be a truly dedicated soldier. He declined two promotions as he did not want to be transferred from the battalion in which he was so happy to serve. Máirín, who was then a lecturer in University College Galway, joined the Red Cross and was soon an officer in that organisation. Vivion had by then been promoted to captain and continued to serve with his unit. Éamon had become the Assistant Master in Holles Street Hospital, and Emer had become engaged to her college friend Brian Ó Cuiv.

Apart from the extensive renovations and repairs carried out on Herberton under the watchful eye of John J. Robinson, there was also the question of security. The Army Corps of Engineers, in conjunction with the Office of Public Works, arrived to erect special fencing around the perimeter, with barbed wire entanglements, armoured guard houses and various defence points. The S Branch presence was also greatly increased. There was a plan for a permanent army presence but this never materialised.

There was also the question of building an air raid shelter. One day, while Vivion was home for a few hours' leave, he spoke to me about the shelter. He said that he would ask Eamonn Coughlan to call, as he was now a captain in the Corps of Engineers. Coughlan called and gave Willie Felton and me instructions to dig a huge hole in a spot he had chosen. Willie and I set to work at once, spending several days digging – a dangerous occupation as we had no timber to act as shoring once we got below six feet. But we pressed on, as time seemed to be of the essence. Willie was a powerful man with the shovel. Before he came to us, he had been a gravedigger in Deansgrange, an occupation to which he returned when he left my parents' service. He had a beautiful technique with the shovel and showed me how to balance the handle across the left thigh, then use the shoulders and arms to get the maximum thrust and lift. I never knew a man as strong as Willie Felton, although he was not a great height or weight. He was in the LSF (Local Security Force, later the LDF), unit in Deansgrange, and as we worked, he told me, through the slight stutter in his speech, that he had been issued with a few rounds of ammunition (as indeed we all were, as it was in short supply). He was determined that each round would account for one of the enemy in the event of an invasion. His face was grim as he said this; he obviously meant it. The LDF was issued with American Springfield .300 rifles, an accurate but heavy weapon. The LSF was later split into the LSF and the LDF (Local Defence Force) the former being a policing body with the latter assuming a military role.

Our task on the shelter complete, I awaited the return of Captain Coughlan so that he could give further instructions. He never came, having been posted elsewhere due to the tenseness of the international situation. The shelter was never completed. The huge hole lay there for years until my father had it filled in, lest one of the grandchildren might fall in, especially since it often filled with water.

But there was more serious secret work to be done. I have already referred to the deep trust which Father placed in Master O'Hanlon and John J. Robinson, and it was Mr Robinson who was asked to design a special secret 'hideout' for Father. Johnny Robinson lost no time. He and O'Hanlon secretly ferried in the required material and carried out the work with their own hands. O'Hanlon was particularly gifted in woodwork; I was roped in to act as their assistant. By night, they worked feverishly to complete the project.

This hideout was very clever. It consisted of a revolving wardrobe, the rear of which was covered with armoured plating. A further escape route from there was planned but never executed. It was only after my nephew had inherited Herberton and sold the old home that the hideout was discovered, more than fifty years after it had been built.

Security arrangements did not end there. The Army Corps of Signals installed a radio in the attic, and I was instructed in its use and given the responsibility of ensuring that it was in proper working order. Compared with the radios of today, this was a rather primitive apparatus, a large box which was all dials, wires, batteries and valves. The plan was that the radio would relay to the local garda station in Blackrock. There was no question of any code. I would simply state 'Taoiseach's house calling Blackrock… Taoiseach's house calling Blackrock.' The gardaí in Blackrock would reply and a message would be relayed.

In fact, the only calls I ever transmitted throughout the entire war were purely test calls to ensure that the radio was in working order, something I was required to do regularly. One night, however, I had been studying for my matriculation and did not go to the attic until near midnight. I sent out the usual call but received no answer. I repeated my call several times, saying 'Come in, Blackrock… Come in, Blackrock.' As I could get no answer, I reported to the S Branch on duty, and they in turn took up the matter with the Corps of Signals. Nothing more happened, so I went to bed. My parents had long since retired for the night. Somewhere about 2 a.m., I was awoken by pebbles being thrown at my bedroom window. I looked out: the guards were beckoning me to come down and let them in. I opened the hall door to find a commandant and corporal of the Corps of Signals. They enquired about the radio and I took them up to the attic. We crept along the corridor, passing my parents' bedroom, then up a flight of stairs to the attic. They fixed the defect in the radio and left. Father knew nothing about this until the following morning.

Years later, I heard the sequel to this story. The radio I used was supposed to have a range of only five miles. The night in question had been calm and frosty, and it seems that my repeated calls had been picked up by a British air force base in Anglesea. They immediately relayed the message to Dublin, believing that it was something much more important than a test call. The army came to Herberton that night, not, as I thought, because the S Branch had reported the defect but because of the prompt action of the British forces.

My bedroom then was a veritable arsenal. My first recollection of what we children called 'real guns' was when Vivion arrived in Springville in 1932 with the Smith & Wesson. In 1940, however, I had charge not only of the Smith & Wesson but also a Parabellum, another .45 and a shotgun, as well as Father's personal weapon, a .38 revolver. Shortly afterwards, I added my service rifle. There was also a considerable quantity of ammunition. I was trained in the use of these guns and was a better shot with a revolver than with a rifle. My duty was to clean and look after these weapons, making sure that they were always in a state of readiness. I was also responsible for seeing that the appropriate gun licences were in order. Father hated me having to handle these guns. He constantly said that I was to take the greatest possible care in handling or cleaning them, and I soon learned to have a wholesome respect for this weaponry. I was required to sleep with a loaded revolver under my pillow – I shudder to think that I was the 'last stand' between Father's room and my bedroom. From then on, when I was out with him, I was always armed. Vivion insisted that I carry the Smith & Wesson. I obeyed his command, for this is what it was.

There were two instances which could have ended in tragedy. Ruairi was home on short leave; his room was opposite mine. In the middle of the night, I thought I heard someone in the house, so I took my gun from under the pillow and roused Ruairi who asked me for a loaded revolver. At his command, we took up our position to cover the staircase. Father and Mother were in their room and presumably fast asleep. In a low but clear tone, Ruairi said: 'Do not fire until I do.' We then saw a figure descend the stairs from the floor above, and to our enormous relief it was a familiar one: Annie the housekeeper. She had come down to get a match for her beloved cigarettes but did not want my parents to know that she smoked. Ruairi and I did, and we kept her secret. On this occasion, she was lucky that she did not go up in smoke from another source. Poor Annie, she often slipped me a cigarette which seemed to appear from nowhere when I had run out of them. Eventually Father found out that Annie smoked. He said that he would not have objected if he had known, but he was cross with her for smoking in the dead of night on the top floor. He told her, very gently: 'Annie, you could have sent us all up in smoke.'

I had however another narrow escape. One night, I had been fast asleep with the Smith & Wesson under my pillow as usual. I awakened to see the door of my bedroom open slowly in the early dawn and glimpsed the figure of a woman approaching my bed. I thrust my hand under the pillow, seized the gun, and pointed it at the approaching figure. Mercifully, just at that moment, Annie called out: 'Its alright, Master Terry. I have come to check the time from your alarm clock.' I was very shaken. Seeing a female figure dressed in a night-dress, my memory instantly returned to the woman in Elm Villa. In fear, I could have fired, no jury would have accepted the real source for my fear. It was indeed a narrow escape.

Other Emergency matters required immediate attention. I remember the local Air Raid Precautions Warden, George V. Collins, calling to fit us with gas masks. He lived nearby. Father took the matter seriously, but Mother disliked the procedures. She said that the masks were suffocating and hoped that we would never have to wear them. Mercifully, this turned out to be the case. This warden was very conscientious and came to see me on a number of occasions to advise on what to do in the event of an air raid. He gave me a stirrup pump for use in the event of fire and showed me how to operate it. Thousands joined other emergency services, including Leslie Mellon, whom I had not yet met. He was active in the local Auxiliary Fire Service and took his duties seriously.

I had obtained my first driving licence for my seventeenth birthday in June 1939, and by 1940, Father wished me to become his auxiliary driver. He was indeed exacting, demanding utter concentration on the task. If I moved my head from right to left, even to the slightest degree, he somehow spotted this despite his poor sight and said harshly: 'Keep your eye on the road!' He had then the long seven-seater Dodge. In addition to driving this, I had to remember the escort car at the rear, ensuring that it could keep right behind us at all times. For instance, if I were about to overtake a tram, I had to judge that both cars would get safely past.

I remained his auxiliary driver until the war was over. I have held a driving licence continuously since June 1939, even when all private motor cars were off the road during the greater part of the Emergency, and thus must be unusual in my generation for holding a licence throughout this period.

The summer months of 1940 were indeed anxious. We never knew from day to day, indeed from hour to hour, when an invasion might take place. Yet amid these anxious times, Father tried to find a little time to help me with my mathematics for my matriculation. Things became more tense with the approach of August when the Germans dropped bombs on Campile in Co. Wexford, causing casualties. Nor did the tensions ease or subside for the remainder of that year.

Mother remained calm and cheerful, always trying to show the bright side no matter what her inner feelings must have been. She was a pillar of strength to my father as she had been in the past. It was at this time, as in former ones, that the bond between them showed so clearly. Father depended on her in so many ways, particularly her deep faith in the power of prayer.

The popular view today, and for some time past, is to create the impression that the only threat of invasion of Ireland during World War II came from Germany. This is far from the truth. Invasion by the British was just as likely, if not more so, and it is now known that the British had drawn up detailed plans for this. What is so terrifying to realise, is that had Germany invaded, Churchill, on the advice of his air chiefs, was fully prepared to order and sanction the saturation of large portions of the Irish population using mustard and phosgene gases, calculated to cause maximum pain, suffering and a lingering death to countless Irish people, both in the south and in the north. The consequences of such diabolical action would have been horrific. It appears that there were no such plans by the Germans to use gas against the Irish. It should not be forgotten that the British, and Churchill in particular, were quite prepared to wipe out large portions of the Irish population by using the most ghastly methods imaginable. This Churchill would do simply to satisfy his own selfish imperial aims and personal lust for power.

Things came to a head again with the approach of Christmas, a time that is very vividly etched in my memory. To add to his difficulties, Father was recovering from a serious eye operation. On Christmas Eve, invasion seemed inevitable. The defence forces were on full alert. Germany was then putting pressure on the Irish government to increase its diplomatic representation, a pressure which Father strongly resisted. It was feared that the move was a prelude to invasion, with Shannon being attacked first. Such happenings would have provoked the British. The question was: would the British try a pre-emptive strike?

It had been the custom for some ten years previously for the family to attend midnight mass on Christmas Eve in Blackrock College. Máirín and I accompanied my parents, and when we returned home, Father asked me to come to his study. He closed the door and told me to sit down. He stood, as he always did if he was about to give serious instructions. He began by asking me if I understood how serious the situation was. I said that I did. As usual, he was calm and controlled, speaking in quiet, measured tones and enquiring if the radio was fully operational. I confirmed that I had checked it and that it was. He then told me that he feared that a British invasion was imminent and I would receive further orders. He added: 'I know I can depend on you to carry out your orders.'

He then moved towards his desk on which there was a parcel wrapped in brown paper. It was not a very well made-up parcel; obviously he had bound it himself and had difficulty with his poor eyesight. His tone of voice then changed and he said, with a somewhat forced smile while at the same time taking up the parcel and handing it to me: 'Here are a couple of bottles of whiskey which I want you to bring to Vivion tomorrow.' Then his tone became more serious and he gave me the following instructions. 'Tomorrow [Christmas Day], I want you to take my car and drive alone to Greystones and hand this parcel to Viv.' Following this, and with considerable force, he added: 'Under no circumstances whatsoever are you to hand this parcel to anyone else. If by any chance you cannot see Viv, bring it back.' He went on to warn me to take great care on the roads as there might be roadblocks, but that I was to proceed to Greystones come what may.

Vivion was then in command of his company which was stationed in the old International Hotel. Next day about noon, I set off alone for Greystones with the parcel next to the driver's seat. Father came to the hall door and saw me off as I drove down the avenue. The journey itself was uneventful, nor did I encounter any roadblocks. I arrived at the avenue leading up to the hotel and had not gone far when I was challenged by a particularly alert sentry. I stopped the car and said I had a message for the commanding officer, Captain de Valera. He transmitted the message to the hotel. Within a couple of minutes, Vivion's second-in-command, a lieutenant, came out and told me that the captain would be with me shortly. He asked me if I understood that they were on 'stand to'; I said I did. Vivion arrived and sat beside me in the car. He first words were to enquire if I knew of the serious situation. I assured him that I did, as Father had told me. I then gave him the parcel, which he received with a somewhat strained smile. He told me that the expected attack was from the British, and in the event, his first duty was to arrest a well-known person in the locality who was known to be a British spy. He revealed the identity of the spy to me, but this shall remain my secret. If an attack came, he would have no alternative but to have the spy executed. He then said that he must return to his men, apologising that even though it was Christmas Day, he could not bring me into the officer's mess for a drink. Should the invasion come, he told me that I would receive orders from Father. He did not say what they would be, nor did I ask. We shook hands. He said that this could well be our last goodbye. He wished me luck, as I did him. He got out of the car, and as he walked away, he waved. I drove home at once, reporting immediately to Father. I confirmed that I delivered the parcel into Vivion's hands when we were both alone in the car. Father said no more, once he was satisfied that I had completed my mission.

Ruairi had been given two hours' special leave from his commanding officer. It may well have been at the request of my father. He was then stationed in the RDS in Ballsbridge with his battalion and other units and had been promoted to lieutenant. Father, Mother, Máirín, Ruairi and I sat down to what turned out to be a rushed and rather miserable Christmas dinner. The atmosphere was tense. Only Mother tried to keep the conversation going, although we knew what thoughts were going through her head: she had known such crises before. Soon it was time for Ruairi to return to Ballsbridge. Before he left, he had a quiet word with me. He had been talking privately to Father and confirmed that the expected attack was from the British. He told me that he had had no sleep as he and his men sat in the trucks all night, waiting for orders to move northwards. It was time for him to go. As he went to the hall door, my parents, Máirín and I followed him to see him off. I can still see his tall, fine uniformed figure as he walked down the avenue, turned and waved. We waved back.

I knew the thoughts that went through my parents' and Máirín's mind. They were as mine – we might never see him again. The rest of that day passed quietly. I tried to play the piano but my thoughts were elsewhere. So also did St Stephen's Day pass, always waiting for the phone to ring or for a message or an order. The next couple of days went by but nothing happened. It seemed then that the immediate crisis had passed.

Many years later, long after the war was over, I picked up courage and asked Father about the famous parcel and whether it contained more than whiskey. I was, and am still, convinced that in a situation such as I have described, Father was deeply concerned with other matters than Vivion and his fellow officers enjoying a glass of whiskey on that fateful Christmas Day. Father instantly remembered the incident, but no matter how I pressed him, he would neither confirm nor deny that I had been carrying something very much more vital and important than a couple of bottles of whiskey. No matter how I pressed him, he steadfastly refused to elaborate further. Later I tackled Vivion, but he would neither confirm nor deny the parcel's full contents. When I further pressed, Vivion did add, that there was, what he called a 'doomsday situation' and that I would have received my orders had this become necessary. He added with a smile: 'All I can tell you is that our parents would be gone and you would have had to stay behind with the radio.'

In later years, indeed not long before Vivion's death, I again raised the question and begged him for a satisfactory and conclusive answer. He only repeated: 'If it came to a doomsday situation, you would have received your orders.' On reflection, it could have been that my father did not wish me to have information, lest I might have been captured. What I did not know, I could never reveal.

It proved futile to elicit further information, no matter how I pressed. The real contents of this parcel must remain for me and my readers one of those mysterious and unsolved questions which occasionally occur in history.

# CHAPTER X

*Experimental Flights on the Atlantic*
*The Commencement of World War II*
*Lessons with Col Sauerzweig*

Ever since my early childhood, aircraft and flying had fascinated me. In 1936, Colonel Charles Lindbergh visited Ireland to advise the government on the possibility of opening up transatlantic routes which would operate from the west coast, particularly from Foynes in Co. Limerick and Rineanna (later Shannon Airport) in Co. Clare. During Lindbergh's stay the government gave an official dinner in Dublin Castle for the colonel and his wife, who was also an experienced aviator. Although my father knew that I would love to meet one of my heroes of the air, he explained that I was too young (I was then fourteen) to attend the dinner. He promised, however, to let me meet the colonel once the dinner had ended and arranged for a car to collect me.

I arrived at Dublin Castle well ahead of time, so the caretaker took me on a tour of the castle until the guests had assembled in the drawing room. When the time came to bring me to the drawing room, Frank Aiken met me at the door and brought me to where Father, Colonel Lindbergh and his wife were seated. Father introduced me to Lindbergh and his wife and then the colonel sat me down beside him. I was very excited to meet the great man, who was still quite young, with a fresh and boyish face. He chatted freely, telling me of his fears as he flew alone across the Atlantic and the immense relief when he spotted boats (currachs) off the south-west coast of Ireland. He knew then that the main hazards of his voyage were past. As how he touched down near Paris, the crowds came rushing at his machine and he feared that he would mow them down. He laughed and said that this was the worst part of the flight. I listened in awe as this brave man described the first solo flight across the Atlantic.

When the colonel had finished recounting his experiences, Frank

Aiken took over the conversation, referring to Father's time in America during the 1920s where pressure was brought to bear on him to fly. He reminded Father of how he had diplomatically avoided the question by saying that he would only fly with Lindbergh. The colonel smiled and reacted immediately, extending an invitation and saying that he would be only too happy to give Father his first flight. This took place the next day from Baldonnell aerodrome when Colonel Lindbergh took him for a flight lasting about fifteen minutes. Father was dressed up in a fur-lined flying suit, complete with helmet and goggles. The plane, a two-seater, had open cockpits. Alas, I had to return to school and was not present. Had I been there, I too perhaps, could have had my first 'flip' with Col Lindbergh. Father described the flight and how the colonel kept turning his head gently from side to side as the aircraft went on its course. Father obviously enjoyed the experience.

I was to have a further disappointment associated with the Lindberghs. Mrs Lindbergh had published an excellent book entitled *North of the Orient* in which she chronicled her husband's and her own flying adventures in the Far East. The colonel gave a copy of the book, autographed by both himself and his wife, to Father who in turn gave it to me. For years, it lay in the old home, but when I came to claim it later, it could not be found. I have regretted the loss of this precious work ever since.

A few years before this, another great pioneering aviator, Sir Alan Cobham, had brought his famous air circus to Ireland. Cobham had gained fame from the time of his epic flight to Australia in 1926. I attended these air displays in the Phoenix Park and was accompanied by Don Cotter. These circuses were truly amazing and well organised, with a loudspeaker system to keep the vast crowd informed of all that was happening. Cobham himself gave a rousing and spirited commentary. He was quite a showman.

The stunts performed were breathtaking, including wing-walking, dangerous and daring close-formation flying, aircraft flown upside down only a 100-150 feet or so above the crowd. One stunt which particularly thrilled the spectators involved one of the dare-devil pilots picking a handkerchief off the ground with a hook attached to the lower wing of his plane. It was there that I saw the novel Autogiro, in a way, the forerunner of the helicopter. Another novelty was the flying flea, a midget aircraft which was shortly to be condemned as unsafe.

The aircraft themselves were all of the 'string and canvas' variety. Pleasure flights called 'flips' were available for those who dared or could afford them – they were expensive at ten shillings for a very short flight.

Parachute jumps were one of the highlights of this fantastic show. Parachutes in those far-off days were not anything as reliable as they are today. The star was 'Birdman' Harry Ward. He was dressed like the Batman of today, with his black suit, goggles and helmet, with canvas stretched between his legs and arms. Duly announced by Cobham, 'Birdman' Harry took off in a plane, and then jumped from a height of almost two miles, spreading his legs and arms as he plummeted to earth. A man in the crowd beside me commented in a strong Dublin accent: 'If he flaps those wings, he'd fly away!' Fly! In fact, poor Harry was a little black dot, falling like a stone at considerable velocity. It seemed that he was doomed. But just before he came to earth, he opened his parachute and made a safe, but rather bumpy landing, to the great cheers of the crowd. This was an immensely dangerous stunt. His predecessor in a circus, Ivor Price, had been killed when his parachute failed to open in a similar display in England only a short time previously.

The pilots and members of the circus seemed to lack any sense of fear or danger. Many had been pilots in World War I and could not find alternative employment in a period of economic depression. One thing is certain: they were brave and daring, their lives constantly at risk.

When Father heard than Don Cotter and I had attended the air show, he was very cross. For a moment he thought, quite wrongly, that we had been up for one of the flips. The truth was that Don and I did not have ten shillings between us to spend on such an adventure. Father, of course, was right. There were great risks, even for spectators. Indeed there had been fatalities in such shows, including one in which the Air Corps was involved when one of its planes crashed, in which both members of its crew died.

Little did I know then that a few years later I would meet Sir Alan Cobham. In still later years, I would meet another celebrity of the air, Douglas Corrigan, known as 'Wrong-way Corrigan'. He claimed that he had flown across the Atlantic and landed in Baldonnell aerodrome, all by accident. He never confessed that his 'mistake' in flying eastwards across the Atlantic, instead of westwards across the United States was purely a stunt which brought him great notoriety. I met him through the kindness of my friend, the late Captain Joe Barrett, himself a distinguished pilot and a retired senior captain with Aer Lingus. Corrigan was then advanced in years, but still very much the showman.

The year 1938 was an anxious one with war clouds gathering in Europe. Although war had looked a real possibility, this period had its triumphs for my father. It was then that he negotiated his famous agreement with Neville Chamberlain, which had such enormous and far-reaching benefits for the country. His greatest triumph in these negotiations was securing restoration of the ports which the British still occupied under the terms of the treaty of 1922. Were it not for the restoration of these ports and cancellation of other ceded facilities to the British, it is certain that this country could not have remained neutral during World War II. Had the country been involved in the war, the devastation, loss and tragedy which would have ensued would have certainly been as bad, if not worse, than the fate suffered by smaller nations such as Poland, Belgium and Holland. The skill and adroit negotiating skills displayed by my father, and his securing the excellent outcome, must be regarded as one of his greatest and lasting achievements.

Ruairi and I accompanied Father to see him off on his way to London. On one journey, he travelled on board the brand new ship the *Munster*, which left the port of Dublin. This beautiful, but ill-fated ship, was sunk in 1940, having hit a magnetic mine. Another ship on which my father sailed, at this time was the *Scotia* which left from Dun Laoghaire. She was later lost at Dunkirk, with great loss of life, when a bomb went down one of her funnels.

Mother delighted in the restoration of the ports and was justly proud of my father's great achievements. She remarked that it was the undoing of an important aspect of the treaty, to which she was so vehemently opposed. Her own record states: 'The year 1938 was a very fateful one for Ireland. The ports were given back. I always think that the Irish people never appreciated what Dev did for Ireland in this connection. Chamberlain will always have a kind place in my memory. He and Dev arranged things so well. It is a pity that people do not understand what they have got. It is extraordinary how little mention is made of those wonderful happenings.' Eamon de Valera has been the only Irish leader since the treaty of 1922 to have succeeded in the restoration of territory ceded to, or rights retained by, the British under the treaty.

The first of the ports in Cork was due to be taken over on 8 July 1938. Vivion and I accompanied Father and, as usual, we stayed with the Dowdalls. When the day for the take-over arrived, Vivion and I were in Hugo Flynn's very attractive house on the shores of Cork harbour and were to join Father on Spike Island. We set out in a small rowing boat to rendezvous with a launch which would bring us to the island. As the launch approached, it misjudged its distance and struck the boat rather heavily, almost throwing us into the water. Vivion, who was in uniform, top boots, spurs and all, grabbed my arm and almost pushed me over. If I were the only solid thing he could grab, he was mistaken – if I had gone into the water, I could not swim! A little shaken, we arrived on the island and awaited the take-over ceremony.

Father took up his position beside the flagstaff. The Union Jack was lowered slowly while the British and Irish troops presented arms. The British and Irish sentries interchanged. Then the Tricolour was attached to the rope, Father took hold of it and very slowly pulled as the Tricolour was raised to the head of the mast as the troops presented arms. It was a glorious moment, seeing Father look up as the Tricolour fluttered proudly in the summer breeze. Moments later, the sound of cheering crowds in Cobh came across the still waters. The port was now in the rightful command of the Irish army.

The take-over ceremony complete, we were taken on a tour of the island and its installations, to be shown around by an old retainer, an English civilian. He said he had been there since 1907, or as he said, 'ought seven'. It was sad for him, for he had come to the end of an era and his career. Later, we watched the British troops board a ship, waving and cheering as they departed. As the ship sailed out of the mouth of Cork harbour, a British destroyer, *Acastra*, weighed anchor. With its siren sounding in salute, it made passage for the mouth of Cork harbour. *Acastra* was also an ill-fated ship. Less than two years later, she was sunk with the loss of her entire crew, save one, in a fierce battle between the German battle cruisers *Scharnhorst* and *Gneisenau* in which the British aircraft carrier *Glorious* and another British destroyer were also sunk.

When we arrived back on the mainland, the streets of Cobh were thronged with jubilant crowds who gave Father a tumultuous welcome. The people were wild with excitement, dancing and singing in the streets for hours, until well into the early hours of the following day. Later that evening, we arrived at Hugo Flynn's house for further celebrations and the drinking of many a toast. My father enquired about one of his cabinet who was missing. (I will not reveal which one, he was celebrating elsewhere!) Father laughed and remarked: 'He can certainly have a dispensation this day.'

As the evening progressed, I recall seeing Seán MacEntee sitting Buddha-like, with his legs crossed, on top of a turf basket with a large whiskey in his hand, wreathed in smiles and contentment. Father had a special affection for Seán MacEntee and joked that at the cabinet table, he was nicknamed 'The Leader of the Opposition', especially when he was the Minister for Finance. I found him charming but sometimes a little difficult, and, like Frank Aiken, prone to contradiction and argument. Oscar Traynor was so different with his gentle manner. Father knew his worth when he appointed him Minister for Defence during the war. Whatever their different personalities, all father's cabinet colleagues showed unswerving loyalty and devotion to their Chief.

In the autumn of that year, the anxiety increased with the Munich Crisis. Father was obviously depressed: despite Neville Chamberlain's efforts, war did not seem to be far off. Ruairi discussed the situation with me, saying that it now seemed that war was inevitable. It was merely a question of time.

Notwithstanding the worsening international situation in 1938 and the following year, the question of transatlantic commercial flying was moving apace. While Seán Lemass is rightly credited with overseeing these operations, it must not be forgotten that Father took a keen personal and active interest and was the driving force in opening up transatlantic routes. This is clearly demonstrated by his many visits to Foynes, Co. Limerick and Rineanna, Co. Clare. I had the pleasure of accompanying him many times, and he had several conversations with Vivion, Ruairi and me concerning the project. It is true that he was highly motivated by his American connection which was always something of great importance to him and of which he was so proud. With Clare being a proposed transatlantic base, he was also keeping a keen eye on his own constituency and his close association with this county, a place which was always very close to his heart.

One day around this time, Father and I were standing in the fields at Rineanna with a number of other people who were discussing the proposed airport. It was a particularly wet and gloomy day with a heavy mist and rain. The land itself was mostly reeds and the ground was so wet that the rain came in through the uppers of our shoes. One of the party, who spoke with a distinct English accent, (he was a specialist of some kind) remarked: 'They'll never make an airport here!'

In those days, the emphasis was on flying boats, land-based aircraft were not yet sufficiently developed for transatlantic flights. The British operated their four-engined 'Short' flying boats, while the Americans used their equally attractive 'Sikorskys'. Certainly their aircraft crews were brave men, setting out on flights lasting fifteen hours or more. From midway across the Atlantic or thereabouts, they were on their own, with the most meagre radio contact with land. There, they found themselves above the vast, empty ocean and all its unpredictable weather.

Father was frequently present to see these crews depart or arrive. The British chose to alight on the main channel at Foynes, claiming that it was safer and more suitable. The Americans, however, wished to score a point. Piloting a Sikorsky aircraft, Captain Harold E. Gray made the most beautiful landing on the water between the island and the mainland. The plane scarcely made a ripple as he touched down, raising a cheer from the waiting crowd. Captain Gray, later became president of the now defunct airline, Pan-Am. He made friends with Father and they corresponded even up to the time when Father was president. I still have his autograph.

An even more beautiful and larger aircraft flown by the Americans was the Boeing *Clipper*. As I saw while on board, she was fitted out in the greatest luxury, with a half-deck at the rear to a lounge or suite, complete with a bar, approached by a small carpeted staircase. It was one of these aircraft which marked the end of a development period in transatlantic air services, As far as the Americans were concerned, the use of flying boats came to an end on 29 October 1945.

Meantime, the British had been experimenting with a novel idea. They designed a sea plane called *Mercury* which would be mounted on the back of the one of the Short flying boats called *Maia*. *Mercury* was too heavily laden with fuel to take off on its own, so *Maia* took off with *Mercury* on its back. Once safely airborne, *Mercury* was released for the transatlantic flight. *Mercury* itself could only carry a limited amount of mail and, of course, no passengers. It was purely an experimental operation and indeed a brave one.

The British were also experimenting with refuelling in the air. Sir Alan Cobham had been a pioneer of this novel but dangerous experiment. I was present with my father to see such an operation being carried out. A land plane based at Rineanna, a 'Harrow' bomber, was converted into a tanker. *Canopus*, one of the Short flying boats, was due to be refuelled in the air and then set out on its transatlantic flight. *Maia* was anchored off the pier at Foynes while *Canopus*, which was also anchored, was being prepared for its flight.

We were first driven to Rineanna to see the Harrow being made ready. As we stood around in a group, one of the British officials thought that it would be a good idea if Father and his party were to view the operation from the air. Father was very reticent. He thought we were going up in the Harrow and he knew well the risks and great dangers attending the refuelling operation. Sean Lydon, however, was close by and quickly reassured him that neither he nor his party would be aboard the Harrow or the aircraft being refuelled. Sean Lydon was particularly nice to me and he knew of my great interest in flying, especially the transatlantic trials. He was a man who rendered stalwart service to the country and was a trusted and indispensable help and friend to Seán Lemass.

Once we had seen the Harrow tanker, we made our way back to Foynes where we boarded a motor launch to *Maia* which had been stripped of all its seats and internal fittings; there was nothing but a mere shell on the inside. We walked along a narrow catwalk and sat on the bare hull and awaited the take-off. There were, of course, no safety straps. The plane was to be captained by Captain Wilcockson, a senior pilot of Imperial Airways who went on to have a distinguished career during the war. His colleague was Captain D. C. T. Bennett, an Australian who afterwards found fame as an Air Vice-Marshall in the British air force. Although unpopular with many in the British establishment during the war, his rapid promotion was assured once he caught the ear of Winston Churchill.

The engines started up and off we went across the water, the spray almost obscuring our view. The roar of four great engines increased, and after what seemed to be a very long time, we rose slowly into the air. The climb was slow and laborious as the huge craft continued upwards. Soon we sighted the Harrow tanker and *Canopus*. Our pilot, Captain Bennett, took up station well to port of the two other aircraft, then moved in somewhat closer. We all gazed out the portholes to our starboard. Then I saw the Harrow take up position slightly higher than *Canopus*. The portholes in the Harrow had been knocked out, leaving an open hole. The next thing, a man put half his body out of one of the Harrow's portholes and proceeded to guide the hose downwards. Beneath him in *Canopus*, a member of its crew also stuck his body out and reached for the dangling hose. He caught it and pulled it in. Then the Harrow pumped the fuel down into the tanks of *Canopus*. When the refuelling was complete, the hose was withdrawn and hauled back on board the Harrow.

The great danger was the moment of disconnection, as a residue of fuel in the hose could spill down on the engines of *Canopus* with disastrous results. All went well, however, as I observed many gallons of fuel fall harmlessly into the Shannon estuary.

Captain Bennett wished to move in on *Canopus* so we could wave farewell as its crew set off on their transatlantic flight. He banked the aircraft gently to starboard, and for a moment, *Canopus* was out of view. He then turned again and I saw we were approaching *Canopus* at speed. Suddenly, and without warning, the huge flying boat banked violently to port in a sharp descending curve. Before we knew anything more, we were all rolling along the floor. Frank Aiken landed on top of me... and that was no mean weight! Within a short while, the plane was again in level flight and we tried to sort ourselves out. Speaking was impossible with the deafening and continuous roar of the engines but our expression showed that we were, to say the least, surprised, if not, shaken at the method of saying goodbye to Canopus. Still showing tense expressions of surprise, we soon heard the engines throttle back and we prepared to make our landing.

As *Maia* was now on its final glide path, many locals had come out in row boats to see the refuelling operation. Captain Bennett had already committed to the landing when a particularly stupid local began to row across the flight path. The aircraft continued on course, descending fast. I can still see the bald head of a man sitting in the boat, gazing up in terror as we sped past with little space between us.

When we landed, the anchor was dropped (a ridiculously small affair) and a launch came alongside. In single file along the narrow catwalk, we awaited our turn to board the launch which bobbed up and down in the none too calm waters. The engines were now silent and we heard nothing but the lapping of the water against the hull of the flying boat. As we stood in the queue, I could see Captain Wilcockson in the cockpit to my right, with Captain Bennett to his left. Oscar Traynor's son Colm, then in his early teens, was the youngest of the party on board. Amid the silence he called out: 'What happened up there?' I will never forget Captain Bennett's reply. He turned his head around, looked straight at us and said (I remember well his exact words): 'You are perfectly right, young man. I nearly made a fatal error of judgement.' These were indeed brave words, for we had nearly rammed *Canopus*. His reply was all the more courageous because he had said it in front of members of the Irish cabinet, other Irish officials and, even worse for him, in front of some of his own chiefs. He was always known to be outspoken and fearless in expressing his views.

Sir Alan Cobham was supervising these refuelling operations and was introduced to my father who engaged him in conversation concerning his pioneering flights and congratulating him on his spirit of adventure, to say nothing of his bravery. Cobham listened politely. Father asked: 'How did you do it?' Cobham replied: 'You couldn't possibly do it, sir, without a sense of humour!' So much for the stiff upper lip attitude of that generation of Englishmen.

Such were my adventures with flying boats, but my first flight had been some time earlier. Father was due to make another trip in connection with transatlantic operations and again, he took me with him. We flew from Baldonnell with Aer Lingus on an aircraft known as the *Electra*. The plane was full to capacity as it moved out on the grass and prepared for take-off. It seemed ages before we were airborne. We set course for Rineanna, flying between three and five thousand feet. I still have the note passed around by the pilot showing our speed, altitude and bearing as we passed over Nenagh. We landed on grass at Rineanna as there were no concrete runways then. I must now be among the comparatively few passengers still alive who can claim to have flown with Aer Lingus before the war.

Ruairí had come to see us off at Baldonnell. He said there was a gasp from the crowd as they watched the take-off; they thought they we would not make it. Of one thing I am certain. Just as we became airborne, the perimeter fence was very close.

Not long before the war, the German warship, the cruiser *Schleswig-Holstein*, paid a courtesy visit to Dublin. It was at anchor in Scotsman Bay, just south of Dun Laoghaire harbour and I, in common with many others, was anxious to visit the ship. She was an old-timer, having served in World War I, but she was in top condition, all spick and span. Many of the young sailors spoke English. I remember one of them, he was a lad about my own age, proudly showing me the guns which had fired in the battle of Jutland (31 May–1 June 1916) . As we were on the deck, the sailors politely pressed us to one side to await the arrival of the captain, accompanied by other naval officers, on their way to an official reception in Dublin. The captain looked so handsome, resplendent in that attractive German naval uniform complete with his decorations. Over his shoulders he wore a black cloak with red lining.

It was the *Schleswig-Holstein* which took part in the opening bombardment of Danzig, now Gdansk, and the guns I had seen were among the very first to fire at dawn on that fateful day, 1 September 1939, when World War II began. In recent years when I visited Poland, some of the younger generation of Poles were surprised and interested to hear me say that I had seen, indeed had my hands on, the guns which had fired the first shots of the war, beginning the ruthless and savage invasion of their motherland.

As August 1939 arrived, it was clear that war in Europe could break out any day. Máirín had been in Sweden for two years on a travelling studentship in Lünd University. That summer, Emer was in a finishing school in Paris. My parents became concerned and both were summoned home. Emer arrived home in good time, although Máirín had more problems with the greater distance to travel. She said that as she was passing through Germany the officials were discourteous, believing her to be English.

On the morning of Friday, 1 September 1939, I had accompanied Mother to town to do some shopping, something she usually disliked. As we came out of Todd Burn's shop in Henry Street, we saw a newsboy holding a placard on which was printed, one simple word: 'War'. I well never forget the expression on my mother's face. She had been through so much. Was it to be repeated, perhaps worse, with sons of military age?

Then came the news of the massive invasion of Poland as the German army smashed its way through. On the Saturday, there was still a slight hope that a full-scale European war might yet be averted. Then came Sunday morning, 3 September, which was overshadowed by a brief thunderstorm. Ruairi and I sat with Father in his study as we awaited Neville Chamberlain's broadcast. We listened in total silence. The moment it was over, my father's expression looked glum and sad. His first words, which he spoke softly, were: 'Life will never be the same again.' When Mother came into the room, he said: 'With God's help we will all be spared to see its end.'

By this time, Vivion had built up a fine practice at the Bar. He was to now leave it, and was called up to join the 11th infantry battalion. The defence forces had been mobilised. By the end of the month, a partial blackout was imposed in Dublin and other emergency powers began to emerge. Otherwise, life on the surface seemed to go on as before, although we knew this could not last for long. Two boys who had been in the national school in Booterstown with me joined the British navy and appeared in uniform at mass in Booterstown. I reported this at once to my father and almost immediately, the wearing of uniforms by belligerents was forbidden as such displays clearly violated neutrality. One of these young men, Tony Toft, was a stoker on the aircraft carrier *Courageous*. He was lost when the ship was sunk by a U-boat that October. He was only seventeen years of age.

Towards the end of 1939, I joined the group of Scouts which was set up in Blackrock College. A bugler was required, and when I mentioned this to Father, he approached Maudie Aiken, herself a highly qualified musician. She, in turn, spoke to Commandant Sauerzweig, the second-in-command at the Army School of Music. The commandant immediately contacted me, saying he would be only too glad to give me instruction and fixing a date to meet him at his home in Donnybrook. The commandant did not expect Father to be with me, and came out to the car wearing a well-worn military tunic and trousers. Very respectfully, he came to attention in a Germanic manner, despite the fact that he was wearing an old pair of slippers!

Lessons began on the bugle calls that day. Quite soon afterwards, however, I saw that I had no taste for scouting; it was nothing more than another form of a religious society in the college. I resigned. Later, when the college unit of the Local Security Force was set up, I joined at once. I enjoyed this training and derived much benefit from it. When I told Commandant Sauerzweig of my decision to leave the Scouts and that I had joined the LSF, he suggested that I continue learning the bugle calls. To my surprise and joy, he presented me with an almost new military bugle and proposed that I should learn the trumpet or cornet.

Not withstanding the huge age gap, a strong bond of friendship grew up between us and from then on, we kept in close touch. Later, he saw my desire to try my hand at musical composition. We spent many hours together and he wrote down my efforts in a musical shorthand which he devised himself.

Frederick Christian Sauerzweig was a quite remarkable man, a musician of the first rank whom I was privileged to know. He was born in Saxony in 1881. Even in his earliest childhood, he showed a great talent for music. He went to the Royal Academy of Berlin in 1910 and soon showed a remarkable distinction playing several instruments. He became a frequent soloist with the Berlin Philharmonic Orchestra and soon received the highest commendation from the director and the conductor of the orchestra who stated they were 'regrettably having to forego his services' for he had joined the German army. He was appointed band master to an artillery regiment stationed in Swinemund on the Baltic Coast. He served throughout World War I, mostly in France. For the most part, his duties consisted of playing at the burial of his dead comrades. Small wonder that he had little liking for either Handel's or Chopin's 'Dead March'. His services were mostly well behind the lines, where, however, his band did suffer casualties when two members were killed in a British air raid.

After the war, Sauerzweig sought a civilian post but still longed for the military life. In 1923, he was invited to come to Ireland with Colonel Fritz Brasé to establish the Army School of Music. He was commissioned a captain and became second-in-command and chief instructor. In 1923, acting as a civilian, he gave a remarkable concert in the Queen's Hall in London. Sauerzweig must be one of the most versatile musicians of all time. Although this may seem an exaggerated claim, he was truly remarkable and played the violin, viola, cello and oboe, clarinet and trumpet, all with amazing virtuosity. There was no instrument upon which he did not excel. He had an outstanding knowledge of theory and possessed the gift of absolute pitch. The English and Irish newspapers raved about his performance in the Queen's Hall, remarking on his great virtuosity on no less than fifteen instruments. There are dozens of critiques which vied with each other in praise of his amazing talents.

One newspaper remarked: 'Virtuosity in many forms, something without precedent'. Another compared him to Richter, Wagner's director and conductor, who was supposed to be able to play every instrument in the orchestra but never demonstrated this in public. As far as Sauerzweig was concerned, the report goes on: 'This is where he, Richter, must yield the palm to Captain F. C. Sauerzweig – he played one and all and quite excellently.'

In 1945, I went to him with a piece I had composed. He was pleased, and with his aid and that of my future father-in-law, Percival Blake, it was recorded by the pianist Jenny Reddin. A little later, I received a phone call from Sauerzweig. In his usual commanding manner, he said that I was to report to Portobello Barracks (now Cathal Brugha Barracks) at 12 noon the following Wednesday. When I arrived, I was conducted to the School of Music and greeted by the colonel; he had been promoted and was now director of the Army School of Music following the death of Colonel Fritz Brasé. 'Follow me,' he said, as he led the way into the practice room. There, to my surprise, was the Number One Army Band who snapped to attention. The colonel led me to a rostrum upon which were two chairs. 'Sit down,' he said, while he sat down on the other. 'Commence,' he said to the conductor. To my amazement, the band began to play my piece. I listened with a slight degree of embarrassment but with pleasure. When the piece had finished, he said to me in a loud voice: 'What do you think of that?' – or rather, 'Fhat did you tink uv dat?' (for he still spoke English with a German accent). I did not know what to say, although I knew that I must say something. Shyly I said, 'I think, sir, that it may have been a trifle too loud.' 'You're damned right!' roared the colonel. 'The way you lot played, it was like a bloody shindig in a pub!' This only led to my further embarrassment, but when the unfortunate band had to play it again, there was a mutual feeling of satisfaction. This great compliment did not end there, for he arranged the same piece for an ensemble and had it played at an official function in Iveagh House. He even went further and included the piece in a broadcast by the Number One Army Band.

Colonel Sauerzweig knew no other life but music. His god was work, so much part of the German character. His only recreation was an occasional cigar. He was a strict disciplinarian, yet his pupils loved him;

deep down, he had a soft and sympathetic heart. To supplement his meagre army pay, he taught every night in the Municipal School of Music. He never accepted that anyone might become exhausted. Once he said to me: 'If you are really tired, you sleep for a while, and then you are fit to start again.' The truth is he had almost impossible high standards.

Our friendship continued, and in time, I became his legal advisor and made his will. He pressed himself too far, however, and collapsed when giving a lesson in the Municipal School of Music. He had suffered a stroke and was taken to St Bricín's military hospital where he remained for some time. While I visited him, I found him frail but his great spirit was unbroken. He called the matron and said that he wished to have his great coat and cap. Members of staff helped him to put the coat on over his pyjamas. Matron and an orderly led him slowly, as he made his way to the recreation room where he knew there was an old battered piano. I followed behind. Very slowly, he moved towards the piano and with considerable effect, played E above middle C, saying as he did: 'That's the damned note I was trying to play when I collapsed. I was determined to play it, and now I have.'

He was later brought home and had to resign his commission. He lingered for a considerable period but died peacefully on 7 April 1953. Although he was no longer a serving officer, both his son Bernard (now alas too dead) and I prevailed on the then chief of staff to have the Number One Army Band play at his funeral. Permission was granted and he was buried in Mount Jerome Cemetery with military honours. It was my task and sad duty as executor to erect a tombstone over his grave. I chose words from Schubert's immortal song 'An Die Musik' but felt that the text be best in English: 'Ah music my dearest consolation' – fitting words, I feel to sum up the life of a great and quite amazingly talented man and a dear friend.

# CHAPTER XI

*War-time Experiences*
*I Become a Solicitor's Apprentice*

By the early days of 1941, the immediate crisis of Christmas 1940 had passed. On the surface, life at home returned to normal, or as normal as it could be at such a time. By then, the country was experiencing shortages and suffered many restrictions.

It was in January 1941 that I first met Conor Maguire at a party in his home, the delightful 'Ashurst', Merrion Avenue, Blackrock (now alas demolished, with a large apartment complex on the site). It was there too that I met were Katriona Delahunt and her sister Mary (now alas deceased). Years later Conor married Katriona. We have remained close friends ever since. Conor is the eldest son of the then chief justice, Judge Maguire.

By Easter of 1941, I had joined the LDF proper and was attached to a unit in Dun Laoghaire. I was posted to the Intelligence and Observation Section, although why I was posted there, I never found out. There were only about twelve to fifteen in the section, among whom was a young medical student who was a cousin of William Joyce, 'Lord Haw Haw'. How this quiet and likeable young man was jeered about this connection.

I very much enjoyed the training and parades. We were issued with the earlier type of uniforms and christened 'The Chocolate Soldiers' by John Burke as the tunic, pants and forage cap were of a light chocolate-brown colour. It was only in 1942 that we were issued with a green 'Bulls Wool' uniform. Our DAO (District Administrative Officer) had a rank roughly equivalent of sergeant major. In his earlier years, he had served in the British army in one of the guards regiments. Adams was a great drill sergeant and instructor. I was not long attached to my unit when a parade was held on Easter Sunday 1941 to commemorate the twenty-fifth anniversary of the Rising of 1916. Father took the salute at the GPO in

O'Connell Street and it turned out to be the biggest military parades ever held in Dublin, taking two hours or more to pass the saluting base. My unit was to march off from Portobello Barracks. The LDF units were to form the rear of the parade, with the regular troops taking precedence. Vivion was towards the front of the march-past. Ruairí was with his battalion while I was far in the rear. In spite of his poor eyesight and the many, many thousands of troops who marched passed, Father was proud to tell us later that he could pick out all three of his sons. Ruairí joked about this: he said Vivion could have scarcely been missed due to the size of the large Parabellum pistol which he sported in a huge holster. I was carrying Cathal Brugha's Smith & Wesson, Ruairí his service revolver.

We all assembled in Herberton that afternoon where Máirín took a photograph with her famous old Brownie box camera which she purchased in 1931-32 for 10 shillings and 6 pence. She did not have her Red Cross uniform with her (she was an officer in this organisation) having left it in Galway, where she was then living, so she decided that she should not appear in the photograph. This picture is of some historical significance. We persuaded Father to put on his 1916 uniform, or at least as much of it as had survived. We had quite a task to persuade him to wear his 1916 medal. He agreed, but point-blank refused to wear his other decorations. This historic photograph has never been published before.

One afternoon in May 1941, I was at home in the garden when quite suddenly, I heard a plane, and then saw an aircraft fly low and at considerable speed in a south-easterly direction. In the LDF, aircraft recognition was part of my training. We were provided with colour charts showing various types of aircraft, both on the Allied and German sides. While I had a good view, I could not recognise the plane. Vivion was at home and he too saw it and said that he thought it was an Air Corps 'Anson'. I replied: 'That's no Anson – much too fast, and its outline is quite different.' Later that day, I heard that a British aircraft had crash-landed in Leopardstown. I made my way there on the bicycle; in those days, it was a place far out in the country and with few houses. The first person I questioned happened to be a German – an old man who had long before settled in Ireland. Eventually I came across someone who knew where the plane had crashed. Within about ten minutes I found it. It had made a belly landing on 'the gallops' to the south-west of the racecourse, and by the time I had reached the scene, the army had arrived and was dismantling the damaged plane. The LDF had been first on the scene and took charge of the crew until the army arrived. The crew was taken to the Curragh for internment. It turned out to be a British 'Beaufighter', a new aircraft which was taken off the secret list following this crash. It seems that the crew had come from Malta, lost their way, and thought they had landed in France.

I will not easily forget the night of 31 May 1941. The weather that evening had been pleasant but the sky was somewhat overcast. I went to bed about 11.30, but at 12.15, I was awakened by the sound of aircraft. I knew they were German; for it was not difficult to recognise the sound of German planes due to the de-synchronisation of the engines. To my surprise, I heard a few rounds of anti-aircraft fire. Following this, the sound of the planes faded and I went back to bed. I fell asleep again, but just before 2.00 a.m., I was wakened by the sound of aircraft, again the unmistakable sounds so typical of German planes. The noise grew louder and louder; then I heard the whine of a bomb, followed by a massive explosion. Almost at once, the guns opened up, sustaining an intensive barrage for about ten minutes or more. In the midst of all the noise, the exploding shells and sweeping search lights, I heard an aircraft flying almost directly over the house. Judging from the noise, it was comparatively low. I knew this had all the signs of attack, perhaps a prelude to invasion. I thought that the house could well be the next target, but within minutes, the sound of the plane disappeared and firing ceased. When I heard the bomb drop (it turned out to be a mine), my first thought was for Ruairi, as I suspected that the target may have been the RDS in Ballsbridge where he was stationed. I could hear the phone ringing and Father's voice as he spoke, but he did not call me nor did I dare go into his room. It was only early next morning that I heard that a bomb had fallen on the North Strand, causing many casualties and considerable damage.

Father's anxiety was only too apparent as he ate a hasty breakfast and made for the scene of the bombing. As usual, he was calm and resolute. Before he left, he told me what had happened. Éamon was in Holles Street Hospital that night and foolishly viewed the spectacle from the roof. He said, quite innocently, that he was aware of several pieces of metal which fell around him, shrapnel from the anti-aircraft fire. Next day, Éamon visited the Mater Hospital and said that he was shocked by the wounds and injuries received by so many of the unfortunate victims of this bombing. He said: 'I have never seen wounds like them. They were horrific'. Vivion came home next day and questioned me closely about the events of the previous night. Anti-aircraft ammunition was in very short supply and he was concerned about the number of rounds which had been fired.

Katriona Delahunt was spending her last days of school in Mount Anville and we sometimes exchanged letters. She wrote to me two days after the bombing and gave her account of that fateful night. She wrote: 'Did you hear the air-raid on Friday night, Terry? I suppose the anti-aircraft guns awoke you, the noise was terrible, even out here. The whole house rocked with the explosions. I can see right over the city from my window and I awoke just before the first bomb was dropped – the flash lit up the sky for miles around. The planes flew just over the house and of course awakened everyone. However, the school was remarkably quiet. The silence was really wonderful, and I suppose to you surprising, considering that there are 140 girls and 90 nuns in the establishment. I was never so frightened before.' Even then, I could see that this letter was a piece of history and I kept it throughout the long years since.

Appalling as this bombing was, my father explained that this action by the German air force was not a deliberate attack on Dublin. Dr Hemple, the German minister, and the German government apologised and in due course, substantial compensation was paid. Even Churchill indicated that this attack could be attributed to other reasons, as the British had been successful in 'bending' radio beams which put the German planes off-course. This has been confirmed by one of the crew of the German planes engaged, who established the cause of the bombing beyond doubt.

I matriculated in autumn 1941 and finally emancipated myself from the hated mathematics. It was then that the question of a career came into focus. For a year or two previously, I had thought of law, especially since Vivion had had such success at the Bar, which of course he had to abandon during the Emergency.

Master O'Hanlon had by then taken a special interest in me, indeed treated me like a son. He suggested to my parents that I become a solicitor.

When he asked me if I would like this, I enquired: 'Is there any mathematics in it?' 'No,' he replied. 'Well, only simple arithmetic.' I agreed.

In addition to his long-life friendship with John J. Robinson, O'Hanlon was equally friendly with Johnny Robinson's younger brother, Tommy, who carried on a fine practice as a solicitor in O'Connell Street under the style of O'Hanlon and Robinson. Robinson had taken over O'Hanlon's extensive practice when the latter was appointed Taxing Master. The master said that he would speak to Tommy Robinson, and Robinson agreed to take me as his apprentice. Tommy Robinson never made any secret about his strongly held unionist views and the fact that he was opposed to my father's politics. He had serviced with distinction in the Royal Flying Corps in World War I. He seldom spoke of his flying days, but did so to me, which one of his friends said I could take as a compliment. He still felt the loss of many of his comrades who had been killed in that war. Tommy Robinson never referred to my father as anything but 'Your Governor'.

Before I was formally apprenticed, I had a short holiday and was invited by my friends, the Cassidys, to spend time with them in Parknasilla, Co. Kerry. I left by train and journeyed first to Mallow, then by lines alas gone, from Mallow to Hedford Junction and then on to Bandon. What a wonderful scenic route these lines were – a tragedy that they were abandoned. It took twelve hours or more to reach Parknasilla where I enjoyed a most pleasant holiday with my friends.

With the acute shortage of coal, maintaining the limited railway services was quite a feat. Some enterprising person ran a stagecoach, a real eighteenth-century coach-and-four, from O'Connell Street to Limerick. I remember seeing it begin its journey from a spot opposite the Gresham Hotel. The story goes that this coach and the only train of the day heading south started off about the same time: the coach reached Limerick before the train. This could well be true, as the locomotives often lost steam due to the poor quality of the coal. Long hold-ups were not uncommon.

My friend Charles Lynch, the pianist, told me of an experience with a train which he had in those years. One day while travelling from Cork to Dublin, the train made very poor progress (again due to the lack of proper fuel) until it reached Tipperary when it came to a dead halt. The passengers alighted and Charles walked up to the engine driver who told him it could well be an hour or even more before he would get up a proper head of steam. Charles asked if it would be alright for him to go for a walk. 'Oh, yes, a long walk. I'll whistle when we are ready to leave,' the driver replied. Charles set out on his walk and returned in about an hour – and still the steam pressure was not sufficient to haul the train. With his wonderful dry sense of humour, Charles remarked that he had thought of a splendid motto and song for CIÉ: 'I'll walk beside you!'

The war had not long set out on its awful course when vital supplies such as grain began to be in short supply. In the main, the country depended on British ships to transport essential material and supplies, and some solution had to be found to overcome this acute difficulty. Seán Lemass, with his unique skills, applied himself to the task, and Irish Shipping was created in March 1941.

A number of foreign ships had been marooned in Irish ports since the outbreak of war, and following protracted and difficult negotiations, these vessels were acquired to form the Irish Merchant Fleet. The last ship to be acquired was the *Caterina – Gerolimich*, an Italian vessel of 7,031 tons, which was renamed the *Irish Cedar*.

I accompanied Father to the port of Dublin when this vessel was commissioned in 1943. Due to his extensive knowledge of matters nautical, Master O'Hanlon came with us. We boarded the ship and set out for a trial run, then sailed beyond the twelve-mile limit. The many guests on board were given a free run of the ship, so some of us went below to watch the engines at work. While there, the engines stopped but no one thought there was anything unusual in this. Having spent some twenty minutes below, our group moved up on deck where we were surprised to learn the reason why the ship had stopped. A British plane had circled the vessel a number of times at a very low attitude to check the identity of the ship which had large tricolours painted on its sides and deck, with the word 'Éire' painted in large bold letters on the ship's sides. Those who had seen the plane told us that these were anxious moments, as they feared we might have been attacked.

Once the 'all clear' had been given, the engine started up and we proceeded on our way. Lunch was served in one of the holds, on long tables covered with spotless white tablecloths. We were amazed to see masses of fruit, including oranges and bananas, which we had scarcely seen for years. The whole trip lasted about nine hours up to when we docked in the River Liffey.

This vessel was luckier than its sister ships in the fleet, as both the *Irish Pine* and the *Irish Oak* were sunk with great loss of life; more than 160 seamen lost their lives in Irish merchant ships during the war. The sailors who perished had bravely given their lives, endeavouring to ensure essential supplies for the country. Without these ships and their heroic crews, Ireland would have been near starvation or at least in great want.

With the demise of Irish Shipping, it is sad to reflect that this maritime country now has no merchant fleet of its own, to say nothing of the loss of employment. It can be only hoped that this loss will not be sorely missed at some future time.

Another summer's day in 1942, I accompanied Father to Dun Laoghaire to see a demonstration in which the army's Ordinance Corps and the Corps of Engineers successfully exploded sea mines which they had designed and made in conjunction with commercial undertakings.

With the Japanese attack on Pearl Harbour on 7 December 1941, it was clear that this action would add another dimension to the war, inevitably bringing the USA into the conflict. This action was bound to have repercussions for Ireland and its stance on neutrality. I could see that Father was perturbed, but he remained calm and resolute.

I went to bed as usual on that night of 7 December. About 1.30 a.m. I heard the telephone ring. Father had an extension at his bedside, and shortly after that, I heard a noise in the corridor outside my room. I got up immediately and went to investigate, and there I saw Father wearing a dressing gown over his pyjamas. He was not wearing his glasses and his hair was somewhat dishevelled. He looked in my direction and said in a strong, stern voice: 'Go back to your room and do not come out unless I call you.' From his expression, I knew that something really serious was afoot. I obeyed his command and returned to my room at once. Within twenty to twenty-five minutes or so, I heard a car coming up the avenue and stopping. Then I heard a man's voice and the hall door opening. A moment later, there were voices in Father's study which was on the floor beneath my bedroom. While I could not hear the exact words, it was clear to me that Father and some man were deep in conversation. Within half an hour or so, the voices moved to the hall, followed by the sound of a car driving away. Father then came up the stairs, walked into his room and closed the door.

Next morning, he told me that the mysterious caller was none other than the British Representative, Sir John Maffey. He went on to say that Maffey had been sent to deliver a special message from Churchill – the famous 'Now or never note'. Father's first reaction was that this might be an ultimatum, but even before Maffey handed him the note, he (Maffey) said that Churchill was in very high spirits celebrating America's almost certain entry into the war. In fact, Father told me that Maffey told him that Churchill was highly intoxicated and was sending telegrams in all directions. As always in serious matters, he remained calm and decided to let some days pass so he could examine the contents of the note more closely and discover what its true intention may have been. (For further details of this incident, the reader is referred to Father's official biography by Lord Longford and Thomas P. O'Neill, Part IV Chapter 30.)

Some commentators have tried to maintain that Father turned down an offer by Churchill to end partition when he used the words 'Now is your chance, now or never, a nation once again.' Such a theory is without foundation, grossly misleading and patently false, for to take one important point alone, the unionists in the North had not been consulted. Certainly I can confirm that when Father told me the story of Maffey's visit, he did not mince his words in describing Churchill as being 'drunk' the night in question. The use of such strong words as 'drunk' would not have been used by Father unless he was quite satisfied that it was appropriate to the circumstances. I have always known his passion for accuracy in the use of words. Father was, however, much more concerned that this note was some form of threat or ultimatum. As he told me, his primary worry and concern at this point in time was not the solution to partition but rather the grave danger of an imminent invasion by the British or some pretext for such. Like other serious crises during the war, this one too passed.

Robinson enforced an almost military discipline in the office and demanded the highest standards, but he was just, and equally hard upon himself. From the day Master O'Hanlon introduced us until I last spoke to him shortly before his death in 1967, I never addressed him as anything but 'Sir'. When I reported to him each morning, standing to attention while I received my orders for the day, I looked straight at a photograph of him standing beside his plane during the 1914-18 war. He warmly approved of me being in the LDF and had strong views about the value of military training and discipline.

While Robinson was quick-tempered and demanding, he was fair and absolutely devoted to the interest of his clients, with the highest standards of integrity. I was only in his office a matter of days when he said: 'Ask that nice mother of yours to get you a hat'. He explained that I must wear a hat while I was out with him or when going to court or public offices. I was to be dressed properly and to be in a position to salute my seniors and superiors. Mother duly purchased the hat. Robinson became very fond of my mother and quite a rapport struck up between them, including a mutual love of Charles Dickens' work. Being in the service of Tommy Robinson was difficult, but he was equally strict with his son Harry, who later became an apprentice. Harry in time succeeded to the firm and brought it to a very high point in the profession. The name of the firm was changed to T. P. Robinson in 1942.

T. P. Robinson lost his court clerk within a year of the commencement of my apprenticeship. This man was brilliant, but he had been in an accident in which he received severe head injuries. One day he simply disappeared with papers belonging to the practice. The poor fellow had taken to drinking heavily, and his departure caused upset. Robinson never replaced him, and I was given the task of being court clerk. This necessitated my being out of the office for long periods, which meant I was unable to do or learn much 'inside' paper work. In after years, my father resented this but in the long run it may have been an advantage. I learned procedures and the general run of the courts and other offices in a way which might not other otherwise have been the case and which stood to me in great stead when I became Taxing Master.

Tommy Robinson was quite different to his brother Johnny. Although similar in appearance, Tommy lacked Johnny's relaxed soft-spoken manner and the kindly attitude which lay beneath his brother's rotund figure, bald head and rimless glasses. In later years I discovered that Tommy Robinson was quite shy. Deep down, he had a heart and was capable of real affection and gratitude for the loyalty and service I had given him. I was told that when he scolded my successors, he said one day in somewhat of a temper 'This would not have happened if Terry de Valera had been here.'

Tommy Robinson was to know great sorrow and tragedy. His eldest son, Bobby, a gentle, quiet, young man and a quantity surveyor, was cruelly murdered.

In those far-off days, there was a difficult Irish examination which had to be passed before one could be an apprentice. There was also a much more difficult examination called the 'Second Irish' which likewise had to be passed before one could be admitted to the roll of solicitors. These examinations had been the brainchild of Ernest Blythe under the Cumann na nGael government in the 1920s and it was accepted in my day that 70 per cent had to be obtained to be sure of a pass.

Having matriculated, I had but seventeen days to cover the entire course for the first examination in Irish. Mother, however, was at hand and she took over. We both put our utmost into the task and in the event, I obtained first place, although a 'place' as such was not recognised as the statute merely required qualification. Years later, when it came to the 'Second Irish' which included technical law, with the teaching of my mother, I again obtained first place in the oral and second in the written. It is sad to think that the standards which then applied have lapsed greatly as far as these examinations are concerned. It was, however, unfair as these high standards were not applied to students reading for the Bar.

A great number of Robinson's clients were unionists. Some were from the North, while others would have had little or no sympathy with the name de Valera. In the public service, especially the court officers, several had been there prior to 1922. A few had been appointed because of their service in World War I and some retained their military titles such as 'Captain this' and 'Major that'. For the most part, the remainder were appointees of the Cumann na nGael government in the 1920s. Practically without exception, all showed me kindness and were anxious and willing to help in my daily work. Some, I feel sure, wondered at the office to which I had been apprenticed and perhaps felt a little sympathy for me in the surroundings, so different from those in which I had been brought up.

As a solicitor, my duties often took me to the Land Registry. One day in the late 1940s, perhaps a little later, I had a query and was directed to a senior examiner. When I entered his room, I was warmly greeted by Neville Griffith who dealt with my query and proved himself to be most co-operative and courteous. When our business had concluded, we chatted for a little while and he said that he had just returned from holidays. I asked him where he had been, to which he replied 'Hungary'. When I remarked that this seemed a strange place to choose, he smiled. I then realised my *faux pas.* I should have remembered that he was the son of Arthur Griffith who had such strong association with Hungary and had a profound knowledge of that country.

One of Tommy Robinson's closest friends was John A. Costello. He was always briefed in major cases as Robinson's leading senior counsel. I came to know Mr Costello well, and from the day I was introduced to him, he showed me nothing but kindness and consideration. My master even entrusted me to carry personal messages and to work for the Costello family. I was once allowed to attend a pre-trial consultation in a very important case in which John A. Costello was the leading senior counsel; the late Kevin Kenny (afterwards admitted to the Inner Bar) was the junior counsel. The clients and witnesses were present, and some discussion came up regarding a document to be filed in court. Robinson was somewhat uptight about the case and became quite excited, wrongly accusing me of failing to file the document. Mr Costello knew that I had and he roared at his friend, springing to my defence despite the other parties being present. Robinson felt quite chastened by the 'attack' of his friend.

In later years, I myself briefed John A. Costello as my leading senior counsel, and a more learned, loyal and conscientious leader one could not have. When leading in a case, he had a rather fatherly approach which I found both helpful and encouraging. But there were cases in which he also opposed me. I recall one very difficulty chancery case in which new law was made and which remains the law of the land to this day. My counsel was my friend, Tony Hederman, later a judge of the Supreme Court. He was then at the Outer Bar, but through his skill and dedication, we won the case. Notwithstanding this, the question of costs arose. Following much argument, Mr Costello succeeded in prevailing on the judge to have a portion of the costs abated or disallowed. This was not good news for my side, although I had an award for the greater part of the costs. When we came out of court, both sides stood in separate groups, talking about the result. Mr Costello caught my eye and beckoned me to speak with him in private. As we stood aside, he said in a very sympathetic tone: 'I'm sorry about the costs, Terry, but you know that I had to do my duty.' This was a gracious remark from an esteemed adversary. While I know that he was quite different in his political views, he privately had a wholesome respect for my father as my father had for him. I will therefore never understand the reasons which prompted him to speak on television in such a disparaging way, the night my father died. Perhaps the lawyer in him came out and he was simply speaking to what he regarded as his brief. At heart, he was a lawyer first and perhaps a somewhat reluctant politician, although a dedicated one. He would have made an outstanding chief justice, if such had been his wish.

By 1942, we all began to feel the pinch of war-time restrictions. Rationing came fully into force, including a complete ban on private motoring. However, I continued to be my father's auxiliary driver and often drove him on shorter journeys. Father was strict in the extreme. One day, I took the car out of the garage to drive it to the front door as I knew that he would be going out. He mistakenly thought that I was driving out to the road and scolded me severely. It was only when I explained what I had done that he cooled down. He accepted my explanation and apologised, saying, however, that under no circumstances whatsoever could the car be used except at his command and when he was in the car.

Clothes rationing came in during that year, and Ruairi rather flippantly remarked that Dublin had never been so well-dressed. People who were unfamiliar with the rationing system could not understand that, once they had parted with the precious coupons, they then had to pay for the goods! To steal a bicycle was a very serious offence and carried a jail sentence. There were 'cycle parks' in town where bicycles were hung up from the front wheels on meat hooks. These parks were often situated close to air-raid shelters which stood in most of the principle streets of the city. There were 'emergency powers' which covered almost every aspect of life. Any breach of these carried stiff penalties, including jail sentences. Yet there was a great spirit, for everyone was in the same boat. There was a feeling of togetherness in very trying circumstances.

Grafton Street was on my rounds and I came to know the street, its shops and cafés, but especially the people who frequented what was regarded as Dublin's most fashionable street. The thoroughfare itself was partially blocked by air-raid shelters which stood adjacent to the path.

I frequently had a quick lunch in Bewley's. In the basement, there was a 'Men Only' section where businessmen and professionals met for their 'wartime' lunch. I remember what I usually had: rissole and mash, a plain bun and a cup of coffee, all for the price of two shillings and three pence, inclusive of tip. Following this, I made my way to attend lectures in the

Four Courts. Grafton Street was frequented by many well-known people, a number of whom have since become famous. I saw Micheál MacLiammóir and Hilton Edwards stride down the street. Micheál was generally dressed in black and wearing his full stage make-up, his clearly died black hair showing in the light. I might spy the poet Austin Clarke as he moved shyly along the pavement, wearing his characteristic black hat which always seemed too large for him. He never seemed to speak to anyone. I often saw the prima donna Margaret Burke Sheridan, for whom Puccini had such a high opinion and affection. She walked there practically every afternoon. I recall her dressed in a well-worn light brown fur coat and those awful platform shoes, her once beautiful face showing the years, her hair obviously peroxided and her bright red lipstick in a Cupids' bow. She delighted in the curious glances of the passers-by and loved to stop and chat with friends. By then, she was a friend of my father's private secretary, Kathleen O'Connell, and it was through this connection that my father came to know her. She had also been a patient of my brother Éamon. I knew her less well, but if she saw me, she always stopped for a chat. When speaking to her, I always felt that she was still on the stage, still giving another of her magnificent performance, but in speech, not song.

Occasionally, I saw Patrick Kavanagh coming around the corner from Duke Street on his way to Davy Byrne's pub, wearing a slouched hat as he ambled along. I might also see Charles Lynch, whom I had not yet met, bouncing along with a quick footstep and invariably carrying an old-fashioned leather music case. I might per chance see the smiling cheerful face of Jimmy O'Dea accompanied by Harry O'Donovan as they made their way to the Gaiety Theatre for a rehearsal. There too I might see Sean O'Sullivan making his way for his too-frequent visits to Davy Byrne's or some other public house. Lord and Lady Longford were frequently seen in the street. One could hardly miss Lord Longford (generally known as 'Teddy') with his extremely rotund figure. Occasionally through the milling crowd I saw Sean Keating. He always looked the same: his dark bearded face, strong staring eyes, his head covered by a wide-brimmed hat, and the inevitable blue or black polo-necked jersey. I only met Sean Keating once, at a brief encounter at the annual exhibition of the RHA. I knew that he had been a pupil of Orpen and that Orpen thought very highly of him. I asked him to tell me a little about Orpen, and he summed it up very briefly by saying: 'I loved the man.' At that time, he felt that Orpen's genius had been sadly neglected, especially in Ireland.

On a few occasions, I remember seeing an unruly fat figure with an open-necked shirt, the collar of which was in a style worn by the poet Byron. He walked along the pavement with an unsteady gait, speaking loudly or shouting to some acquaintance. I did not know then who he was; he was simply someone decidedly the worst for drink who attracted the disapproval of his fellow pedestrians. He was clearly courting attention. It was only later that I learnt that it was Brendan Behan.

I dined only twice at Jammet's famous restaurant, once with my brother Vivion when he brought me to dinner with some of his business friends, and again with Dr Thomas McGreevy, who at that time was director of the National Gallery. Dr McGreevy was a friend of both my parents and had a special regard for my mother. Knowing of my interest in art and painting, he took me to lunch one Saturday and then we walked back to the National Gallery where he gave me a fascinating private tour. He showed me the Titian painting, 'Ecce Homo'. I was stunned at its beauty and remarked that I thought it the most beautiful thing I had ever seen. He smiled and was pleased. Unknown to me, a controversy was then raging as to whether this work was a genuine Titian or not. Since then this exquisite work has been confirmed to be from the hand of the great Italian master.

There were other restaurants in Grafton Street, far less expensive than Jammet's. Most notable were Roberts' Café, the Monument Café, Fullers, and at the lower end of the street, Mitchells, the latter being a rendezvous for middle-aged matrons with distinctly 'West Brit' accents.

Brian Maguire (Conor's younger brother) was then a young medical student, and we frequently met at Roberts for coffee on a Saturday morning where we consumed that awful wartime coffee substitute and nibbled biscuits made from 'black flour'. A trio of none-too-young ladies provided music, comprising a violin, piano and cello. Their music was always pleasant but alas, few paid much attention. One of Brian's companions was a fellow medical student, Dan O'Herlihy, later to become the well-known film star. He was somewhat odd, for in the course of a conversation, he kept on repeating, half to himself and half aloud, 'Boom,

boom, boom'. We never found out what he meant.

In August 1942, I was returning home very late – it was almost dawn – when I heard an aircraft overhead. I recognised at once that it was German. Next day, I was driving south with my father and Frank Aiken. We had not gone far when Aiken said that a British plane had been shot down in Meath and that its pilot had later died of wounds in St Bricín's military hospital. The pilot was Polish, Flying Officer Boleslaw J. Sawiak, a member of the Polish squadron in the British airforce stationed at Kilkeel, Co. Down. Aiken remarked: 'Those planes [the Germans] have a sting in their tail.' I later learned that two other Spitfires of that squadron followed the German plane, a JU88, down the east coast and shot it down. The German crash-landed and the crew was uninjured, save one. The surviving Germans were interned.

That summer of 1942 dragged on with no mention of a break for me. During that period, the army was to carry out extensive manoeuvres in Munster, and Father was anxious that I should accompany him. Robinson agreed, so my holidays were arranged to coincide with the manoeuvres. We set out for Cork where, as usual, we stayed with the Dowdalls, leaving each morning to follow the exercises and troop movements and not returning until late at night or even the early hours of the morning. We were often joined by the 'top brass', including the chief of staff, Lt General Dan McKenna, who was seldom far from Father's side.

The story of his appointment dates back to 1932, when an eminent scientist, Professor John Nolan, was lost in the Wicklow hills while carrying out some experiments. He had been caught out in the great blizzard which occurred in the early part of the year. As time passed, there was considerable anxiety for his safety, and Father, Vivion and others set out as a rescue party. When they reached Enniskerry, they found all the routes completely impassable. Even men on horseback could not move as the horses became stuck up to their bellies in the deep snow. The army was called out to join the search, and Father was greatly impressed by the organisational skills and initiative of the officer in charge, Major McKenna.

Eventually Prof. Nolan was found safe and sound in a cottage. When the appointment of chief of staff was made during the early part for the war, a number of names came before Father, who remembered the incident in 1932 and the way in which Major McKenna had used his head in an emergency. Father was obviously impressed and chose him to be chief of staff. I was but a mere volunteer in the LDF and of course kept my distance but he was always most courteous to me. I had a great respect for him as had all those under his command.

We returned to Cork in September and again Father was anxious that I accompany him. He went ahead of me, so the difficulty arose as to how I would join him. Apparently he mentioned this to the general who said that matters should be left to him. I subsequently received a phone call from Colonel Devlin in army headquarters who told me that he had orders from the chief of staff to take me to Cork; he would call for me the following afternoon at 5.30 p.m. sharp. I remember the brand new Chevrolet staff car, complete with driver, arriving at the house. We proceeded at some speed, but I noticed that the colonel was rather sullen en route and spoke little. I, of course, did not speak until I was spoken to. I later discovered that Col Devlin was furious that the general required his presence in the south when he thought he could have a quiet time remaining in Dublin. When we reached our destination, Col Devlin practically frog-marched me to the general who smiled and extended his hand in greeting. Returning the colonel's salute, the general gave him a wry smile. It was clear that the general knew that I was acting as a personal aide to Father, and that I could do things for him which he did not wish to delegate to strangers, not even to his ever faithful aide, Commandant Sean Brennan.

During the course of the military manoeuvres, we found ourselves deep in the heart of south-west Cork. We were journeying through desolate and remote upland when we suddenly came across a small party of soldiers. The cars stopped, we got out to investigate, and found a young corporal with his section. They had been lying in the ditch, and looked worn out and dishevelled. The embarrassed corporal could hardly believe his eyes when he saw us. He jumped up, pulled himself together, buttoned up his tunic and snapped to attention, as did his men. The chief of staff and his aide, Lt

Col Bobby Childers, were with us, as was the Minister for Defence, Oscar Traynor. Father said nothing, then the general enquired about what the corporal and his men were doing there. He explained that he had been cut off from his unit, an infantry battalion. They had been ordered to hold this position and had had no rations for two days. He spoke with the strongest Northern accent. Hearing this, the chief said with a somewhat sarcastic smile: 'I see, corporal, you are from Cork.' Like a flash, the corporal replied: 'Yes, sir, like yourself.' The general was a native of Tyrone and the corporal from Derry city!

I was with Father in the headquarters of the 2nd Division when news came through that two soldiers had been drowned in the course of the manoeuvres while attempting to cross the River Blackwater. Father was visibly disturbed by this news.

While we were in Cork, I accompanied Father on a run on the motor torpedo boat MI with the new naval service. Father also carried out an inspection of the forts in Cork harbour which he had not seen since they were taken over from the British in July 1938.

The Air Corps had pressed a Lockheed 'Hudson' bomber into service. It had been in the service of the British and had survived many operational flights. It was quite evident from patches on the fuselage that the plane had sustained damage from gunfire or shrapnel. After repairs, the plane was taken over by the Air Corps.

Father told me that he was going to have an aerial inspection of a large part of the country. He did not specifically mention any details, and I knew that I should not enquire further. We took off from Baldonnell and flew due south and then west to land at Shannon. We were not long airborne when I decided to inspect the interior and made my way to the gun blister mounted on top of the fuselage. I climbed inside where I had a splendid view of the countryside. Flying astern was an Avro 'Anson'. I waved a greeting to the pilot of the other plane who acknowledged my wave. Suddenly, and without any warning, the guns reared upwards and jammed my legs so I could not get out of the seat. I had the elementary sense not to touch anything, being quite ignorant of the mechanisms of these guns, but at the same time I could not communicate with our pilot or anyone else aboard. There was nothing for it but to stay there. In time, we lost height and prepared for our final descent into Shannon, to land on grass as there were no concrete runways then. As we touched down and as the tail wheels hit the ground, I was violently bumped, hitting my head repeatedly off the roof of the gun blister. I did my best to protect myself but could do little until the aircraft came to rest. Then, of course, I could not be found. When I was finally rescued, the pilot was absolutely furious. I really don't think he accepted my explanation, that I had been accidentally jammed in and certainly not through anything I had done; nor had I the slightest wish to stay there while we landed. He went on: 'You could have broken your bloody neck! Crew do not land there, even on active service!' I'm sure he was right but I had simply no alternative. I was indeed lucky, particularly that this unfortunate incident was kept from my father. After lunch, we took off again. This time, I made sure to remain in the body of the aircraft. We flew north over Galway, then on towards Donegal, turning east along the border and then south to Baldonnell. It had been an eventful day.

# CHAPTER XII

*War-time Transport*
*Meeting my Future Wife*

In 1943, invasion seemed less likely than heretofore. Although the Emergency was still in full swing with all its restrictions, certain, what can be called normal, activities did take place. One of these was the making of the film *Henry V* with Laurence Olivier in the lead. Much of the filming took place during the summer in Powerscourt Demesne, Enniskerry, Co. Wicklow. Father was invited to watch as some of the film was shot. He took me with him, and we arrived on a rather dull, overcast day. Lord Powerscourt received Father and we were then led to a tent to meet Olivier and several members of the film crew. We had lunch in a large tent at a long, narrow table with Father on one side, accompanied by senior members of the undertaking, including Lord Powerscourt. Olivier sat opposite, resplendent in his costume, and entered into conversation with Father. With his knowledge and love of history, Father began to speak to Olivier about the Battle of Agincourt in 1415 and in particular the near invincibility of the English archers. Olivier became quite enthusiastic and his replies showed clearly that he had an intimate knowledge of this famous battle and of the period.

Later, someone remarked about Olivier's make-up, which was stunning. His face was heavily made-up and his hair exactly like the colour of red ink of the time. These were the early days of colour films, hence the exaggerated tones used. Olivier smiled and said to Father: 'You know, sir, my nose is not as well-shaped as may now appear.' He then began to pull rather violently at the bridge of his nose and painfully removed a 'build up' of some plastic substance which had been applied by the make-up people. Having done so, he said with a broad smile: 'You see, my nose is not as well formed as you may have thought!' Someone asked him why Vivienne

Leigh was not present. He laughed and said that she was working elsewhere. All through the lunch, he was friendly and showed that he had a good sense of fun but was obviously conscious of his own fame as an actor.

Afterwards, we were brought out to see the great cavalry charge. A week or more before, every poor horse within a radius of many miles had been rounded up – it was said that up to 600 horses were involved. Members of the army had also been released temporarily to take place. Olivier spoke of his gratitude for this and remarked on their great discipline, as it was no mean task to organise and manage such an undertaking. In due course, the 'French' Cavalry lined up about a quarter of a mile away and the order to charge was given. It was an awesome sight to see them approach at full gallop, their lances flashing as they came on with a great thunder of hooves, to say nothing of the shouts from the French who were eager to join in the fight. As they approached nearer and nearer, the English released a shower of arrows – a dangerous operation, although no one was hurt.

Before we left, Mrs Norah Maguire (wife of the President of the High Court) was standing beside Lord Powerscourt. I was by her side. The Lord of the Manor began by saying that it was so good of him to have given the facilities in Powerscourt. 'Good?' she said. 'Aren't you being well paid for it!' She was always someone who could express her feelings forcefully.

When Lord Powerscourt heard that Father was coming, he refused to fly the Tricolour but flew what he called the 'Green Ensign' instead. Another actor of note, whom my father met at the time, was Leslie Howard. He called on Father in Government Buildings and the pair chatted briefly. Father told me that he was much impressed by him and his pleasant speaking voice, but I cannot say whether or not he suspected that Howard was in fact a British spy or agent, who shortly afterwards lost his life in the air in mysterious circumstances. Maureen O'Hara was another film star whom my father met. He thought her charming and sincere. Regrettably I never met her, but I knew her brother who had a practice at the Bar for a short while.

By now I had become quite accustomed to my life as a solicitor's apprentice which for the most part consisted of being at best law clerk. In fairness, Tommy Robinson allowed me time off for the LDF when this proved necessary, although he was openly quite pro-British in his views. If I was lucky, and depending on the work of the day, I often managed to get a lift home to lunch with Father, although he could not always manage to get home when the Dáil was sitting or for many other reasons. Robinson saw to it that my nose was kept to the grindstone, even to the point of delivering letters and documents by hand rather than having them sent by post.

One day, I pointed out that I had no less than nineteen letters to deliver, in addition to all my other work. Robinson was not in good form and his reply was curt: 'I wish you had twenty-nine. Continue with your work.' These duties were obviously time-consuming, particularly since Robinson did not wish me to use my bicycle. He said he would not take the responsibility, even though the traffic was light, with no private cars whatsoever. Altogether this exercise kept me very fit and healthy, there were times when I felt quite exhausted. Indeed I wore out a new pair of shoes in less than a month from all the walking. The purchase of a new pair meant the use of more precious clothing coupons.

While at home for lunch with Father on one occasion, he asked if I could do a message for him in town. I was particularly pressed that day as Robinson required me to be back in the office not later than 4.30 p.m. to attend a consultation. I was naturally anxious to accommodate Father but concerned that I must have my work finished before I returned to the office. In a quiet, somewhat hurt tone, I said to him: 'Oh Dad, if you had as much on your mind today as I have, you would not ask me to do this message!' Father instantly burst out laughing and I realised what I had just said. However, I managed to get his message done and complete my work. Father told me later that he often told this story which he enjoyed immensely.

One Sunday in the summer of 1943, I had just returned home from duty with the LDF. While I was waiting for a meal, I went into the garden and walked around to the front of the house. I was about to go in by the front door when I heard the noise of cars coming up the avenue. Thinking that it must be Father returning home, I waited to greet him. His car came around the bend, closely followed by another. The two cars and the escort car then stopped. I had clearly been seen and I could not make my escape. Out of the first car stepped Father, accompanied by Frank Aiken and Father's aide, Commandant Sean Brennan. Out of the second emerged Lt General McKenna with his aide Lt Colonel Bobby Childers. I quickly donned my beret, snapped to attention and gave my smartest salute. As Father went up the steps he did not notice me. Frank Aiken simply grinned, but the general saw me and returned the salute. Then with a smile, he half-whispered: 'At ease, Terry.'

On a summer Saturday afternoon in 1943 at about three o'clock, I was sitting at a seat in the garden, having a quiet smoke outside the breakfast room window. Father never approved of me smoking and certainly did not like it in his presence. Father was inside when quite suddenly, I heard the roar of an aircraft. I looked up and saw a Liberator bomber in British air force livery fly very low in a south-easterly direction. It was so low that I could clearly see the helmeted pilot and his companion. I immediately rushed in to Father and told him what I had seen. To my surprise, he looked up and said, quite sharply, 'Get out the car.'

Father got in, accompanied by one of the guards, and told me to drive. He asked in which direction the plane had flown. When I replied that it was heading in the direction of Dalkey and Killiney, he told me to proceed there. As we drove, he repeatedly asked if we could sight the aircraft which we could not. Having reached Dalkey and Killiney, he told the guard to keep a look out, especially towards the sea, but the guard saw nothing. After a while, he told me to return home. When we reached Herberton, he told me to put the car away and nothing further was mentioned. I thought it very odd indeed that we should attempt to chase a plane by car and had no idea what was in Father's mind. But I also knew that, on occasions such as this, it was not for me 'to know the reason why'.

The war had been over for a number of years – perhaps it was 1947 – when I was sitting at dinner with Father. Suddenly he turned to me, and in a tone so typical of him when he used a deliberate understatement, he said 'Do you remember when I asked you to drive me when you saw an aeroplane pass over the garden?' 'Indeed I do,' I replied, 'and I can tell you now that I thought it very odd to attempt to chase an aircraft in a car.' This answer only made him smile. 'Well,' he said, 'I can now tell you about it. When we came home, I telephoned Maffey [Sir John Maffey, later Lord Rugby the British representative during the war] and told him what you had seen. He took a very serious view and said that he would have the matter investigated at once.' And it seems that he did.

Maffey contacted London and by an elaborate chain of command, the aircraft was traced to a squadron based in Wales and the crew identified. The pilot was a young Irishman who lived in Dublin, and he thought that he would chance his arm by flying over Dublin to buzz his folks who lived in a southern suburb. Father looked at me and said: 'The unfortunate pilot was, I believe, court-martialled and reprimanded.' That momentary sighting had triggered off events and enquiries right from the top. Concluding his story in a way that was very typical of him, Father added 'If I had known that the poor fellow was about to be court-martialled, I would have sought to intervene on his behalf.'

A year or so before this, Master O'Hanlon thought that I should learn something about sailing. He himself had already spent a good part of his early life at sea and as we have seen was a master mariner. He was the owner of a fine yacht, *Evora*, which was berthed in Dun Laoghaire; his two sons, Ruairi and Desmond were keen and accomplished sailors as was his wife Ethel. I was detailed to present myself in Dun Laoghaire each Saturday. On the first occasion, I was inadequately dressed for the voyage, although this was quickly put to right by the master. We rowed out to *Evora* and boarded her. There was an important race that day and to my great embarrassment, I was to be part of the crew. The master was friendly with 'an old salt' who joined the crew. O'Hanlon was our skipper and gave me some elementary instructions about what to do – more particularly what I was not to do. The race commenced, and as we sailed out into a stiff wind which swept across Dublin Bay, *Evora* pitched and tossed while the master called out his orders. To his annoyance, I became suddenly violently seasick and he promptly sent me down below, saying: 'You have got to get used to this sort of thing.' There I remained in misery for a considerable time. *Evora* had a particular rival on her way across the bay, but due to the skill of O'Hanlon, we gained first place, taking the wind out of our rival's sails as we rounded the final buoy.

A dinner for the winning crew was given by the Howth Yacht Club. Still in my borrowed nautical gear and feeling anything but a sailor, I was especially embarrassed to be included in the congratulations. I dreaded the return journey to Dun Laoghaire and timidly suggested to the master that

I would make my way home by bus. He would have none of it. 'Don't worry,' he said, 'you will be fine on the way back.' The wind had now risen and the sea quite choppy as we sailed for Dun Laoghaire but I had found my sea-legs as the water broke over the gunwales and the sails strained against the rushing wind. While the master knew that I had no great call for the sea, I came to enjoy those trips. Attitudes were different then. The master, his wife and two sons were very poor swimmers. I could not swim at all. They believed in the philosophy that if the sea is to claim you, it will.

*Evora* was destined to be an unlucky ship as tragedy struck some years later when Desmond, the younger son, was lost off her while on a solo voyage to Angelsea. The exact reason for his death was never established but it appears that he must have slipped overboard. In time the master sold *Evora*. The boat itself had a mysterious end. Without warning, it burst into flames at its moorings in Dun Laoghaire and became a total wreck.

Robinson allowed me time off in the autumn of 1943 as I had to face my first serious law examination. Known in those days as the 'Intermediate', it took place half-way through the apprenticeship. I got down to my law books and attended lectures and grinds, which in those days offered the only practical way of preparing for an examination. These were conducted by the well-known and much respected solicitor, the late Brendan P. McCormack. Generations of solicitors' apprentices would never have qualified had it not been for his skilful teaching. He always displayed great interest in his students but worked them to the limit. I sat for my examination in October 1943 and passed without difficulty, although not with any particular distinction.

A fellow apprentice of that period was Leslie Mellon. We became close friends and have remained so up to the time of his unexpected death. He was destined to have a profound influence on the remainder of my life, for it was he who introduced me to my future wife. Leslie attended the now defunct Avoca School which he left with academic distinction.

Although Robinson would not allow me to ride my bicycle on office business, he had no objection to my using it to come to and from the office. Leslie Mellon was an enthusiastic cyclist and always used his bicycle. We frequently met and cycled home together. If the weather was poor, we met and went home by train, leaving our bicycles at the station.

I particularly recall Halloween 1943. We met as usual and as was our habit, we stopped at Donnybrook where Les bought the *Evening Mail* (long since defunct) which consisted of only four pages in those days, as was the case with all newspapers due to war-time restrictions on imported newsprint. We sat for a while on the cross-bars of our bicycles while we smoked our cigarettes before resuming our journey along the Bray Road, then almost devoid of traffic.

The reader will have noticed my various references to smoking, but in those days, almost everyone smoked. One was entitled to a ration of five cigarettes a day and you felt cheated if you did not obtain your ration at six old pence for ten cigarettes. While modern medicine frowns upon and indeed wholly condemns cigarette smoking, it served its purpose then and helped to fill in the many gaps with the acute shortages of food and many things which the generation of today simply take for granted.

Attitudes were quite different then. If a person met with an accident or received a shock, the first thing you did was to offer the victim a lighted cigarette and, if you could, a drop of brandy or whiskey. This was very much the norm in England during the Blitz. Today's medicine would utterly condemn such practices.

As Les and I sat on our bikes, he pulled a bundle from his inside coat pocket, saying that he had something very interesting to show me. He was apprentice to a well-known and long-established firm of solicitors, T. W. Hardman, and on this particular day, his master had asked him to search the basement of 14 Molesworth Street for some deeds. In the course of his work, he came across all sorts of his documents going back to the eighteenth and nineteenth centuries; some even dated from the seventeenth century. Among these papers were some original letters from the Sheares brothers, including a long letter written by Henry Sheares on the night before his execution in 1798. This letter, which is of considerable historic interest, is a pathetic outpouring by poor Henry which tells how he and his brother John were betrayed by the infamous Captain Armstrong, and his grief at leaving his beloved wife and family. In the event, Henry was not properly hanged but choked to death the following day, 14 July 1798.

I asked Les if I might take this to read more carefully, on the strict undertaking that I would return it to him the following Monday. He agreed to this condition and accepted my solemn promise. That evening, I read the letter with ever-growing interest and then asked my sister Máirín to copy it, as my own writing was so poor. She copied it, and as a well-trained apprentice, I compared the copy with the original and certified it to be a true copy. I showed this and some other letters to Father who remarked that these precious documents should be given to the National Library.

Leslie and I met as usual the following Monday. I returned the letters and told him of Father's views. Leslie passed these on to his master who, however, took little or no interest in the affair. Years later, John Denny Stokes, a fellow apprentice and contemporary of Leslie and me, succeeded to the firm and I took up the matter with him. He was enthusiastic about the idea but as there some difficulty in the library accepting them, he presented them to Trinity College where he had been a distinguished graduate.

More recently, I used these letters as a subject of a paper which I delivered to the Old Dublin Society of which I have been an active member for a considerable number of years. But when I came to inspect the letters in Trinity, I was shocked to learn that the last letter, and by far the most important, was missing. By good fortune, I had my certified copy. I showed this copy to Christina Dowager Lady Longford, a great authority on the Sheares brothers, and she had no doubt about the authenticity of these documents and their great historic interest.

By the spring of 1944, Leslie Mellon and I gave up our bicycles as a means of transport to and from the office. We preferred the trains, leaving the bicycles at the station. Those wartime trains were really quite something. They were hauled by stalwart locomotives, many dating from the nineteenth century and often with gas-lighted six-wheel carriages. Much of the rolling stock was from a bygone era, and it was most romantic to be in a Victorian or Edwardian setting. With the passing of steam traction, so much of the romance of railway travel has been lost forever. With the limited transport available, these trains were invariably crowded to capacity. Indeed more passengers were allowed on than were within in the strictest limits of safety and we were at times packed like sardines. Yet everyone was cheerful and there was a good camaraderie among the passengers whose age groups varied from quite young to those of advanced years.

There was a famous train which left Westland Row every evening, known as the 'ten-to-six' (its correct time was actually seven minutes to six). An express, its first stop was Blackrock. One special journey for me on this famous train took place on a dark and blustery winter's evening. My carriage was one of the older type, with separate compartments. The facing seats were fully occupied, while the narrow aisle was crowded with standing passengers. I was standing at the end of the aisle right beside an open window. Even though it was winter-time, it was necessary to keep the window open because of the lack of air and overcrowding. Just as we passed Sydney Parade station, I was accidentally jostled and my head went slightly out the window. The wind was blowing strongly and with the train doing about forty-five miles an hour, a gust of wind caught my hat and off it disappeared into the darkness. I felt a bit foolish but there was nothing I could do. My fellow passengers grinned sympathetically. Once again, my poor mother came to the rescue and a new hat had to be purchased with the loss of clothing coupons.

Those war-time trains proved to be invaluable. In addition to the trams, they provided vital links. Without them, the transport position would have been quite hopeless, since buses were few in number and depended on vital diesel fuel.

While the trams and trains served the southern suburbs, western parts of the outer city were less fortunate, although these suburbs were not as extensive then. The only tram routes remaining were O'Connell Street/Nelson's Pillar to Dalkey, and Nelson's Pillar to Dartry and Terenure. All other routes on this highly efficient network had ceased before, or in the first year of the war, many as far back as 1938, including all routes to the northern parts of the city. Some parts like Howth were lucky and well served by the former Great Northern Railway. I had married and moved to Foxrock before I started using the now defunct Harcourt Street–Bray line which was closed in 1958. It is difficult, if not well nigh impossible, to understand the mentality that led to the closure of this valuable commuter line, particularly that of Dr C. S. Andrews, then chief of CIÉ. He remained deaf to all protests and arguments against the closure. But it must be said that he was not the only one who remained deaf to all pleas. As I was active in endeavouring to retain this valuable railway, I spoke to the Minister for Transport, Erskine Childers. He was actually hostile and said that I was, like other people, suffering from 'railwayitis' and that the line was out-of-date. Even then, it seemed obvious that the southern suburbs would expand, which has indeed proved to be the case. The closure of this valuable line was erroneous, unjustified and singularly lacking in elementary judgement.

Dublin's tramway system was an institution in itself. The trams expressed so much of the atmosphere of Dublin during the first half of the twentieth century. With their passing, the city lost a great deal of its character. I travelled on nearly all of the thirty-one routes which made up the network. Many of the vehicles dated back to the earlier part of the 1900s, with the famous 'luxury' trams being introduced in the 1930s. While these later models were more comfortable and faster than their predecessors, they somehow lacked the romance of the older trams, especially the open-topped ones. The model known as the 'Balcony 8-Wheeler', was a giant. Both ends of the top deck were open to the elements, and if the weather was not too bad, it was a favourite spot for children and courting couples who snuggled together, shielding themselves from the rushing wind and isolated from the passengers in the 'saloon'.

The introduction of the luxury trams caused quite a stir. They were so much publicised when they first appeared that they were worthy of a sketch in one of O'Donovan's pantomimes in the Gaiety Theatre. Jimmy O'Dea and his friend, Frank Dunne, were the dames and there was a great banter between these famous pair. In their strong Dublin accents, the dialogue went like this: Dunne said: 'So poor Mary is gone.' 'Ah, yes,' replied Jimmy. 'Terrible, terrible sad, but, oh, she had such a beautiful death, killed by a luxury tram!'

Several stories are told of the conductors, so many of whom were real characters. They were very much in command of their 'ship' and enforced strict discipline aboard. On at least two occasions which I remember, when a passenger was unruly with too much drink taken, the conductor looked out until he spotted a garda, then stopped the tram. The garda entered the tram and removed the offending passenger to the nearest garda station.

I remember two stories, both true, about the conductors from my boyhood. The trams ran in the middle of the roads and the passengers had to walk from the pavement to board them. One day in the early 1930s, a tram stopped at the corner of Holles Street and Merrion Square. A middle-aged lady, very prim and with a grand accent, walked out and called to a conductor: 'Will this tram leave me to Kingstown?' As he pulled the strap to ring the bell so that the driver would proceed, the conductor replied:

'Twenty years too late, madam!' Another conductor, while passengers lined up to board the tram, saw that the vehicle was full. Among those standing in the crowd was a lady who called out: 'Where will this tram leave me?' 'Precisely where you are, madam,' came the reply as the conductor pulled the strap!

These luxury trams were capable of a great turn of speed. On a winter's night in the mid-1930s, I was a passenger with Christy Cruise as he drove behind a tram making its way to Dalkey. At that moment, the tram was running between Merrion Gates and Booterstown. In the normal way, Christy would have passed it but he noted that it was travelling at just under fifty miles per hour. This was remarkable, considering the massive bulk and weight of such a vehicle.

The last tram I ever saw running was a Luxury 8-Wheeler, Number 8, making its way to the depot in Blackrock, still known to the older generation as 'the stables' in memory of the horse trams. It was a sad sight to see the vehicle being taken away to be scrapped or sold. This was in July 1949, the day after the last tram had run in Dublin.

Now the new era of trams in Dublin will soon be upon us with the Luas system. But I very much doubt it will ever have the romance and thrill which we knew with the old Dublin United Tramway Company.

One bright evening in late March 1944, Leslie asked me to meet a special friend who travelled on the 'ten-to-six'. We boarded the train and alighted at Blackrock where he spotted his friend, a very attractive, well-dressed young girl walking smartly along the platform. Leslie stopped her and introduced me to Phyllis Blake. We crossed the footbridge together. The Blake and Mellon families had known one another for years and I had known Phyllis to see since childhood when she lived in Booterstown and later in Blackrock. She remembered me, as a young boy, walking along Cross Avenue on my way to a music lesson, swinging my violin case as I strolled along.

Phyllis lived in 'St Kilda' in Avoca Avenue, while Leslie lived in nearby Glenart Avenue. From then on the three of us met regularly on our way home and thus began the romance between Phyllis and myself.

Her father, Percival C. Blake, was one of a large family. He entered the civil service as a young man and quickly gained recognition for his fine brain, the mastery of his work and his capacity to execute a task properly and quickly. During World War I, his special gifts came to the attention of Lord Granard and he was awarded an honour in the service, rarely given at that time. Later he was awarded the OBE for his outstanding service.

With the creation of the Free State, Percival Blake chose to remain in the Irish civil service, although strenuous efforts were made in London to entice him to the British Post Office with a promise of certain and immediate promotion, to be followed by a knighthood. All this he strongly resisted. He told me that he never regarded himself as anything but Irish and wished to remain in his native land. Above all, he did not wish to bring up his family in England. He had a singular gift in design and architecture and was also splendid with figures. It fell to him to re-design the GPO after its destruction in 1916. In later years, he designed many other post offices throughout the state. He was known and acknowledged both at home and in England as a highly skilled negotiator, and for having considerable business acumen.

Percival Blake also had a marvellous sense of humour and once told me a story of how he was negotiating a matter on behalf of the Post Office with the Department of Finance. Things got difficult and he found Finance very resistant, so he remarked to an his opposite number: 'You are like an inverted Mr Micawber, waiting for something to turn *down*'. Among his varied achievements was his work at his golf club in Dun Laoghaire, of which he became captain, and later president. His memory is still cherished there to this day.

Due to wartime restrictions, life took on a simple pattern and our recreation was necessarily confined. My first 'date' with Phyllis was cycling with her to Ballyogan in Lehaunstown, then unspoiled, open countryside. Our main recreation consisted of going to the pictures, either in the local cinema in Blackrock or Dun Laoghaire or else by tram to town. We also enjoyed the 'hops' at the Law Society. These dances were confined to solicitors' apprentices and their friends and were strictly supervised under the ever watchful eye of William the Porter. They took place in the lovely old hall which had been the library of the Law Society until comparatively recent times. When the dancing had finished, we had to catch the last tram or bus, and this was well before midnight. Occasionally we went to more formal dances in the Gresham Hotel which were dress–suit affairs. If it happened to be a special occasion, we used a taxi, but these were expensive. At other times, we had to use our bicycles.

Phyllis' parents made me welcome from the beginning. Her mother soon became my champion and our rapport grew from that time. Phyllis also met my parents and Mother took to her at once. Father too was very fond of Phyllis and had an affection and respect which grew as the years passed by.

Unlike me, Phyllis was fond of sport. She played a fair game of tennis but excelled in table tennis and won several cups. Alas, the more she was with me, the less she was able to play. Certainly I would have been a useless partner. She had inherited her parents' gifts and was very useful with her hands, especially in needlework and knitting. Like her father, she showed a great gift for design and had an accurate eye. In those days, she had a sweet true voice and was active in her church choir. We spent many pleasurable hours together in our respective houses. In summer, we played a little tennis and even archery with Ruairi in Herberton.

Life for me as a solicitor's apprentice was now becoming a serious matter with my final examination not too far off. As part of our course we attended special lectures in the Law Society. One of these was by a well-known Dublin solicitor, the late Frederick Gilligan, who also travelled on the ten-to-six. He often saw Phyllis and me together, with Les Mellon sometimes making up the trio.

I had not done as well as Mr Gilligan had hoped in a test at Easter. He was a splendid lecturer, but his passion was for 'future interests', one of the most difficult and complex aspects of the law of property and the dread of most students. He explained to me where I was wrong, for he had always taken an interest in my work. Then he remarked that he was disappointed with the latest test: 'Perhaps you have been seeing too much of Miss Blake.' Perhaps he was right: in fact I know he was. Like the other passengers on the ten-to-six, Gilligan made his way to and from the station on his bicycle. Alas, he had a bad heart and died suddenly from a heart attack some years later. We had all a great respect for him.

In the spring of 1944, the threat of invasion, as far as the ordinary citizen was concerned, seemed to have abated. Life proceeded smoothly, notwithstanding the many limitations and restrictions of the Emergency which continued as heretofore.

Suddenly in February, like a bolt from the blue, another crisis erupted with the delivery of the so-called 'American Note', the brainchild of David Gray, the US diplomatic representative in Ireland. He was obsessed with a hatred for my father and his government and their stance on neutrality. Further, he was violently opposed to any move which might lead to the ending of partition. He went far beyond the parameters of his diplomatic position by approaching some members of the opposition in the Dáil in an effort to induce them to depose Father and bring down the government. In this, however, he failed, as members of the opposition, to their great credit and sense of integrity, rebuffed such overtures or at least refused to co-operate.

Gray's primary intention was to secure the ports and establish bases and other facilities for the use and occupation by Allied forces. The consequences of such a move would have provoked appalling bloodshed and disaster for the country, as such an occupation would have been resisted. At first, the British connived in this plan but their cabinet was divided, with Churchill and Herbert Morrisson in favour and Anthony Eden opposed; the latter remarked that the proposal 'would be likely to give rise to acute difficulties'. In the event, the British showed more sense. Seeing the dangers of a forced occupation, they acted as a restraining factor on the impulsive, at times naïve, but always mal-intentioned Gray.

Although the 'American Note' as presented was modified, it still contained a serious threat and could have been interpreted as an ultimatum. It had demanded the removal of the German and Japanese diplomatic missions to this country. The British supported this note fully and confirmed their support of the American demand.

True to his nature, Father held his nerve and stood firm, rejecting the contents of the note, but not without the greatest fear that the US and British might well attack. In the event, they realised the folly of such a move which would destroy their moral claim for fighting the war. After all, was not the invasion of Poland the pretext for the British to go to war? Further, were both Britain and the USA not claiming to be at war to defend the rights of small nations and the liberation of countries such as Belgium, Holland, Denmark?

Once Father had made his attitude and position quite clear, showing that he would not yield to the demand, the crisis mercifully passed. Gray and his colleagues had failed. Yet again Father had demonstrated his adroit handling of what could have been a disastrous situation. The State's defence forces were put on full alert, including the LDF. Special exercises took place in which I played my own very small part.

When the war was over, Father spoke to me of his dealings with the British, German and American diplomatic representatives. He spoke with a degree of warmth for Sir John Maffey for whom he had a great respect; he always acted correctly and honourably, at times even proving helpful. Father spoke equally well of the German representative, Dr Eduard Hempel, and said that he was honourable and forthright in his dealings, with an understanding of this country's attitude towards neutrality. For David Gray, however, he had totally different feelings. To put it bluntly, he regarded him as nothing short of a mischief-maker, indeed a downright enemy of this country. This particularly grieved Father, especially because of the long historical connections between Ireland and the USA. He would quite reasonably have expected a much more sympathetic approach. Gray, on the other hand, never spared himself in his endeavours to sour this connection, deliberately misrepresenting Ireland's reason for remaining neutral. In the end, in spite of all his cunning, devious ways and guile, Gray failed miserably. He was no match for Eamon de Valera. A lesser man might well have yielded to the might and strength of the US and Britain, both then and in the earlier part of the war. Throughout the centuries, Ireland has had its enemies who bitterly opposed the country's struggle for freedom and independence. David Gray must, if he is remembered at all, be regarded among those enemies by his attitude and so many of his unworthy actions.

My father was always conscious of the value and importance of the American connection and his own natural affection for that country. I am quite sure, however, that he would not have had the same admiration for the US today, especially its government's foreign policy over the last few decades. Like all other large and powerful states, it has become bluntly and distinctly imperial, both in its attitude, but above all, its actions, using the time-worn excuse that it must use force to protect its 'interests' and this regardless of the fundamental rights of lesser and weaker states and nations, their lawful governments and their national assets.

The US is now following the trail of history where so many other states or countries have in the past coveted and by force taken over that to which they had no moral right. To make matters worse, the US, with its undoubted power and might, tries to bully the UN for its own selfish gain and in particular where oil is concerned of which the US itself, has plenty and great reserves. Despite its protests and gestures, oil is its real concern and all others rights must be subservient to that. No fairminded person can believe the arguments they put forward to justify their piratical activities and those of their lackey allies.

Eamon de Valera, I believe, would not have been happy with the way the European Union appears to be moving. I remember well speaking to him at the time of the entry to the EEC. While he acknowledged that entry was inevitable, he accepted this with very strong reservation regarding loss of sovereignty. He agreed fully with the concept of the development of trade and commerce and the more desirable aspects of culture from the continent of Europe. Political union or the diminution or loss of sovereignty was quite a different matter in which he felt the smaller nations would fare worst. I believe he would have opposed a situation whereby we were ruled or governed by faceless unelected officials, which already seems to be the position and which affect us and against which our European elected representatives or our ministers seem to do little but slavishly agree. Irish sovereignty, after centuries of strife and enormous sacrifice, has been too dearly won to be taken away or diminished by foreign politicians or their officials. This would not be by war or invasion, but in a more subtle way, by stealth. Such would clearly be to the detriment of this little nation. Time will tell.

From the end of May 1945, my final examination was in sight and I obtained a leave of absence from the office so I could devote all my time to study. Again I attended the indispensable grind of Brendan McCormack. Pressure built up as the summer wore on; I broke out in a rash caused by strain and nerves, and the doctor I attended was none other then Dr McCarville, the man who had saved my life when I had pneumonia in 1925. Without several injections a week, I could not have continued. Dr McCarville assured me that once the examination was over, the rash would vanish and I would be back to normal. He was right, for within days of completing the examination, the rash vanished. I sat for the examination and passed in all subjects but again, much to the disappointment of Brendan McCormack, I did not receive a merit. Examinations were always my bug-bear and seldom did I do justice to the work which I had put in. The only examinations I ever enjoyed were those which involved music, although I enjoyed the debates in the Solicitors' Apprentice Debating Society and acted on the committee of that society for some time. I had won distinction by winning the silver medal for legal debate, and was beaten, I believe by one mark, for the gold medal by a fellow apprentice, a brilliant student from the North, Jack McNally, who tragically died young from a heart attack very shortly after he qualified.

Having passed the legal examinations, there remained another hurdle to cross: the compulsory 'Second Irish' examination. It was entirely thanks to my mother's tuition I passed, obtaining first place. Again, actual placing was not recognised by the statute under which this examination took place: one either passed or failed. Until you passed, your name could not be entered on the Role of Solicitors.

Having qualified, I remained in Robinson's office for a further year as a junior qualified assistant. Life was now less stressful for me, with the dreaded examinations a thing of the past and I had more time for recreation.

In November 1943, there was the annual event in the Law Society buildings in the Four Courts when the auditor of the Solicitors' Apprentice Debating Society made his annual address. By tradition, he invited prominent people to speak following his address. Members of the diplomatic corps were important invited guests. I was then a senior apprentice and also a member of the committee.

That year, Father was invited to be the principal guest speaker. This function was quite a formal affair at which we were required to wear white tie and tails, and a great deal of work went into preparing for the society's most important annual event. One of the duties of the committee was to receive the guests particularly the speakers and members of the diplomatic corps. When Dr Hempel arrived, he was brought to a specially reserved room where drinks were served. The room was not particularly large and Dr Hempel was not long there when the door opened and who should come in but Sir John Maffey. He looked around and his eye lit on Dr Hempel. He took one further look and bolted from the room. Dr Hempel simply grinned. It was a great *faux pas*: Sir John should have been brought to another room and instructions had been given to separate the British, German and Italian diplomatic representatives. The event caused a stir and embarrassment, but it was shown that the fault did not lie with the members of the committee, and the unfortunate gaff was passed over.

Lord Rugby, as Sir John later became, had a good sense of humour. The story is told that one day he was motoring along Northumberland Road (where the German legation had its headquarters) with his escort car. Dr Hempel was travelling in the same direction. Maffey is supposed to have said to his driver: 'All right, let him pass on petrol protected by the Royal Navy'.

With the war at an end, my LDF unit was disbanded and wartime duties were over. The radio was dismantled and taken away, with only its small mast remaining on the gable end of the house as a reminder of more anxious times. We had our last public parade on the 'Old Victoria Pier' in Dun Laoghaire harbour. Quite a crowd turned out to see us. It was a sad affair, although the parade was not regarded as the official 'stand down'. Apart from the interesting experiences of the time and the friendships I had made, I had two lasting mementoes. One was receiving the Emergency Service Medal; the other was two brand new tyres and tubes for my bicycle! Tyres and tubes were indeed precious during the war, so when the State rewarded us by giving us new ones, it was something of real value. Slight as this gift may seem now, it was a very welcome one with the acute shortages of those days.

Looking back on those wartime years, I feel strongly that not enough credit has been given, or acknowledgement made, of those who served, particularly in the regular forces who sacrificed years of their life in the service of their country. So many of them voluntarily gave up promising careers in professions, trades, business and other occupations and all for the highest motives. Alas, there were others more selfish, giving little or no service. Limited as were the armed forces of the State were, and lacking so much in military equipment and stores, history has shown that those who served played a vital role in keeping this country neutral, thus sparing its people the anguish and ravishes of war. For this, we remain in their debt.

Lt General M. J. Costello always contended that weak in equipment as the army was at that time, it was sufficient to deter a would-be invader as such a move would cost the invader dearly, and that the price to be paid for such a move would well exceed any advantage to the aggressor.

In Father's, now world famous, speech which he delivered on 16 May 1945 (the one in which he made his masterly reply to Winston Churchill) he made a special point of thanking the army and other security forces for the invaluable service which they had rendered to the Irish nation, ending his speech with words of praise and gratitude and expressing, in truth, the feelings of the entire country when he said: 'The nation is profoundly grateful'.

Both Vivion (now with the rank of major, which was later changed to lieutenant colonel) and Ruairi completed their service, although Ruairi remained in the Reserve for some time to come. Máirín had completed her service with the Red Cross. Vivion returned to his practice as a barrister and was called to the Inner Bar. Ruairi resumed his studies in archaeology and eventually became Professor of Archaeology in UCD. Éamon's practice as a doctor continued to flourish. Emer, Vivion and Éamon had all married during the war years. Emer had married her old college friend, Brian Ó Cuív, who later became a professor and director of the Institute of Advanced Studies. Vivion married Brid Hearne, a gifted graduate of science whom he had met in the College of Science while carrying out experiments on explosives in the earlier part of the war. Éamon married Sally O'Doherty whom he met when she was a theatre sister in Holles Street Hospital. All three weddings were quiet family affairs, something my parents desired especially during those anxious times so full of limitations and restrictions.

# CHAPTER XIII

*The War Ends • Learn to Fly*
*Pursue Interests in Chopin & John Field*
*My Practice as a Solicitor*

I remember so well the day the war ended on 5 May 1945. Strangely, there was a brief thunderstorm, just as there had been the morning the war began. I remember phoning Phyllis and remarking that it was the first time we had spoken in peace-time, or at least with the cessation of hostilities in Europe. I mentioned that I hoped life would now return to what we knew in pre-war days.

The future now looked brighter. But on 13 May, Winston Churchill gave his famous victory speech in which he made a wanton and bitter attack on my father and the Irish nation. The country's reaction was instantaneous as even those of different political opinions united in a massive wave of indignation and anger. The entire country, indeed the world, awaited Father's reply.

Three days later, Father made his now famous broadcast. He began with a prayer thanking God for saving the nation from the ravages of war. He then thanked the political parties, the defence forces and all sections of society for their constant maintenance of neutrality. Still, the nation awaited his reply to Churchill. Then it came. In calm, quiet, controlled and masterful tones, he admonished the British prime minister's wholly unworthy and petulant attack, thereby routing Churchill's onslaught. (For a full account of this speech, the reader is referred to the biography of my father by Lord Longford and Thomas P. O'Neill Part IV. For the full text of the speech, refer to *Speeches and Statements by Eamon de Valera (1917-1973)* edited by Maurice Moynihan.)

The effect of the speech was electric. The entire country stood behind the sentiments expressed. Messages of congratulations poured in from all parts of the country and the world, especially the USA. Later in the Dáil,

Father received a standing ovation, a unique demonstration of approval and spirit of unity. It was, to quote Churchill himself, Father's 'finest hour' – or at least one of them.

It is said that Randolph Churchill, the prime minister's son, had advised his father not to attack de Valera and this country, but foolishly, the British prime minister did not take this son's advice and paid the price. As far as my father was concerned, his reputation was never higher. This speech was one of the great triumphs of his long life. Mother was 'immensely' proud of him. She gave her characteristic dance which she did when she was overjoyed or greatly elated.

While rationing and shortages remained into 1946 and beyond, private motoring had been permissible from November 1945. Many pre-war cars were put back on the road, although petrol was still rationed and in short supply. Shortly after this, I asked Father to lend me his car to take Phyllis to a formal dance in the Gresham Hotel. He was surprised at the request: he had not realised private motoring was again lawful. I assured him it was, and when this was confirmed by Vivion, he willingly loaned me the car. It was a lovely feeling, being able to use a car again for purely private purposes.

Tommy Robinson had always made it clear that there was no long-term future for me in his office, so I had to look for another position. I obtained a post as junior qualified assistant in the office of P. J. Ruttledge, then the General Solicitor for Minors and Wards of Court. Ruttledge had given up his position as a cabinet minister as he wished to return to the law. He was one of my father's closest friends; Father had a particular regard and affection for him. For his part, Ruttledge revered my father and was completely loyal, remaining one of the closest to 'the Chief'.

My years with Ruttledge were happy ones. He turned out to be a kindly boss with a paternal interest in his staff. He suffered from poor health, not least from wounds he had received in the troubled times from 1921-22 where he had been a fearless soldier. It was quite obvious that he still suffered pain from these wounds which he bore with great fortitude. His poor state of health prevented him from working in the office as he would have wished; he was still a TD and active in politics. One of the most attractive sides of his character was his wonderful sense of humour.

He had a great facility for making friends, even among his political opponents. He told a story well, loved a joke and enjoyed a drink with the 'lads', as he called his friends in Leinster House. Father, despite his deep affection for him, thought that Ruttledge was at times consuming more alcohol than was good for him. Very gently, Father chided him, suggesting that perhaps he could drink less. Ruttledge listened and when Father had finished, he replied in a soft, gentle Mayo accent: 'Ah Chief, one swallow never made a summer!' Father giggled when he told me this story, adding that his friend's reply had totally disarmed him.

Underneath Paddy Ruttledge's gentle manner and soft spoke voice lay a tiger. While opposing the solicitor Arthur Cox (then very prominent in the profession), Cox phoned him to offer terms of settlement which were quite unacceptable to Ruttledge. When the conversation ended, Ruttledge put down the phone saying: 'There's the old fellow Cox trying to slash me across the face with an olive branch!' During the trouble times, he was nicknamed 'Padraic the Ruthless'.

In my time, Alexis FitzGerald was a senior solicitor on the staff and for practical purposes, he ran and managed the office. I always found him most courteous, friendly, understanding and willing to help and guide where this proved necessary. He had an excellent mind and a very thorough knowledge of many aspects of law. He had married Grace, the eldest daughter of John A. Costello, who tragically died young. He later became the senior partner of the firm McCann Fitzgerald Roche and Dudley.

My work during the next few years consisted of dealing with what were then called, 'lunacy cases' – dealing with the estates of persons of unsound mind, as well as the estates of minors. The law then was that a person did not obtain their majority until the age of twenty-one.

By then, Ruairi had a car, a pre-war Morris 8. He was very generous and often loaned me this attractive little vehicle when I had a date with Phyllis. Petrol was still in short supply and we had to measure it out in milk bottles. Our favourite runs were to Co. Wicklow, particularly the Devil's Glen near Ashford. In those times, the glen was quite unspoiled and one could find peace and beauty among the giant beech trees. Even in the blaze of a summer's day, the foliage almost blotted out the sky. Only by the lakeside did the bright sunshine shine through. Tragically, theses lofty and noble giants were later felled and the glen was never the same again. True, it was replanted, but it will take many years to recover its former majesty and beauty.

Nun's Cross church (Church of Ireland) and its surrounding graveyard was another of our haunts. The church had its own peculiar feeling of peace. I loved to linger there, reading many plaques which adorned the walls, relating to the history of Anglo-Irish families who lived in the neighbourhood, including Major Casement, a cousin of Roger Casement. This too was the parish church of the Synge family whose estate, Glanmore, was close by. John Millington Synge knew this church and the surrounding countryside intimately.

In much later years, I obtained permission to play the organ in the church. One beautiful summer's evening, I played a number of hymns and pieces while the sexton, Richard Bradshaw, stood beside me, singing in a loud tenor voice with a distinctive Wicklow accent. When we had finished, Bradshaw said: 'I think you would like to be one of us.' Perhaps from a musical point of view he was right.

Some years later while walking up the churchyard path, I suddenly saw Bradshaw rise up from a table tombstone. He was startled when he saw me and perhaps a little embarrassed. When by rights he should have been mowing the grass or cleaning the churchyard, he was lying on the flat of his back on the tomb with the sun beaming down on him. 'I am lying here thinking,' he said. 'I hope that they are a great deal happier than I am.' A short time before, he had lost his wife who was buried not far from the spot where we were standing. Bradshaw joined her soon after and I hope that they are indeed a great deal happier than in this vale of tears.

Another pleasant memories of playing the organ occurred not long after I was appointed Taxing Master. Through Leslie Mellon, I was introduced to the late Canon Marcus Taylor, rector of St Brigid's Church (Church of Ireland), Stillorgan, who kindly gave me permission to play the church organ.

On several Saturday afternoons, I went to the church, locked myself in and there, in perfect solitude, played music of a liturgical character. I loved the atmosphere of that church. I felt at peace and happy to be alone as I go to bits if I have an audience. Only the poor old organ itself could protest at my sometimes poor playing.

I had a curious experience there one afternoon. I had been playing some pieces for a considerable time, but then thought that I would try my hand at a little improvisation. Quite suddenly, I found myself playing music which would normally be far beyond my limited capacity. I felt that my fingers had been taken over, that someone else was playing. This continued for some three or four minutes, perhaps a little longer. Then, almost as soon as it had come, the 'inspiration' vanished. It was all very strange but pleasant. Try as I might, I could not recapture those moments. I never played so well before or since.

Notwithstanding many other activities, the burning desire to learn to fly had not deserted me, nor had my interest in aircraft. I was now earning my own money and resolved to accomplish my ambition. I was advised to contact the Weston Aero Club where Captain Darby Kennedy was the owner. I did so, again borrowing Ruairi's car to make the journey to the aerodrome.

Even then, Captain Kennedy was a legend. He had spent some time as a pilot with Imperial Airways and later Aer Lingus. Even now, in his eighties, he is still flying. There were a number of aircraft at Weston; the plane used for my training was a BA Swallow, a lovely little single-engine monoplane built in the late 1920s, very much a canvas and wood affair. I had borrowed a helmet and goggles and an old leather jacket – I was all set for my first lesson.

The day arrived. Captain Kennedy walked me to the aircraft and told me to occupy the rear cockpit. He then climbed into the front. (Open cockpits were quite common in light aircraft of the time.) As I attached my safety harness, my instructor began explaining the controls and the few instruments. Long before my first lesson, I had read manuals dealing with elementary but vital information for a pilot. Captain Kennedy started the engine and taxied to the spot where we were to take off. We slowly lifted into the sky. When we reached about 1,000 feet, I heard Kennedy's voice coming through the intercom which was nothing more than a speaking tube attached to the helmets. Very calmly, he said: 'You have her.' I knew that if I did nothing, the plane would simply fly straight ahead, but Kennedy noticed this and began to give me more instructions on how to bank the aircraft. We did this for about fifteen minutes when he again took over and landed the plane.

That was my first lesson, and yes, I had actually flown a plane.

Depending on the weather, the lessons continued and I made further progress, including many landings and take-offs. I was well advanced in my course when Captain Kennedy said my next lesson would be the stall. I took off with him and we climbed to about 3,000 feet. It was then that he told me to cut the throttle. The engine stopped and all was silence, save for the rush of winds. Then he prepared me for the stall, saying that as we lost speed, one of the wings would drop. It did, but suddenly my head was flung forward and dashed against the side of the cockpit. I was dazed and could see the ground spinning vertically below me. I heard Kennedy call out instructions but while I could hear him, I could not move my hands or feet. We had dropped about 1,000 feet when he realised what had happened. He quickly took the controls and pulled the aircraft out of the spin into level flight while I tried to pull myself together. He told me to climb again and chose whatever landmark I liked, then dive down in its direction. 'This will clear your head,' he said quietly.

I saw the tower of the Spa Hotel in Lucan and commenced my dive. I had the most extraordinary feeling that I wished to fly straight into it. As we descended at speed (this particular plane was not to be flown at more than 120 miles an hour), I seemed to be whizzing through space. I kept on going until Kennedy ordered me to pull out. As we passed over the tower, he chuckled: 'That was close enough.' When we landed, he told me not to worry about what had happened in the spin as this sometimes occurs with beginners.

The part of flying I liked best was skimming over the countryside at low altitudes, almost hedge-hopping. To quote Robert Louis Stephenson yet again, indeed it was like 'over bridges, houses, hedges and ditches', all very exciting but perhaps somewhat dangerous.

At the end of one lesson, a group of qualified pilots were standing around; one of them was a young air corps pilot. He said he was taking an aircraft up and asked whether I and 'your girlfriend' (as he referred to Phyllis) would like to go up for a flip. I jumped at the idea. This aircraft was much more powerful than the Swallow, a four-seater. I sat beside the pilot while Phyllis sat at our rear. We took off and flew towards the borders of Co. Kildare. We had no earphones – the only means of communication was through signs or shouting very loudly. The pilot thought I was qualified and certainly I may have looked the part, complete with my helmet and goggles. He beckoned to me to take over, I did, but did nothing except let the plane proceed on its course, thinking he would soon take over the controls. He, on the other hand, thought that I was trying to go off for a long flight and get the best value out of the trip. He beckoned that I should bank to the left. I did, but to my amazement saw a CIÉ train vertically below me. Phyllis panicked and beat me on the shoulder. Luckily, the pilot took over immediately. He brought the plane to level flight and made for the aerodrome. Just as we were on our final glide-path, another madcap pilot did not see us and flew straight across our flight-path. Thanks to the skill of our pilot, we landed safely. Shortly afterwards, I learned that the aircraft in which we had been flying required special skill in a left-hand bank. From what another pilot told me, this machine knew its own mind in such manoeuvres: technique and experience were essential to overcome this difficulty. We of course told Captain Kennedy nothing of our adventure but Phyllis had a sore tummy for some time afterwards.

Not long after this incident, I had the most vivid premonition that I should crash and be killed or severely injured and that I should not continue with my flying. In addition, Phyllis and my parents were very much against my pursuit of such adventures. Father had his own idea, and while he himself took enormous physical risks in his life, he was very much against any member of the family doing likewise. I told Captain Kennedy, who was disappointed. He was not a man of many words but said that my progress as a pilot was 'above average' and that it was a pity that I would not pursue my flying. I, however, felt that common sense must prevail. I had already survived a number of incidents in the air – any one of which could have proved fatal – and this reinforced my view that I should stop. I felt strongly that I should not push my luck any further. I was then in my mid-twenties, but had I been younger, I am sure I would have continued.

In 1948, Ruairi married Eithne Smyth, a native of Co. Down. The pair first met when they were university students. She qualified as a solicitor and ran a successful practice in Down: Smyth & Boyd. Eithne was a person of quiet disposition but the possessor of shrewd judgement and definitive ability. I was Ruairi's best man at his wedding, as later he was mine.

Having put further thoughts of flying behind me, I returned to safer interests and decided to take a serious interest in the life and work of Chopin. I set out to become an expert and contacted, among others, the great authority on Chopin, the late Arthur Hedley, an Englishman who had devoted his life to the study of Chopin and possessed souvenirs and manuscripts of the composer. We corresponded frequently and he was most helpful in my research. He was very generous with information and directed me to many valuable sources.

Due to the expertise I had acquired, I was chosen by Radio Éireann to give an hour-long broadcast on Chopin and his music the night of the centenary of his death, 17 October 1949. Ruairi, as usual, was active in encouraging and helping me with this undertaking. This was indeed an honour, for radio stations throughout the world broadcast similar commemorative programmes that night. It was also at this period that I resolved to research the life and works of John Field. He had been very badly neglected, especially in Ireland, the land of his birth. Since Field had spent over thirty years in Russia, it was almost impossible to obtain biographical and other material under the communist regime.

Father knew of my interest in Chopin and Field and encouraged me in every way. I told him of the difficulties about obtaining information from Russia, then the Soviet Union, and he promised to do what he could to see if material could be obtained. This, it should be remembered, was when the Cold War was at its worst. Father later told me that he approached the British, as Ireland then had no diplomatic mission in the Soviet Union. The British were delighted to co-operate, explaining that it was vital to keep the lines of communication open at all costs. Field seemed to them an excellent and subtle means of doing this.

They requested information about Field which came through regularly and was used as a diplomatic tool. It seems that the Soviets were also anxious to keep the lines of communication open and regarded John Field as a safe *modus operandi*. The result of these political manoeuvres was that I obtained a great deal of information and music which had been denied the western world from the time of the Russian Revolution. This gave me a marked advantage in my research on the composer. A Russian lady living in Greystones, Co. Wicklow, who had fled from Russia after the 1917 Revolution, was happy to translate everything I received. I had planned to write a book on Field and his music, but before I could do this, I was married with a family to bring up. With the further responsibility of running a solicitor's practice, I soon realised that I did not have the necessary time. Shortly afterwards I met my friend, the Englishman, Patrick Piggott, the distinguished pianist and musicologist. I gave him a great deal of the precious material I had collected which he used in his definitive life on the work and music of John Field. He acknowledged this and dedicated the book to Phyllis and myself. If I did not use the valuable material in book form, it was later used in many broadcasts, articles and lectures.

In the summer of 1949 I bought my first car, a Baby Austin, made in 1931. I purchased it for £55. Its seats were stuffed with horse hair which stuck out in places so I called the vehicle 'Jenny of the light brown hair' or 'Jenny' for short. This was followed by a Fiat 500 and, just before I married, a Morris Minor. I now had independent transport and the famous bicycle was laid up while the use of trams or trains became much less frequent.

About this time, I became friendly with a neighbour, Ken Chapman, a graduate in engineering in Trinity who was employed in a well-known firm of Dublin engineers. Ken was a gentle and clever young man, the same age as myself. His great interest was cars and he started building his own racing car. Alas, he would never see it finished, for he drowned while on holiday at Brittas Bay, Co. Wicklow on 11 September 1949. My mother had quite an affection for Ken and felt a void at his passing. His sister Lorna, like her mother, was very artistic and painted charming watercolours. Lorna was married to Rex Sharp, also an engineering graduate of Trinity. While he had considerable independent means, he held the post of chief fire officer for the county of Wicklow.

Lorna knew of my interest in art, and as a resident of Bray, she came to know Yann Renard Goulet RHA and his family. A committed Breton nationalist, he had to flee France where he had been condemned to death for his political activities. He was almost destitute when he reached Ireland, and Lorna and Rex befriended him and did their best to encourage and support him. Lorna became his pupil for sculpture and suggested that Phyllis and I join the class. We spent almost every Saturday in his little studio which he had made with his own hands from the most basic material. Renard proved to be a hard task-master but an excellent teacher. He also painted, but his works are in expressionist mode and vivid style. In time, he became a respected artist and a full member of the RHA. The work for which he first became known was the Custom House Memorial in which he used Phyllis' neck as a model. Renard was also commissioned by the government to execute the beautiful bust of John Field in the National Concert Hall. I was able to provide portraits of Field and other material concerning the composer, which he acknowledged to be of great value. One of my personal favourites is his bust of Parnell, now in the House of Commons in London.

Yann Renard made us spend many hours working on a piece and was quite liable to tear off the clay if he felt that any portion of the work was not up to standard. When the model was complete, he himself did the casting in plaster. Casting day was always something special when he and his class spent many hours learning the mysteries of this art.

In the spring of 1951, he suggested that we submit our work to that year's RHA exhibition. I entered my work – the head of his eldest daughter, Armelle, then about twelve – and was lucky enough to be accepted. Phyllis and Lorna also modelled Armelle. I considered Phyllis' work superior to mine since her's represented the true age of the sitter, while mine seemed to be of an older girl. Phyllis did a fine head of a boy who used to come and sit for us in an attractive composite called 'Icarus'.

Later I submitted a composition of my own, 'The Dying Warrior', based on Oliver Sheppard's 'Cuchulainn', to the Oireachtas exhibition and it was likewise accepted.

Lorna had her own studio in their house at the top of Bray Head. The house was called 'Clouds Hill' and commanded panoramic views of the Sugarloaf Mountain. In later years, she produced a fine head for the Lifeboat Institute. Lorna died of cancer when she was comparatively young, Rex survived her by many years but he too is now dead, and likewise Lorna's parents whom I also knew.

Renard, although a Breton, also spoke French. One of the many difficulties with which he had to contend was his limited knowledge of English. Phyllis and I became officially engaged in December 1950 and were attending his class as usual. Yann heard about it and called the class together, saying he had the most important news. He put his arms around Phyllis and me and exclaimed: 'Listen, listen. I have news. My dear Phyllis and Terry have to get married!' We all burst out laughing, especially Lorna Sharp, who simply could not contain herself. She always saw the funny side of things. She explained to Yann what he had said and he too then joined in the laughter.

I, and other members of the family, commissioned Yann Renard to paint a portrait of my mother. Somewhat reluctantly, she agreed to sit; she positively disliked having her portrait painted. Yann himself was pleased to undertake the task and put his heart into the work. His style of painting is bold and he loves to use strong, bright, vivid colours. The finished painting is striking, professional and technically excellent, although it has not pleased some who have seen it. It must be remembered that Mother was advanced in years when this work was undertaken. She herself felt that it made her look somewhat haggard; she particularly did not like her neck as painted. Yann knew this, so he painted a scarf across her neck and shoulders. This object is somewhat out of character as it gives the impression of affectation, which most positively was not a facet of my mother's character. Since those far off days, Yann Renard became an Irish citizen. He too, like so many of my friends, is now alas dead.

Phyllis and I planned to be married in the summer of 1951 and our thoughts turned to where our new house would be. We had often gone on cycle spins through Foxrock and Carrickmines. In those days, Foxrock was considered remote and unspoiled countryside, similar to Carrickmines, which had, up to recently, changed little since Beatrice Elvery (later Lady Glenavy) described it as 'a wild and lonely place'. We secured a site on the former Kilteragh Estate on lands once belonging to Sir Horace Plunkett. By then, I was part of the Blake family and had built up a strong rapport with Phyllis' parents, especially her father. He offered to design our new house and applied himself to the task with all his skill and knowledge. Building had commenced by May and we hoped to be married in August. But then a tragedy happened which meant we had to postpone our wedding. The health of Vivion's wife Brid began to cause concern and she was diagnosed with an aneurysm in the brain. Her condition was indeed serious, so the decision was made to move her to London where it was hoped her life could be saved. Despite the best medical attention, all efforts proved futile and she died on 19 June 1951; she was only thirty-nine. This was a shattering blow for Vivion and his two young children, indeed for the whole family. Vivion had just decided to leave the Bar. He wished to devote his talents to being chief executive of the *Irish Press* and continuing his life as a TD, having been a member of Dáil Éireann since 1945. Mother was sorely grieved at his loss and she, despite her age, took over the rearing of Vivion's two young children, Ann and Éamon. My last summer in the old home was therefore a sad one.

Phyllis and I were married on 1 September 1951 in Booterstown church by Canon Flanagan, a distant relative on my mother's side. It was a quiet family affair with only the immediate families and a number of close friends as guests. The late Gerard Shanahan, the pianist and organist, played a number of my own compositions for the organ. Phyllis and I spent our honeymoon in Paris and London, and I had the privilege of visiting the Maison Pleyel, through the good offices of the Irish ambassador in Paris, to see a piano which belonged to Chopin. I also made a pilgrimage to lay flowers on Chopin's grave in the Père Lachaise cemetery, Since Chopin's death in 1849, flowers are put on his grave no matter what time of year.

At the end of our honeymoon, we went to London where I spent some time on research in the British Museum. Phyllis told the story that she had to spend part of her honeymoon there, researching the lives of Chopin and Field. My luck in research did not end there. Some years before when Máirín was on a travelling studentship to Sweden, she became friendly with a fellow student, a kinsmen of Thomas Tellefesen who had been a pupil of Chopin. (Tellefesen was an interesting composer and Chopin thought highly of him. He is still remembered in his native Norway.) This friend proved to be most helpful and sent me interesting information and music concerning Tellefesen and his music. I used this material in a broadcast about the composer with Gerard Shanahan as the pianist.

Towards the end of September 1951, we moved to our new home and began married life. Until then, I had only a mild interest in gardening but it soon became a serious hobby and a wonderful form of exercise. Phyllis played a major part in the design of the garden and together we tackled the virgin soil. It was from this period that I acquired a love of trees and shrubs. Our home became our castle.

We had not long moved into our new home when one afternoon, Mrs Alice Mansfield called on Phyllis. She had lived in the house 'Hainault' in Foxrock since the early part of the twentieth century and had been a widow for years. In her younger days, she moved in high society and had been presented at court. Phyllis returned her call, and in the drawing room she noted two large photographs in silver frames, one of King George V and Queen Mary. Beside these was an equally large photograph, also in a silver frame, of Eamon de Valera whom she admired greatly. When I met her, she told me a curious story. One warm, sunny evening in 1920 (probably in June), Sir Horace Plunkett had been entertaining A. W. Cope, the assistant under-secretary for Ireland, in his home at Kilteragh

Mansions. After dinner, the pair went for a walk and Plunkett thought that they should call on Mrs Mansfield. Little did her visitors know that, just at that moment, she had a member of the old IRA, a local postman, hiding in her attic where she had kept him while he was on the run.

Sir Horace Plunkett entertained many famous people in Kilteragh Mansions – Michael Collins, Lady Lavery, AE Russell and the artist Nathaniel Hone. The house was burnt down in the Troubles but later partially re-built.

While I was still an assistant solicitor in P. J. Ruttledge's office, he allowed me to commence building up a private practice. I was not, however, destined to remain in this position for long as Ruttledge's health was giving cause for concern towards the end of 1951. By the following year, it was obvious that he would not live long, as cancer had been diagnosed. As the spring approached, his condition deteriorated and he died on 8 May 1952. Paddy Ruttledge had an extraordinary way with animals. He was well-known in racing circles and considered a good judge of horse flesh. Even as he lay dying in that beautiful house, Ardagh Park, his faithful dog remained at the foot of his bed.

Ruttledge's death created a serious situation for me as I was now without a job. A decision was quickly made, however, and I set up in practice on my own in Dame Street. Percival Blake was again at hand to help, designing the layout of my modest new office. My parents, true to form, gave financial help. In a short time, I built up a good practice which increased steadily as time progressed.

Veronica Rock had been P. J. Ruttledge's secretary, and she came with me when I set up in practice. She proved absolutely invaluable. Without her skill, expertise and loyalty, my practice would never have been as successful as it turned out to be. I relied heavily on her help, her devotion to her work, her experience and her integrity. She remained with me until my appointment as Taxing Master of the Supreme and High court in 1969. In 1975 she became my sister-in-law when she married my eldest brother Vivion.

Life as a practising solicitor was arduous and exacting. In those days, competition was less keen and there was a much higher standard among practitioners, as well as fewer solicitors and barristers. At that time, most of the best businesses were still in the control of large Protestant firms. There were some exceptions, but the most lucrative work remained in the hands of the older, long-established Protestant firms. I got on splendidly with them and received nothing but friendly co-operation. There were higher standards then and one's word was one's bond. While there were a few exceptions to this, we knew them and were on our guard.

Many of my colleagues were a great deal my senior and some expected that we call each other by our surnames. If the older ones used the word 'Mister' they were referring to a clerk, not a qualified person. It was all a throw-back to English public school ideas; a number of them had served in the British forces during World War I. I remember, for instance, one transaction with Ivan Howe, quite an old man at the time. One afternoon he phoned me and said: 'de Valera, this call has nothing to do with a sale, but I was wondering if you were listening to the wireless at lunchtime?' I told him that I had not. 'Oh dear,' he said, 'I thought that you might have heard the latest score from Lords!' This older generation was commendable in the way they approached their work with such dedication and thoroughness. They required every 'i' to be dotted and every 't' to be crossed. They stuck to their desks and moved with caution and care.

I recall closing a sale one day at which Howe was acting for the purchaser. One outstanding point remained, and as was the practice, I offered him my solemn written undertaking that the matter would be dealt with. When I mentioned this, he replied: 'Oh, that is not necessary – all I require is your word as a gentleman.'

As an interesting point: barristers are 'gentlemen' by virtue of their office, whereas solicitors are 'gentlemen' by virtue of statute. In my earlier days in the law, there were very few lady barristers or solicitors, but it would seem to follow that lady solicitors are 'statutory gentlemen'.

A few of the older generation certainly had a gracious way of doing business. I remember closing a sale with O'Keeffe, then the principle partner of O'Keeffe and Lynch, who arrived at his office each morning driven by his chauffeur. He lived in the beautiful house, 'Cranford', on the Stillorgan Road and told me it had been built in an English style for himself and his bride. They were married sometime around 1910. Regrettably, most of the land has been sold, and shops and houses have been built on part of the grounds.

When I arrived at the office, O'Keeffe was seated behind his desk in what was formally the front drawing room of a house in Molesworth Street. His personal law clerk stood beside him, blotting paper in hand, as the old man only used a steel-nibbed pen. When the business was completed, the clerk left the office. At that point O'Keeffe stood up – he was a portly little man – and waddled over to the cabinet in the corner. Slowly he took a set of keys out of his pocket and opened the cabinet from which he took a decanter with two glasses. He moved slowly back towards his desk and quietly poured out two glasses saying: 'de Valera, you will have a glass of sherry before you leave'.

Prominent among the Protestant firms was the Orpen family who had been in the law for generations. Members of this distinguished family had been presidents of the Law Society. I came to know Thomas Jackson, a nephew of Sir William Orpen, and often tried to get him to tell me more of his famous uncle. He was always full of fun and loved trying to shock people, not least with the very strong language he was prone to use. Trying to tease me, he said: 'Very well. I'll tell you about Uncle William, if you really want to know. It's quite simple: wine, woman and song.' Although this was true, I did not expect that it would be put so bluntly, but knowing Tom Jackson as I did, his method of reply was not all that surprising.

On another day, I was with him in office where there were a number of beautiful examples of Orpen's work. He showed me a gorgeous pencil drawing of a middle-aged, rather matronly lady. 'Look at that! I don't know the hell who the old bitch was – perhaps your father would know.' He then wanted me to take the drawing to show it to my father but I declined, saying that I did not want the responsibility of such a valuable item. He seemed to understand and appeared to regret what he had just said, but I knew him and his odd ways, so the matter was left at that. Despite this outward show, he was a sensitive and brilliant man, a splendid lawyer with excellent business acumen and a successful businessman. When he died, I missed his warm-heartedness, his jokes, his sense of fun, his stories, even his eccentric personality.

In those days it was the custom to brief barristers of different political or religious persuasions. I was no exception. I briefed Mr J. A. Costello as my leading senior counsel and frequently briefed his protégé, Desmond Bell SC, a friend of Vivion's from their university days. Desmond had strong political views. He was unashamedly a Blue Shirt and often boasted of this, mostly in a jocose way. He had one of the finest and quickest minds I have ever known and quite a phenomenal memory for fact and case history, apart altogether from his winning personality. His comparatively early death was a great loss to the profession. Others I briefed and for whom I had a great respect were Colm Condon, Roger O'Hanrahan, Vincent Landy and Hugh O'Flaherty.

I had already left practice on my appointment as taxing master by the time my nephew, Éamon, was called to the bar. Since then, he has become a member of the Inner Bar and in June 2001 was appointed a High Court judge. His son Éamon and daughter Atain are likewise following a career in law, keeping up the family tradition. Emer's son Brian was likewise called to the Bar, but did not practice. I also briefed my brother Vivion when he too was practising at the Bar.

I had a particular regard for the late Noel Garland BL. He was acknowledged to one of the greatest authority on conveyancing and had been for some time 'court counsel'. A bachelor and somewhat odd in his ways, he would only accept work from solicitors whom he liked. He was particularly unconcerned about earning fees and was most modest in what he charged. If, as I often did, remind him that fees were due, he would simply say: 'Oh, you look after that'. His only interests in life were law and opera. I gave him almost all my conveyancing work and not once did he fail me.

Noel had a rule that a solicitor must not tell him that a case was urgent unless this was genuinely the position. One day, I called on him with a truly urgent matter and found him sitting in his study, which was covered with books and papers on the mantelpiece, on the floor, on top of bookcases, almost everywhere. One could scarcely see the desk itself with the multitude of papers. 'Is this really urgent?' he asked. 'Yes,' I replied, 'I'm afraid it is'. 'Very well,' he said, 'follow me and bring your papers with you.' He led me to the toilet and when I looked in, there were papers everywhere. 'See that?' he said as he put my papers on top of the toilet tank. 'Understand? I see them when I have a call of nature. That reminds me that they are urgent. I then take the papers and deal with them immediately.' This formula worked.

Another eminent senior counsel I knew well was the late Chris Micks, a most likeable personality. He was well-known in the profession, highly respected as a skilful lawyer and famous for his quick tongue and sparkling wit. One afternoon, some time after my appointment as Taxing Master, I was in the courtyard having finished my day's work. He had just come out from the Law Library, accompanied by his colleague, the late Raymond O'Neill SC. He saw me, he pointed with his walking stick (he was lame). His round, reddish face lit up and with a twinkle in his deep-set penetrating dark eyes, he called out loudly: 'Master, I hear that you have become expert in division and subtraction. But for Heaven's sake, work up your multiplication!' He was referring to the taxation of barristers' fees.

Occasionally I appeared in the District Court to plead my case, without the aid of counsel, and those cases which came before District Justice Kenneth Reddin come to mind. He was a very colourful and popular character, a successful playwright and literateur. He loved 'theatre' in his court and was prone to make witty remarks. He wore his self-designed head-dress like a black biretta. I could not help thinking that he reminded me of Jimmy O'Dea at times. On one occasion, I had to bring proceedings in his court on a very serious matter. I was seeking an order to have the defendant committed to prison for contempt of court due to her failure to pay instalments which had been fixed by the court. I was acting for the executor of an estate who was then resident in England, which placed even greater responsibility on me to ensure that the instalments were paid.

The court day arrived. The defendant was a particularly good-looking, well-dressed, woman about thirty-five years of age. The judge put her in the witness box to explain why she had failed to pay the instalments. She looked at him and then across at me. I was a considerable distance away: the Kilmainham court room is a vast one. The sum outstanding was seven pounds and ten shillings. She opened her handbag, took out a £5 note, two single notes and a soiled ten-shilling note. As she did, she glared across the court. In a very loud voice and with a distinctive Dublin accent, she shouted at me: 'Here's your fucking money!' Ordinarily the use of such a word could have been considered contempt of court in itself, but the judge simply smiled and turned to me saying: 'Mr de Valera, do you wish to reply?' I told this story to my father; he knew Reddin and enjoyed it immensely.

On the subject of strong language, my father once asked me: 'Why are some lawyers so coarse?' I replied: 'Because they see the raw side of life.' Too often, they had to deal with the less attractive side of human nature. I did not add, as indeed I could have, that the use of coarse language could equally apply to some politicians and those in other callings. On the whole, although there were notable exceptions, Father did not care for lawyers, perhaps became so many of his political opponents were lawyers. He had, however, a great respect for the medical profession, most prominent among them being his close friend, Dr Farnan.

In another case which came before Judge Reddin, I had taken on the defence of a man who lived in the North and who came south on a spree with his young lady friend (who was not his wife). Both had been drinking heavily and he crashed his car into a house only yards from a garda station, injuring his companion and causing major damage to the house itself. The car smashed through the wall and the bonnet ended up a short distance from an old pair sitting at their fireplace. The gardaí were very quickly on the scene. My client was uninjured and frankly admitted that he was hopelessly drunk. There was but one course to take: plead guilty and hope for the best. I told him in no uncertain terms that there was little chance of avoiding a jail sentence, which he accepted, but he begged me to do what I could and refused to have anyone plead his defence but me. I reluctantly agreed.

The court day arrived, and before the case was opened, I begged leave of the court to address the judge, saying that I felt it would save the court's precious time. I was well aware that Reddin liked to spend the minimum of time in court, and he agreed with his customary smile. I began by saying that my client had come from the North and stood his ground rather than running away; he had willingly submitted himself to 'His Worship's jurisdiction'. He had, I went on, come from 'another shore', so to speak (meaning that he was from another jurisdiction) and that he could have avoided the proceedings by fleeing back to the North. By this time, Reddin had achieved considerable notoriety for his play, *Another Shore*, and my mention of it made him positively purr. I went on to say that my client fully accepted that he had committed a grievous wrong. He knew that his driving licence would be suspended and he was aware of the possibility of a jail sentence. As I continued, I referred to a motto which my master (Tommy Robinson) had given me as an apprentice: if you make a mistake, as we all do, own up, pay up and shut up. I said this towards the bench with great worked-up passion and expressed a wish that his worship will not add 'lock up'.

I could see that Judge Reddin was obviously enjoying the proceedings and smiling broadly, particularly as he saw that the prosecution, led by the much-respected garda superintendent, Leo Maher, (who had been called to the Bar) was livid at the way in which the case was proceeding. Indeed the superintendent tried to intervene, but Judge Reddin would have none of it and told me to continue. I proceeded for a while, and when I saw that the judge was sympathetic, I sat down. Despite Superintendent Maher's protests, and he made them with considerable force, the judge said that he had already made up his mind and would not let the prosecution say any more.

As expected, the defendant's driving licence was suspended. In all the circumstances, the judge suggested that the defendant put the sum of £10.00 in the court poor box. Superintendent Maher could not believe his ears. At that point, my client jumped up and pulled a huge wad of notes out of his trouser pocket. 'It's not enough, it's not enough!' he roared. 'You have treated me very fairly!' 'No, No,' said the judge. 'Ten pounds seems a fair sum.'

Again the defendant responded: 'No, no. I am far too grateful. Here's £100.00.' (A very large sum for those days.) There followed an acrimonious argument between the judge and the superintendent about which charity should received the money. Thus ended this novel case. Superintendent Maher died many years ago. He never quite forgave me for this case but otherwise we got on splendidly.

When I told Father the story, he was not sympathetic that the defendant should have got off so lightly. Perhaps he was right, but I had to do my duty and my plea had worked. Certainly it was clear that the judge had enjoyed his morning and seemed content with his decision. On a more serious side, my client indeed had good reason to be thankful. The point at which he had crashed the car was only yards from the jurisdiction of District Justice Liam Proud, a judge who was always considered fair but strict. Most certainly he would have sent the defendant to jail.

I have special memories of my close friends, Judge Cathal Flynn, President of the District Court, and his wife Mary. They were also great friends of my brother Éamon and my father. To many, Judge Flynn appeared cold and even austere, but at heart he was sympathetic and kind-natured. He had a marvellous mind and made law the very essence of his life. He was uncommonly conscientious, with almost impossibly high standards. He took a great interest in me from my student days and did all he could to further my progress in law. I had a particular affection for his wife, who was most generous. She became a client of mine, as I also acted for the judge in some of his personal affairs and occasionally appeared in his court. I remember a very difficult licensing case involving a dance hall which I had prepared with special care, knowing only too well that I would be sorely tested. The case went on for several hours, and to my great disappointment, the judge held against me. I appealed this decision which then came before the Circuit Court where Judge Flynn's decision was reversed. This instance, however, did nothing to lessen the bond between Judge Flynn and myself.

I was appointed a notary public by the Chief Justice in 1958. Notaries public are important in their own right: their acts are recognised internationally, as one of their functions is to authenticate documents for foreign courts. A great deal of the work was for the USA. At the time of my appointment, the notaries decided to seek permission from the Chief Justice to form a faculty, and a meeting of the country's notaries was convened. (There would have been no more than thirty-five notaries in the State at the time.) At that meeting, a decision had to be made as to the appointment of a dean of the faculty and registrar; the latter would act as secretary. I was the latest notary appointed and therefore the most junior. It was decided that the longest-serving notary, the late Charles Doyle, solicitor, would be elected dean. Doyle was a close friend of Percival Blake; he and his wife were guests at my wedding. He carried out his duties admirably.

My friend the late Peter Prentice, solicitor, and Tom Jackson were present at the notaries' meeting, and Peter played a little trick on me, proposing that I be elected the first registrar without my knowledge. The proposal was put and accepted unanimously. I was taken aback but flattered and set out to make the new faculty a success, devoting a good deal of time to this. On my appointment as Taxing Master, I had, of course, to cease being a notary public, along with being a practising solicitor and commissioner for oaths. My very able successors were my friends Enda Marron and Brendan Walsh. They have continued to work hard and have brought the faculty to the success it enjoys today.

I have always been a firm believer in the 'split' profession in law, with barristers and solicitors remaining quite separate. Each branch has its own special functions and work; being so organised serves the interests of the public best. Where other jurisdictions operate, and where there is fusion of the two, the tendency is to break down into two. There is then the 'desk man' or woman doing the solicitor's work and the 'court' members operating as barristers or advocates.

Another great advantage operated in my time: a barrister could not then be sued for negligence, thus leaving him/her free to offer advice and guidance which might not be the case otherwise. I think this is clearly in the interests of the client. The two branches of the profession have a totally different approach. Solicitors must have a good degree of business acumen – they must be good organisers and administrators – whereas this may not necessarily be an attribute of a good barrister. The latter is much more concerned with the academic side of law and the presentation of a case in court. Neither can I see any merit in the argument that there would be a saving in costs. In my view, it could prove to be quite the opposite. I am likewise a firm believer in upholding the traditions in the law, including the wearing of wigs and gowns in court for both the bench and barristers.

Above all, there must be dignity in a court. I make no apologies for contending that a court ought to be held in some degree of awe, which in turn begets respect for the law itself and the enforcement of rights, constitutional and otherwise. I would oppose most strongly any broadcasting by radio, and especially television, in any court. This reduces the majesty of the law and can turn it into vulgar theatre, as was so clearly demonstrated in the famous O. J. Simpson case in the USA. Such broadcasting is not the function of the law. Instead, it debases it and could, in my view, create a positive injustice.

This attitude towards publicity for its own sake has been greatly emphasised of late in the celebrated Louise Woodward murder trial. Its proceedings degenerated into a cheap circus, a piece of vulgar entertainment watched by millions throughout the world. Indeed it became a highly popular 'soap opera' and was devoid of all dignity, fairness and justice, revealing the US court's shocking procedures and the general *modus operandi* of the trial both in and out of court.

These procedures and practices, which appear to be permissible in America, are at total variance with our court practices and traditions. They are fundamentally contrary to our concept of the administrations of justice. In the above cases, it was an alarming revelation of the basic inadequacies in the American court system, demonstrating that such broadcasting is a retrograde step. The participation of the general news media and its obvious influences acted as a further brake on the attainment of a fair and just trial.

From my earliest days in the law, I had an interest in the history of the courts and its traditions. Barristers carry a curious cloth bag in which they bring their books and papers to court. Upon arrival, they put these bags, made of a black material, on top of their desks in the law library. In the days before 1922, a barrister appearing in the House of Lords was entitled to a red bag. I recall seeing a number of these red bags scattered throughout the law library.

To people who are not lawyers, it may seem odd that solicitors are strictly forbidden to enter the Law Library: they may only go as far as the door where a barrister is called by a 'crier'. The barrister then comes outside to see the solicitor.

In my early days, there was a very famous crier called Campion. He was quite a character who had served no less than fifty-eight years in the library. Campion was a little man with a large walrus moustache which was often covered with jam; he hid his sandwiches in his 'flip-top desk'. He had a powerful voice which rang out throughout the library, although he said that his voice was nothing to that of his immediate predecessor, who had been a sergeant major in the Crimean War and whose voice could be heard at the other side of the River Liffey.

I often quizzed Campion and begged him to tell me stories of the days long ago. Whenever he was in good humour, he obliged. He remarked, in a rather condescending way, that even the most senior men then at the bar were only boys when he first knew them; a number were not even born.

He recollected how, on the death of Queen Victoria, Queen's Counsel (the forerunners of today's Senior Counsel) solemnly placed their wigs and gowns on their desks and walked slowly in procession making their way to the Round Hall under the great dome. There, in perfect silence, they awaited a message from Dublin Castle. Then a messenger arrived, dressed in knee britches, buckle shoes and ornate tunic, and read with great solemnity a proclamation calling them again to the inner bar, to be now known as 'Kings Counsel.'

Another quaint story involved a judge of the High Court who arrived each day in his coach, pulled by two splendid horses. He took great pride in these animals and insisted that they be stabled in a room adjoining his court, the present no. 2 court in the Great Hall. In his droll Dublin accent, Campion added that the stench of horse dung was awful.

He told me another curious tale. It seems that a woman sold apples from a large basket just under the clock at the entrance to the Great Hall. Barristers and others often purchased this fruit; it was known for counsel to eat an apple as he addressed the court. To make a point or impress a jury, he would hurl the core into the vast, open fireplace which heated the courtroom in those days.

There were other more curious tales. Some judges had a large decanter of wine on the bench and freely imbibed as the case proceeded. While this was before Campion's time, they were further provided with a chamber pot under the bench. Campion insisted that he had been told by his predecessor that if a barrister suspected that his lordship had 'the urge', he discreetly raised his voice!

All this seems very odd to us today, but it must be remembered that the court was then a wholly male world. Women were not present, save as witnesses, and when this was so, it is hoped that his lordship was more discreet. In my early days, there were few woman practitioners. There were only a small number at the bar and just one senior counsel, the formidable Miss Fanny Moran. While there were more lady solicitors, they constituted a small minority. Even among the court officers there were very few women. Prominent at the outer bar was the good-looking and gracious Miss Deveraux.

Two prominent ladies in the profession were fellow apprentices with me: Moya Dixon (afterwards Quinlan) and Marie Hughes (who later married the late Professor Thomas P. O'Neill). Moya Quinlan became the first lady president of the Law Society. Marie O'Neill followed her husband's interest and professional calling in history and produced several scholarly works on eminent women in Irish history. She is an active member of the Old Dublin Society which has published her work, and for which she was awarded several society medals.

Campion told me other stories which he insisted were true. Somewhere at the close of the nineteenth century, the court of appeal was sitting, and the case had just resumed after lunch. Suddenly there was a disturbance at the entrance, which came to the notice of the Lord Chief Justice. At first, he took no notice, but then called out to the Dublin metropolitan policeman on duty: 'What's the cause of that noise?' The constable replied shyly: 'My Lord, there are men from the Board of Works and they want to repair the clock.' 'What?' replied the judge. 'They can't possibly do that while the court is sitting.' It was noticed, however, that the court rose earlier than usual. The judges had scarcely departed from the bench when a party of men entered: neither they nor the clock were ever heard of again. According to Campion, it was thought that they were students from Trinity College. Adding that they had done this by way of a bet, they were probably law students!

Campion described in some detail the first day of the legal year, during the days of the British administration. The judges, wearing wigs, ornate gowns and court dress, accompanied by senior court officers, passed in procession through the Four Courts and then took up position under the clock in the great Round Hall beneath the dome. There, the lord chancellor and other senior judges received each member of the bar in order of seniority.

Master O'Hanlon told me that in those far-off days, the taxing masters were keepers of the lord chancellor's purse and carried a purse on a red velvet cushion in the procession. It was the custom for the lord chancellor to place two sovereigns in each purse, and it became a tradition for the taxing masters to keep these coins. This became an expensive matter for the lord chancellor, especially since there were separate taxing masters for each of the old Four Courts.

I once joked with my friend, the late Chief Justice Thomas F. O'Higgins that this ceremony should be revived. He quipped that if I thought this, I was mistaken, as I was not going to make such easy money! The military and the police also took an active part in the ceremonies on the first day of the legal year.

Campion also told me that his grandfather had a bookshop in a laneway, long since disappeared, where the flats in Chancery Street now stand. His grandfather often sold books to barristers on their way to court. One morning in 1803, his father was in the bookshop as usual at about 9.00 a.m. He knew the sexton of St Michan's church who had just come in to see him. In a low whisper, the sexton said: 'Do you know who we buried last night? Robert Emmet.' Later, when Campion's grandfather and the sexton met, he showed the latter the grave. The grandfather showed his son who in turn showed Campion. I was quite excited by this and asked Campion if he would meet me after the library closed and show me the spot. He declined but took care to point out where the grave was supposed to be: the second grave in the top left-hand corner of the graveyard facing west. Later I inspected the graveyard but could find nothing of interest as the spot mentioned was covered with long grass. I had known from my particular interest and study of Emmet that another supposed grave in St Michan's had been excavated, inspected and rejected by experts as being the grave of Robert Emmet. I, therefore, treated Campion's story with considerable suspicion. The grave of Robert Emmet remains one of the great mysteries of Irish history. By far the most likely location is in the Trevor Vault in St Paul's.

In 1946, while I was still living in the old home, Father called me to his study. I had scarcely opened the door when he said: 'I want you to do something for me. It's Bernard Shaw's birthday and I want to phone him to extend my greetings.' He then took his personal diary from his pocket and said: 'The number is written in here – an English number.' As he handed me the diary, he added: 'Under no circumstances do I wish to speak to anyone until you have old Shaw on the line.'

I dialled the number. The phone was answered by a lady, and I told her that my father wished to speak with Mr Shaw. Almost at once, Shaw came on the line. I asked if I was speaking to Mr George Bernard Shaw, and he roared: 'Yes!' I then asked him to hold the line for Mr de Valera, and he again bellowed 'Yes!' I then handed the phone to my father who extended his greetings. While I could not hear what Shaw was saying, it was obvious from Father's laughter that they were both having a jovial conversation. When the call had ended, Father put down the phone and said: 'The old boy is so amusing.'

I mentioned this story for, although it was the shortest of conversations, I can nevertheless boast that I have spoken to George Bernard Shaw!

# CHAPTER XIV

*A Feast of Music*
*Presidential and Royal Visitors*

I had settled into married life by 1953. It was in May of that year that I
met Charles Lynch and began a deep and lasting friendship. I had long
since known of his fame as a pianist and arranged for him to visit my
home. My mother had given me a boudoir grand piano some months
before my marriage, which had been vetted by the pianist and organist,
Gerard Shanahan. It turned out to be a fine instrument which Charles
Lynch loved to play.

When he arrived, I showed him some of my own musical
compositions which he kindly agreed to play, even saying a few nice things
about some of them. We soon turned to more serious music, however, and
I had my first feast of his unique playing of Beethoven, a talent which had
gained him international recognition. Charles obviously enjoyed the
evening and became a regular visitor. Seldom did he partake of meals; if he
did, he ate little and took a long time in the process. His great passion was
for mushy cream cakes, buns and gallons of tea – in between he chain-
smoked cigarettes. He had little or no time for alcohol. Phyllis always made
sure that a supply of tea was at hand. He had a special affection for her, as
he had for my mother whom he met later.

Charles Lynch was born in Cork on 31 October 1907, the only son of
Colonel Lynch, then the most senior colonel in the British army. His elder
sister Violet sang in her younger days. After the troubles of 1920–22, the
family sold their spacious house and lands in Cork and moved to London.
His parents lived beyond their means, in the grand style of the old landed
gentry, but with very little cash to support their extravagances. Despite this,
they moved to a fashionable part of the West End. Violet had been a pupil
of the Webber Douglas School of Singing and Drama where she met and

became friends with the actor, Stewart Granger. Violet acted with him in student productions in the college.

Although Charles Lynch was educated for the most part in England, he recalled a visit to Cork not long after they had settled in London. 'I saw a red glow over the city one night in December 1920 when it was burnt by the British army and my heart grieved at this terrible act. There was more sorrow in the unfortunate Civil War that followed. There was fighting in the fields around our home.'

In London, his great talents were recognised and he began to mix in high society, to be lauded by the most eminent musicians and artists of that period. He became a friend of Sir Thomas Beecham, Sir Adrian Bolt, and the composers Delius and Bartok. Prominent among his friends was Sir Arnold Bax, Master of the King's Music, who dedicated a work to him. He also knew Percy Granger and told some amusing stories about the practical jokes he was fond of playing.

Charles was fêted wherever he went and was soloist with the most famous orchestras of the time. He became a pupil of Rachmaninov who told him that he suffered an almost suicidal depression while composing his immortal Second Piano Concerto. By mere chance, I was able to attend a concert given by this composer in the old Theatre Royal in the late 1930s. I have vivid memories of the occasion, especially the way Rachmaninov showed his marked disapproval for late-comers. He played his famous Prelude in C Sharp Minor as an encore and was most annoyed when the audience broke into applause at the opening bars. Charles Lynch told me that Rachmaninov had grown tired of this piece and almost regretted that he had ever composed it.

During this time, Charles was very much in fashion with the highest ranks of British society. Indeed it is said that the Princess Royal had a crush on him and followed him from concert to concert. Whether this is true, I cannot be sure, but I am certain that Charles did not reciprocate for he was a confirmed bachelor.

There was practically no one of importance in London's artistic circles whom he had not met, so much so that I had a game with him. I would mention someone but invariably he had met them. One evening I said: 'I'll catch you this time, Charles. I'll bet you that you never met Orpen.' 'Oh, yes I did,' came his quick reply. He then went on to tell me that they were fellow guests at a luncheon and was able to name the date and the house where the function had taken place. He found the diminutive Orpen very lively and amusing.

During his sojourn in London, Charles Lynch was in contact with George Bernard Shaw and William Butler Yeats. It was during an interval at Glyndebourne that he was introduced to Shaw. Shaw's wife and Charles' mother had been friends since their girlhood days, and the men spent some time discussing the genius of Mozart's Don Giovanni. He also met Yeats around this time when the poet was in England for a proposed production of some of his plays. Although these plans came to nothing, Charles Lynch would have been asked to play incidental music which had been composed specially by George Anthell. Yeats also asked Charles to compose music for some of his other plays, saying that the music must be on a small scale for the piano and flute. The theatre in question was small, the Mercury in Notting Hill, so it would be only possible to have a small number of instruments. In 1961, Charles Lynch fulfilled this wish when he composed music for Yeats' Death of Cuchulainn which was staged at the Cork Drama Festival.

Charles Lynch had an amazing pianistic ability and a phenomenal technique. He was also an extraordinary sight-reader with a superb musical memory. By the mid-1930s, he appeared to be going from one success to another. But about 1938, something happened which he never discussed with me and he decided to return to Ireland with his sister. By then his parents were dead, and when he arrived back in Ireland, he was practically penniless. He certainly lacked any business acumen and was a very poor manager of his own affairs; in those days, competent agents for artists were few. When it came to everyday living or money, he was practically hopeless but felt that he should be able to live on in the style and comfort which he had known in his younger days. Although he was so disorganised in many ways, he was thorough in the extreme when it came to his art and most reliable in keeping appointments for broadcasts and like engagements.

We had not known each other long when he became aware of my interest in both Chopin and Field. He encouraged me in every way and played so many of their works. His playing of Field was exquisite. He placed great stress on treating the music strictly in the style of the period in which it had been written. In this regard, and indeed with all music, he frequently pointed out that keeping the period in mind was an absolute essential for a proper performance. When playing Chopin, he had a great dread of making his music sound sentimental. He also loved Schubert,

Brahms and Lizst, and was a great exponent of even the most difficult of their works. He also played the composers of an earlier period so well – Bach, Handel and Mozart. Indeed no music was beyond the scope of Charles Lynch. There was practically nothing in the piano repertoire he did not play admirably, often from memory. Charles was equally at home with many modern works, some of which did not appeal to me.

Charles was one of the principle performers at a testimonial concert for Austin Gaffney which took place at the Gaiety Theatre, Dublin on 13 September 1953. I was very touched when he included 'Scherzino', a little piece I had composed, in his programme. In 1954, thanks to our mutual friend, the composer John Kinsella, then head of music in RTÉ, it was arranged that Charles and I would broadcast the entire John Field 'Nocturnes', something which we were sure had not been done before.

As our friendship grew, visits to my home became more frequent. He was always generous with his art and lost himself in the music. One night, he had scarcely got up from the piano and it was well after midnight. Phyllis continued to provide the mushy cream cakes and tea and his favourite cigarettes. He looked up from the piano, a cigarette trailing from his rather large lips, and said in that half-Cork, half-English accent: 'Am I staying too long?' 'Oh, no,' we both replied immediately. 'It is marvellous to have you. We don't care if you stay until dawn.' He resumed his seat at the piano and continued with piece after piece, often stopping to point out interesting and pertinent points. Those joyous hours wore on, and it was after 5.00 a.m. when he finally decided to leave. I drove him to the Royal Marine Hotel in Dun Laoghaire where he was staying, and as we reached the hall door, he looked up at the glorious sky and said: 'Ah, what a beautiful dawn!' As I left him at the hotel, he was quite distressed that I should have to return at once as I had to be in my office that morning. Poor fellow, he had lost all trace of time.

Following the successful series of broadcasts on Field, there were many others which I wrote and presented, while Charles played the music. We did an interesting series on the composer, Stephen Heller, a contemporary of Chopin, which was followed by an ambitious series in which Charles Lynch played the entire set of Mendelssohn's 'Songs Without Words'.

Charles Lynch had a great knowledge of nature and was particularly fond of walking. One windy autumn day, Phyllis and I took him to the Devil's Glen in Co. Wicklow. The glen looked particularly beautiful with all its varied hues. Having enjoyed a long and refreshing walk, we returned home. Later that evening he played a piece 'To Autumn' by his friend, Arnold Bax, with a passage which evoked the last withering leaves being snatched from the trees. It was an enthralling experience, capturing the atmosphere of our walk a few hours before.

Apart from his enormous musical gifts, Charles was a very cultured man, with a knowledge of theatre, poetry and literature, as well as botany. He also had a profound knowledge and love of Shakespeare. Charles had a strange passion for railway bridges and had studied them extensively in both Ireland and in Britain. One of the more attractive sides of his complex character was his marvellous sense of humour. He was a splendid raconteur and had a fund of interesting stories. One of his best, and one I enjoyed most, concerned Richter, Wagner's manager and conductor. Richter was in London to conduct the London Philharmonic Orchestra. He was accustomed to the strict discipline associated with German orchestras, but in London, he was quite unnerved when the players chatted freely during the rehearsals. This was something which Richter would not accept, but he found it difficult to do anything because he spoke little English. Eventually, he became utterly exasperated as the chit-chat continued and shouted: 'Don't spoke! I can stand a little then and now but mine Gott always never!'

Great credit must be given to Charles Lynch for his dedication to the revival of interest in John Field. He knew the value and importance of Field's music, both in its own right and in the history of music for the piano. Some forty years ago, it was difficult to arouse any interest in Field, but Charles Lynch was never wanting in this regard. He partnered me in every way in our efforts to see that the Irish composer was given the recognition he richly deserves.

Charles and I also had a common link in our interest in the occult. He claimed to have had no less than two remarkable experiences, both of them in Ireland. The first occurred when he was dressing for dinner in a friend's large old house in the country. In a mirror, he saw the face and upper body of an elderly man dressed in clothes which were fashionable in the middle of the nineteenth century. As he stared at the figure, the figure stared back at him. Charles assured me that this lasted a minute or so, then the image faded slowly and Charles could see nothing but the reflection of a wardrobe on the other side of the room. At dinner, he told his host of his experience. His description fitted exactly with that of the host's grandfather who had died many years before.

The second story was more dramatic. He often stayed in a well-known Dublin hotel where he knew the housekeeper quite well; she always came to greet him when he arrived. He had not been in the hotel for several weeks when he called to stay the night. He saw the housekeeper descend the staircase, smile at him, then turn and walk along a corridor and out of sight. He was puzzled that she had not stopped to have her customary word with him and commented on this to the porter. The porter looked at him in great surprise: 'Did you not know sir? She died a week ago.'

My interest in Robert Emmet led me to know more about his fiancée, Sarah Curran. Sarah was very musical and was said to have had a fine voice. A friend of her family, the Reverend Crawford said of it: 'She sang with exquisite taste. I think I never heard such a harmonious voice.' It is said that Tom Moore was Sarah's unofficial music teacher and that he taught her a number of Irish airs. She also played the harpsichord, piano and harp, excelling in the latter instrument. She was one of the first in Ireland to recognise the supreme genius of Mozart, and this only a very few years after Mozart's death.

Charles came to know of my interest in Sarah, particularly her talent in music. This aroused his curiosity, as did the Cork connection as Sarah's father came from that county. Together, we broadcast a programme of the music associated with Sarah which ended with Charles Lynch playing a beautiful setting of 'She is far from the Land', arranged by Constant Lambert. It was the last piece he ever recorded or broadcast. It was a strange ending to a wonderful career during which he had played the most famous and difficult music. Yet his final piece would be a simple and beautiful Irish air.

Shortly after we had completed the recording the programme, Charles had a heavy fall and was moved to St Vincent's Hospital in Dublin. By then, in his late seventies, his old friends, Dr and Mrs Petit of Cork, took him into their home and even provided him with a piano. Strange to say, it seems that he did not own a piano since his return to Ireland in 1938. Charles died peacefully on 15 September 1984. Phyllis and I travelled to Cork to attend the funeral, a most moving occasion. Dr Geoffrey Spratt of University College Cork provided the music which included the college choir. During the mass, they performed Purcell's exquisite 'Funeral Sentences'. I had the honour of being one of the pall bearers, who included the late Jack Lynch, the former Taoiseach, and the late Dr Brian Boydell. We bore him along the churchyard path in St Fin Barre's cemetery where his remains were interred in a grave provided by the Petits. At the end of the committal ceremony, the choir again sang the 'Funeral Sentences', their voices singing a last farewell to a noble and learned musician. There he lies in his native Cork, and remembering his profound knowledge of Shakespeare, it is perhaps fitting to say: 'After life's fitful fever he sleeps well.'

Some years before his death, he had been playing some of Beethoven's sonatas at my home. When he finished, he began to talk of the genius of these works. I then turned to him and asked: 'Charles, when you die, how will you feel when you meet Beethoven?' He smiled broadly and responded: 'I think I shall be terrified!' All who had the privilege of knowing and hearing Charles Lynch are sure that his fears are unfounded: few have done such justice to the supreme master.

The birth of my eldest daughter Síle on 17 December 1954 gave an entirely different dimension to life. I had chosen this name as my mother had taken it in its English from for her confirmation. It was Father who suggested that the name be spelled in the more modern Irish form. My mother was Síle's godmother; Ruairi was her godfather.

With this new arrival, there was much less time for interests outside my profession as my practice continued to increase. Towards the end of the fifties, West Germany was making a remarkable economic recovery, with many wealthy German industrialists becoming interested in Ireland and purchasing properties here. I acted for a number of them and quite a few bought substantial properties throughout the State at prices which they considered much lower than in Germany. I had personal reservations about this, lest these acquisitions should become too widespread, returning us to the time of absentee landlords. In the event, this did not happen, especially with the introduction of a penal stamp duty for purchasers who were not Irish citizens. Entry to the European Union changed all this, however, and there are those who think this is not for the better. The Germans could scarcely believe that there were no capital gains tax but they were shocked when I had to explain the heavy death duties which applied at the time.

It was about this time that I met Patrick Piggott, an acknowledged expert on John Field, quite apart from his great gifts as a concert pianist. He was also a respected composer; although I found his compositions far too modern, he was adamant that he would never be an imitator. Piggott soon came to know of my accumulation of valuable biographical and other material on John Field. I still harboured the hope that I would write the composer's biography, but with the ever-growing pressure of work and the added domestic responsibilities, I could see little or no chance of completing such an undertaking. I therefore decided to co-operate with Piggott and gave him a large part of my collection. He, in turn, gave me unknown music by Field and other material which he had found from his research in Russia. Piggott graciously acknowledged my contribution in his definitive work, *The Life and Works of John Field*, and dedicated the book to myself and Phyllis. It remains one of the most important works on John Field, in addition to being a useful contribution to Irish heritage.

In 1953 my father and Sir Winston Churchill finally met. When I asked Father to tell me of this famous meeting, he explained that both he and Churchill had been in Strasbourg when it was suggested that they should meet. He told me that Churchill was at the top of a staircase and about to descend. At the same time, Father was at the bottom about to go up. The first thought which struck Father was that Churchill might seize on the opportunity to snub him, especially since it was such a public place with many of the press in attendance. He decided that he would not give the British statesman such a chance and thus they did not meet that day.

Later, Father was in London when he received an invitation to lunch with Churchill at No. 10 Downing Street. Father gladly accepted and was accompanied by Frank Aiken and F. H. Boland. There was never any question of Boland having to use 'considerable arm-twisting' to get my father to accept the invitation, as has been stated by one writer. Such a statement is simply untrue.

They had scarcely sat down to lunch when Father asked Churchill to tell him about his young days as a soldier; Churchill had taken part in what turned out to be one of the last cavalry charges in history. Churchill was delighted to recall his experiences, and when he had finished his story, he turned to Father and said: 'I believe you too did a bit of fighting.' Father went on to tell him of the shelling of the distillery tower near Bolands Mill during the Rising in 1916, and of the ruse he had played on the British forces, and of his admiration for the accuracy of the gunners on the *Helga*. In spite of his poor eyesight, Father could detect a broad, approving grin from the British prime minister.

When the lunch was over, Churchill ushered Father to seats beside a window where they sat alone together for a serious conversation. Father challenged Churchill on his continued hostility to Irish independence and told Churchill that there would never be a lasting and final peace in Ireland so long as the evil of partition remained. Churchill listened, but replied that they could never put people out of the United Kingdom so long as the majority in the Six Counties wished to remain part of it. There were political factors which no conservative could ignore. Father continued to press him and challenged him as to why he should continue to support the injustice of partition, to which Churchill curiously and somewhat dismissively replied: 'Politics, my dear fellow, politics,' thus showing his disregard for principle, and the proprietary rights and the peaceful living of others.

Their discussion also dealt with the question of the transfer of Roger Casement's remains to Ireland. Churchill himself appeared sympathetic, and although he said he would look into the matter, nothing came of this. It was only when Harold Wilson became prime minister that the patriot's remains were returned to his native land. Despite the strong and deeply divergent opinions and convictions held by Eamon de Valera and Winston Churchill, man-to-man they had considerable mutual respect.

On the day when Roger Casement's remains were re-interred in Glasnevin Cemetery, accompanied by a full military ceremony, the weather turned particularly nasty, with driving wind and bitter showers of sleet. My father was ill at the time, and I had threatened pneumonia, but he resisted every effort to prevent him from attending the ceremony, even going against the advice of his doctor, the late Dr Bryan Alton. Eamon de Valera had made up his mind: it was useless to resist his determination to pay tribute to the dead patriot. Bare-headed, he delivered one of his most eloquent speeches. He was then in his eighty-third year.

Another Churchillian connection was when his daughter, Lady Soames, came to lunch with my mother in Áras an Uachtaráin. Mother told me that she expected this visit to be difficult although it turned out to be quite the opposite. Soon the conversation turned to poetry, and Mother told Lady Soames of her great love for many of the English poets, particularly Byron. Lady Soames at once interjected, saying that her father also ranked Byron among his favourites. The pair got on splendidly, and Lady Soames did not leave until the afternoon was well spent. Mother found Lady Soames friendly, talkative and intelligent. It is known that Winston Churchill himself expressed the wish to re-visit Áras an Uachtaráin where he had spent part of his boyhood in the vice-regal days. It was through no fault of my parents that he did not fulfil this wish.

Our second daughter Jane was born on 22 May 1959. Again, there was the question of her name and much discussion took place. My mother's given name was Jane, although she did not care for it. I did not like the Irish form, Sinéad, so we settled on Jane. Phyllis' mother was Sarah Kathleen, so a compromise was reached by choosing the name Kathleen Jane, but she was to be known as Jane. My father was her godfather and my sister Emer was godmother.

In 1952, a by-election in Limerick was about to take place when Father sent for me. He told me to sit down while he stood, always an indication that the matter was of some importance. Very quietly, he said that I must feel free to reply to the question he was about to ask; he would not bring any influence to bear one way or the other. He continued: 'They [whoever "they" were] are anxious that you stand as a candidate.' My reply was swift and immediate: I had no desire to enter active politics. He looked at me and said: 'That is your considered answer?' 'Yes,' I replied. He then added: 'I think you have made a very wise decision'.

This reply, of course, was open to two interpretations – either he thought I was unsuited for such a life and did not posses the necessary skills, or it would be better for me to pursue the life I was leading. I feel, however, it the latter. I know the stresses of a political life, while continuing my profession would not have suited me. Full-time politicians were rare in those days, and certainly I had no desire to become one. Politics, I am convinced, is a special vocation, and with some almost like a disease, and often an incurable one. A person has to be prepared to give his entire life and time, and too often to a thankless public. Politicians frequently become the butt of unfair and even untrue adverse criticism, and this accompanied by the risks, the strain, the hours spent, inevitably a seven-day week, and the effect these have upon their families. Although it may well have its moments of satisfaction, even glory, it cannot be said that politicians are privileged, as some claim, especially when one compares their lives to many other professions which fare much better.

While I am quite sure that politics was not my professional calling, this did not prevent me from taking part in many elections, nor has it affected the strong political views which I hold. My first experience was in the general election of 1943. Young as I was, I was deeply concerned that my father should remain in power, especially during the war. I took a much more active part in the highly successful general election of 1944 and travelled the entire length of the old County Dublin Constituency which stretched from Balbriggan in the north, to the borders of Bray in the south, and westward to the county of Kildare. The election took place near the Whit weekend when the weather was simply gorgeous. A meeting in Balbriggan which I addressed from the steps of the courthouse is said to have been attended by some 1,500 people. The reception was encouraging and Tony Hederman made a splendid speech that day. Open-air meetings were then a vital part of electioneering, as there was no TV or radio coverage.

I took part in all subsequent elections up to the time of my appointment as Taxing Master when I ceased to take any part in party politics. I was appointed agent for Tommy Mullins in the heart-breaking by-election campaign of autumn 1947 when he was defeated by the leader of the newly formed and now defunct Clan na Poblachta Party with Seán MacBride as its leader. This was a gruelling campaign where no quarter was asked or given.

I found the general election of 1948 demanding and frustrating. Despite its best efforts, Fianna Fáil failed to obtain an overall majority, and I remember being at home with Father on the day the Dáil was to re-assemble. He could see that I was depressed: this was a new experience for me, as he had been in power since I was less than ten years old. We spoke of the proceedings in the Dáil that afternoon and then he said, in a quiet but determined voice: 'Don't worry. I'll get them on the hip.' Later, he did. Remembering his soldiering days, he said of MacBride: 'He'll not get my left flank.' As events proved, he held that flank.

When John A. Costello became taoiseach, one of his friends, a fellow lawyer, was anxious to send a message of congratulations, although he did not share Costello's political viewpoint. He devised a formula which any lawyer would understand and appreciate. His telegram read: 'Without prejudice, congratulations!'

Father's last campaign as party leader was in the general election of spring 1957. It was a resounding victory. As 1958 was drawing towards its close, Father confided to the family that he would be standing for president the following year. The election took place in June 1959, and Jane, who was only three weeks old at the time, still claims that she was granddaughter of a taoiseach even though it was only for a matter of weeks.

Mother had certain reservations about going to 'The Park'. She had always led such a private life but, so typical of her, she said she would do her duty despite her advanced years. She would have much preferred to remain in Herberton, where she had taken over the rearing of Vivion's two children, Ann and Éamon.

I was present at my father's inauguration and the reception in Dublin Castle that night. Among the many distinguished guests were Mícheál MacLiammóir. When introduced to him, I said that we had first met while I was a boy in Blackrock College when he came to give lessons in stage make-up to the principals in our Gilbert and Sullivan operas. MacLiammóir threw back his shoulders, and with that characteristic pout of his heavily made-up lips, he said: 'When was that?' I replied: 'In the 1930s.' His dark eyes sparkled. Placing his hand on my shoulder, he said with mock seriousness: 'Dear boy, you are mistaken. It must have been my father!'.

I had often seen him perform when Mother brought us to the Gate Theatre and came to know him better in later years. When my daughter Síle was studying *The Importance of Being Earnest*, I wrote to MacLiammóir, asking if I might call on him for some expert advice. Almost by return of post, I received a charming reply, inviting Síle and myself to tea in his famous house in Harcourt Terrace. We arrived at the given hour and were conducted by his man servant to the drawing room where Mícheál received us. He was dressed in a velvet jacket and wearing a wine-coloured shirt with a broad white stripe and a tie to match. A pink handkerchief dangled from his breast pocket with exquisite carelessness, and he was all made up for his performance. At first he thought that Síle was to act in the play, but when she told him she was studying it for her Leaving Certificate, he became very interested and talked for a good while about the play and, of course, about Oscar Wilde himself. After about half an hour, the door opened and the man servant brought in tea; MacLiammóir had even taken pains to include Lady Bracknell's cucumber sandwiches. We had scarcely finished tea when Hilton Edwards came in. We had of course mentioned Oscar Wilde many times by then, whereupon Edwards chided MacLiammóir. He said: 'There was a rule in their house that Mícheál has to pay a fine each time he mentioned Wilde.' MacLiammóir reacted immediately. He produced a ten shilling note from his pocket and placed it with great ceremony on the nearby piano.

We then spoke of MacLiammóir's painting and his love of music. He played the piano well and was interested in my love of Field and Chopin. He also spoke of what he referred to as, 'Your dear parents' and of my mother's love of the stage. MacLiammóir showed particular interest when I told him what Yeats had said to her: 'You and the wind were the success of the day.' He kept repeating this with a certain sense of puzzlement and wonder.

Mícheál told us of Lord and Lady Longford's gratitude for the support my mother had given the Gate, and of how Longford was thrilled when Father nominated him as a senator. In the course of our conversation, I told him about my uncle Andy who had a shop in Balbriggan. He was very good to the poor and no beggar left empty-handed. One day an old woman came in, a regular caller, and he gave her a few pence. The woman replied: 'May every hair in your head be a candle to light you to heaven.' My uncle was almost totally bald! MacLiammóir was delighted with the story and said: 'Oh that's marvellous! I'll use that in one of my plays.' I don't think he ever did. It was a most enjoyable afternoon and a memory to be treasured. He wrote two beautiful letters to me on the death of my parents.

My parents moved into Áras an Uachtaráin at the end of June 1959 and began a new life there. My mother made no secret of the fact that she disliked the move. She was lonely in these strange surroundings but determined to make the best of it. My family visited them regularly and spent many Sundays in the Áras. We came to know the place and enjoyed exploring the house and grounds. I was particularly interested in its history. Mother also became interested and loved to take her walks alone so that she could say her prayers. Her favourite place was 'the wilderness', a lonely, wooded area on the north-western part of the grounds. There, a monument, upon which was engraved a poem to the wilderness, had been erected by one of the viceroys of the nineteenth century. This piece appealed to me, although the monument was in poor condition at the time. I mentioned this to Mother, for she too enjoyed reading the poem and had written it down so that she could read it at her leisure. She then spoke to Father and he arranged for the monument to be refurbished.

Other monuments in the grounds included one erected by a viceroy to his deceased wife. Even more interesting is the grave of 'Jack', the favourite Irish terrier of King Edward VII. The king had taken the dog with him on his visit to Ireland in 1903, and poor Jack had only survived three weeks. During my father's first term of office as president, this monument was also refurbished.

Both my parents never ceased to show their love of animals, and on one day towards the end of Father's second term, Mother was missing. She had gone out for her usual walk in the wilderness and had been out longer than usual. One of the *aides-de-camp* went to look for her and found her deep 'in conversation' with a buck deer. The animal had stopped and responded to her but fled at the sight of the newcomer. She did not think it a bit odd that even a wild animal reacted to her greetings.

While Father was president, I attended a number of official functions, the most notable being receptions for President Kennedy, the King and Queen of the Belgians, Prince and Princess Rainier and President de Gaulle, although he had retired when he came to visit.

Phyllis and I were with members of the family, ready to be presented to President Kennedy, but this took some time. Standing only yards away, I was more than an hour in his presence and could observe the American president closely. He made an impressive figure, so tall, continually talking, his large lips often breaking into a smile and sometimes a hearty laugh. I remember remarking to myself that I was only feet away from perhaps the most powerful man in the world. My time came to be introduced. As he shook Phyllis' hand, he said: 'I'm glad to meet you.' As he shook mine, he noted that I was the youngest son of President de Valera.

A great many people were present at this reception and President Kennedy's bodyguard became concerned. I believe there were twelve of them and as Colonel Sean Brennan told me, they were very jittery. He tried to calm them by saying that the president had nothing to fear in Ireland as the only thing which could kill him here was love. Still, they appeared over-anxious. At one point, the crowd pressed in on President Kennedy and the bodyguards reacted immediately. One of them elbowed Ruairi's wife, Eithne, in the chest, knocking her to the ground. President Kennedy saw the incident and shouted in a loud voice: 'Lay off there!' Father could not see the incident. Although it caused some embarrassment, there were no apologies from the bodyguards, nor did President Kennedy realise who his guard's victim had been.

It is so tragic to think that, with all the close attention of his bodyguards, John F. Kennedy would have such a short time to live before he became the victim of assassins' bullets.

I had brought my brand new camera on the occasion and was anxious to take photographs but I knew the protocol was very strict. I sought permission through my father and permission was then granted for me to take photographs of President Kennedy. The itinerary was running late, and both presidents were due to leave to attend another function. Only my brother Éamon and I were permitted to take photographs and we raced towards the hall door in readiness. As President Kennedy and my father appeared and were about to come down the steps inside the hall door, we took our shots. I was not as familiar with my camera as I ought to have been and began to fumble excitedly. President Kennedy saw this and said in a decidedly stern voice: 'If you don't take your time, you'll make a mess of it!'. This only made matters worse, and the photographs were not as successful as I would have wished.

It was well known that President Kennedy took to Mother as she did to him. It is equally well known that he loved poetry and he was fascinated by her knowledge of poetry which she could recall so freely. Shortly before he left the Áras, my mother recited a poem about the River Shannon. He was delighted and wished to use this quotation in his departure speech. He took an envelope from his pocket and scribbled some lines. Seán Lemass, who was then taoiseach, accompanied President Kennedy in the presidential helicopter on their way to Shannon. According to Lemass, Kennedy could not read his scribbles and had to improvise by making up missing lines. On his return to the US, President Kennedy wrote the following personal letter to my mother:

The Whitehouse,
Washington.
July 9, 1963

Dear Mrs de Valera,

I wanted to write you a personal note to tell you how much I valued meeting you. Sitting next to you at the luncheon and the dinner is among the most pleasurable remembrances not only of my trip, but of my term in office.

I admire greatly all that you and President de Valera are doing for your country and share your own people's pride in your lifetime of work for the cause in which you both so strongly believe.

I hope you will not dismiss these words as mere flattery, even though a wise old Irish lady once told me 'a kind word never broke a tooth'.

My very best wishes to you both.

Sincerely,

John Kennedy

MRS EAMON DE VALERA,
THE PRESIDENTS HOUSE,
DUBLIN,
IRELAND.

❖     ❖     ❖     ❖

Among the many guests at the reception for President Kennedy were Sean O'Sullivan and Jimmy O'Dea. O'Dea had been a lifelong friend of Seán Lemass and it was he who arranged that O'Dea be included. Years before, O'Sullivan had made a charcoal drawing of O'Dea which is absolutely superb, especially in the way he captured the character of the sitter. Again I had my camera with me, and this time I was more at ease with it and asked if I might take a photograph of the pair as a memento of the wonderful drawing. They both smiled and posed for me. The diminutive O'Dea was almost obscured by O'Sullivan's massive frame. Just as I was taking the photograph, I said: 'Now I have the subject and the artist,' to which O'Dea quipped: 'No... artist and object!'

My mother often told us of her first meeting with Jimmy O'Dea. She had seen him on the stage when he was very young, around 1917, and was so impressed that she told him he had a great future on the stage. O'Dea never forgot this and referred to and acknowledged her words of encouragement in much later years. Mother took us to pantomimes at the Gaiety in the 1930s. She enjoyed these productions in which O'Dea was always the principal attraction and for her the main reason for going. During one performance, we were seated in a box in the dress circle. In one of the scenes, Jimmy was being chased by the villain and pretended that he could not remember the word that would save him. He ran about the stage in an effort to escape, crying out in a pathetic voice in his immutable way. While doing this, he kept appealing to the audience to tell him the missing word. When Jimmy spotted my mother, he raced across the stage and actually climbed up one of the pillars almost to the level of the box. Looking straight at her as he clung on, he called out in a most appealing tone: 'Help me, help me! Tell me the word – you can help as you did in the past!' Mother of course supplied the missing word. She was quite sure that O'Dea was referring to the words of encouragement she had spoken to him all those years before.

Jimmy O'Dea had a great respect and positive affection for my mother, and in her last years, he sent her a beautiful orchid with a touching message of remembrance. When she showed me this flower, her face beamed with smiles as she recalled the great artist and the performances which had so delighted her.

My experience with royal visitors was more relaxing. The King and Queen of the Belgians paid a State visit, Father arranged for Phyllis, Síle, Jane and myself to be presented. It was quite an informal affair, and again permission was sought to take photographs. The queen insisted that Síle and Jane be included, and put her arm around Jane.

Later that evening, Phyllis and I were guests at a private dinner party after which the royal pair was due to attend a reception in Dublin Castle. I was told that our car would be last in the procession and that I was to take up my station ahead of the others since the itinerary was running late. Scarcely had the dinner ended when Phyllis and I dashed to the private wing to get our coats. On the way back, we passed along a narrow corridor and were surprised to see the queen coming towards us, accompanied by her lady-in-waiting. She was actually running, holding her gown up to her knees as she raced along. We immediately stood aside and as she passed, Phyllis curtseyed while I bowed. She smiled and said in perfect English: 'Thank you, but we have no time for that now!'

During their stay, the king expressed a wish to learn more about hurling. The president of the GAA arrived, complete with hurleys and balls, and the king, my father and Taoiseach Jack Lynch, prepared for the demonstration. Despite his poor eyesight, Father said he would like to try his hand. As he said himself, by sheer good luck, he connected beautifully with the ball and sent it a respectable distance. Mr Lynch was then asked to show off his prowess. By some completely uncharacteristic slip, he failed to connect the first time. This, of course, raised a titter, remembering his great fame on the playing field. It was then the king's turn. He did connect, but the ball veered off at a sharp angle and almost hit the house. This story has been told by others and somewhat embellished, claiming that the ball which the king had pucked had broken a window, but this is only a case of a good story being 'improved' in the telling.

Another memorable night was the visit of Prince and Princess Rainier. Phyllis and I were presented to them in the afternoon and attended a dinner party that evening. As the guests assembled for dinner, the princess chatted freely with Father, while the prince engaged Mother in conversation, although his knowledge of English was limited. I was standing in a group not far away. Earlier that day, perhaps a day or so before, there had been an attempted burglary in Áras an Uachtaráin. An Englishman had been released from Mountjoy Prison and when set free, he had no idea where he was. He wondered up to the Phoenix Park, saw some big house and thought that he would try to 'knock it off'. Although he succeeded in entering part of the Áras, he was instantly arrested. It was just as well that he had not tried the American Embassy as the marines might have given him a very different reception. The other guests in my group were discussing the attempted burglary when the princess overheard our conversation. Very much to my embarrassment, I had to relate the whole tale which amused her greatly.

Time was pressing, so Father extended his arm to take the princess in to dinner, with the prince and Mother close behind. As they passed, the princess was carrying a white mink stole. The next thing I knew, the stole was flying through the air in my direction with the princess smiling and saying to me: 'Take that for me, please.' I successfully caught it and thereby became 'keeper of the princess' stole'.

During the course of the dinner, I had ample opportunity to observe the royal guests, especially the princess. She looked beautiful that evening, and her fine features dominated the scene. She was very natural and full of fun, although I was surprised that she took out her compact and made up her face as the dinner ended. She obviously wore a considerable amount of make-up but her hair was one of her most striking features. Later, my mother told me that Princess Grace was concerned about the upbringing of her children and was anxious to get my mother's advice. Mother gave her advice which came from her own experience over many years.

Phyllis and I attended other official functions in Áras an Uachtaráin and were regular guests at the annual Red Cross party which was usually held in June. Among other events which I recall was a dinner which my father gave for the judges of the Supreme and High courts and former Attorneys General. He was anxious that I should attend, although frankly, I felt somewhat out of place in such exalted legal company. It was a purely stag affair as there were no women members of the High or Supreme Courts in those days. I found that my immediate dinner companion was to be Patrick McGilligan. I scarcely knew him, although I had attended his lectures on constitutional law in UCD. I knew of his strongly held political views and that he had been former government minister. I was also aware of his reputation for having a caustic tongue, at times a bitter one, rivalled only by his predecessors, Tim Healy and Albert Wood and later, Albert Wood's son Ernest.

As we sat down, McGilligan broke the ice by remarking in his crisp Derry accent that he had counted thirteen former attorney generals at the table and hoped that there was no unlucky omen in that. Then he sallied into one story after another, showing himself to be a splendid raconteur with his dry, keen sense of humour. He was a most pleasant companion and made the evening a memorable one. As the dinner ended, my father rose to propose a toast. The company stood. Father held up his glass and said in a strong voice: 'Gentlemen, a toast. To our sovereign lady…' He paused and there was a gasp around the table. Then, in an even louder voice, he continued: 'The law!' We drank the toast amid much laughter.

From the time of President Hyde, it became a tradition that each president and his spouse should plant a tree in the grounds. In later years, the tree chosen was an Irish oak. In addition to her planting oak, my mother expressed the wish to plant a rowan tree. She had a special affection for this species and its association with Irish folklore dating back to earliest times.

My parents used to joke about the pair of Irish oaks which had been planted by President Seán T. Ó Ceallaigh and Mrs Ó Ceallaigh. Although planted on the same day, President Ó Ceallaigh's grew slowly and became a somewhat chubby specimen (he was small in stature), whereas Mrs Ó Ceallaigh was a tall lady and her tree well outgrew the president's.

It was during Father's second term as president that both Síle and Jane learned to drive in the grounds of Áras an Uachtaráin, a splendid and safe environment with its many long and well-surfaced avenues. There was also a 9-hole golf course which the family used very little as none of us were golfers. If we did try, certainly as far as Ruairi and I were concerned, we spent 95 per cent of our time in the rough. Things were quite different when Patrick Hillery became president. A keen and dedicated golfer, he used the course frequently and often played there with our mutual friend, the Irish Open champion James Malone. Malone was someone for whom I had a tremendous regard and affection. In my days as practising solicitor, we had many business connections and had several mutual clients. He was a chartered accountant. One of the cleverest men I have ever known, he was very humble about his many talents. One of the facets of his amiable character was his wonderful sense of humour. His face lit up as he laughed and many is the joke we shared together. His untimely death in August 1987 came as a bitter blow and I, like so many others, missed him greatly. He had reached the zenith of his profession as an accountant. I had known his wife Gay since childhood as we both had music lessons with Clare Hand.

Áras an Uachtaráin had its own peculiar atmosphere, especially in the State apartments. I cannot say I found it particularly friendly, although it was pleasant to gaze out across the park as the sun was setting setting and see the Dublin and Wicklow mountains in the distance. Often on a Sunday afternoon, I spent hours alone, playing the piano in the drawing room. The instrument itself was not a very good one, a baby grand which had been there since President Ó Ceallaigh's time.

My thoughts often wandered to the history of that room and the many famous persons who had been there in bygone times. The private wing, added for the visit of King Edward VII, was somewhat modern in concept and rather lacked atmosphere, at least for me. The oldest part of the house, especially along a corridor on the top floor, was quite eerie. This was near Queen Victoria's bedroom and the adjoining bathroom. (In modern times, an oratory has been built in this part of the house.) Over the years, many people have expressed a feeling of uneasiness in this corridor. At least six claim to have seen an apparition of a young boy dressed in clothes dating from the end of the nineteenth century and who is said to haunt this spot. Some have even claimed that this is why the oratory was built there. One thing I do know is this. When my father visited the oratory, the door leading to the corridor was left open; if not, it seemed to close of its own accord. No rational explanation was ever found. As a boy, Winston Churchill spent some time in Áras an Uachtaráin when it was the Vice-Regal Lodge. Could his spirit still be in this place?

I knew little or nothing of the history of the house until I came to know it in the summer of 1959. With my interest in the occult, I was anxious to learn more about the old place, especially if it had its ghosts, as I would have expected. Certainly I am convinced that there was a strange atmosphere near Queen Victoria's bedroom. I had not then heard the story of the boy ghost. There are further claims that a ghost of a former Dublin metropolitan policeman has been seen on the Royal Walk, a fine avenue to the southern side of the house which is lined with mature trees set by royal visitors when the house was the Vice-Regal Lodge.

General Charles de Gaulle had already retired as president of France when he and his wife came to Ireland on a private visit. He spent some time at the Áras with my father who arranged for the family to meet him. We were all assembled in the Boudoir where each of us was introduced. General de Gaulle was very formal as he shook hands with each of us. He did not speak in English which he disliked doing. Certainly I was at a disadvantage: my knowledge of the French language was only school French – and in that I place no blame on Blackrock College. De Gaulle had been walking the gardens with my father, just the two of them alone, before he came to meet us. He was a man of massive proportions and it was seldom, if ever, that I saw someone walking with Father who was considerably taller. He did speak English with Father whose French, although fair, was not enough to keep up at length or in a detailed conversation. The two men got on splendidly and developed a deep, mutual respect. Father said that the more he knew de Gaulle, the more he admired him. They had a lot in common.

# CHAPTER XV

*A Serious Interest in Painting*
*Appointment as Taxing Master*

Towards the end of the 1950s, I began to take a more serious interest in painting and decided I would like to take up this form of art. I approached my friend, Albert J. Thompson, who had been a client of mine for a number of years. He was a very well-known character in the Dublin of that time. Jack was a skilled draftsman, having spent some time in the Belfast shipyards. He later joined the civil service. When I knew him, he and his wife Pat were running a highly successful business selling drawing-office equipment. Shortly after the war, he was one of the first to introduce photocopying to Ireland.

Thompson explained that he knew a lot about technical engineering and architectural drawings but was not an expert in art, yet he could introduce me to a friend who sold art material and who was himself a gifted painter. This was James Kenneth Kennedy. It was with some feelings of timidity that I went to Kennedy's shop in Harcourt Street and made a modest purchase of basic art material. Although my first efforts were feeble, the more I tried, the more interested I became. I was soon a regular visitor to Kennedy's and a warm friendship grew between Kenneth Kennedy and myself, although he was some twenty-five years my senior. He was always most helpful, giving me many useful tips and always full of encouragement. During the war, he had been a senior officer in the LDF which served as a further link between us. We often romanced about those eventful days.

Kenneth had a particular talent for drawing and painting. He had studied in the School of Art in the early 1920s, where one of his teachers, Patrick Tuohy, gave him particular encouragement. Tuohy was a greatly gifted painter, who tragically took his own life in New York in 1930, aged 36. His father, Dr Tuohy – as we have seen was my mother's friend –

brought my brother Ruairi into this world in November 1916. Tuohy had been a pupil of Willie Pearse in St Enda's prior to 1916. Most of the well-known artists of the day patronised Kennedy's shop in Harcourt Street, including Sean Keating, Sean O'Sullivan, Yann Renard, George Colly, Maurice McGonigal and Tom Ryan. Speaking of eminent artists, Jack B. Yeats remarked to my father that he had nothing but contempt for those who bought his pictures. Whether he meant that he felt they did not understand his work or that the purchasers were only interested in their value as works of art, I am not sure.

I remember going into Kennedy's shop one day and was scarcely in the door when I called out to my friend: 'Hope springs eternal!' To this, Kennedy replied like a flash: 'Abandon hope, all ye who enter here!' He had a lovely sense of humour and we enjoyed many jokes together. Not alone was he a gifted landscape painter, he also executed some excellent portraits. He paid me the compliment of asking me to sit for him and this work was much admired. Later, Frank McKelvey RHA was to say many nice things about this painting. Like me, he was interested in railways. As a native of Bray, Co. Wicklow, he had travelled by train to his school in Dublin in the earlier part of the twentieth century. He knew and loved the now defunct Harcourt Street Railway line and was deeply upset at its passing. He gave me some clever and interesting pictures which he had painted along this old line. For some reason, he did not drive a motor car and had a passion for motorcycles, a subject in which he was quite expert. He knew almost every inch of his beloved Wicklow and often spoke to me of the county, particularly of the Devil's Glen which he had known and loved since the early 1920s; indeed he told me that he proposed to his wife there in 1927. His knowledge of nature was remarkable. His father and grandfather loved the sea and owned a sailing boat. Kenneth too loved the sea and was quite expert in nautical matters.

Kenneth Kennedy's talents and interests extended far beyond his art and business. He was particularly well read and had a knowledge of many subjects. He was the third generation to run the business in Dublin, a firm which had formerly been brush-makers. The nature of the business changed at the end of the 1950s when the firm concentrated exclusively on the supply of art materials.

I had not known him all that long when he asked me to act as solicitor for his family and his firm, which I did until I retired from practice. His firm was a tenant in the Harcourt Street premises, but when an opportunity to purchase arose, I acted for him in this transaction. The former front and back drawing room on the first floor are particularly fine, retaining Georgian stucco plaster work. Kenneth Kennedy had always harboured the hope that this area could be turned into a gallery. Alas, he did not live to see this; his two sons Ultan and Conor – both accomplished artists – accomplished this task. These splendid rooms were converted into a gallery and opened by the then Lord Mayor of Dublin, Bertie Ahern, in May 1987. It has now become one of the foremost exhibition venues in Dublin.

In late 1961, through the kindness of the late John J. Smith, I was given the opportunity to obtain a site not far from my home in Foxrock. My first and immediate reaction was to seek the advice of Percival Blake. As usual, he was willing to offer me his opinion and the decision was made to proceed. This presupposed the building of another house, but Percival Blake agreed to design the new house despite the fact that he was now advanced in years. He threw himself heartily into the project. In time, the new house was built and the first sold, albeit with a feeling of regret as we had been so happy there.

Phyllis and I busied ourselves with the many tasks ahead, including the design and layout of a new garden. My father 'cut the sod' and agreed with my proposal that the new house should be called after Percival Blake. I chose the name Charton, which was made up with part of his second name, Charles, and his mother's name, Antonia. Antonia was also Phyllis' second name, so we brought all associations together to arrive at the name 'Charton'.

It was only after we married that I took a serious interest in gardening, prompted by Phyllis' own interest, and always found it relaxing to commune with nature. Not infrequently, I have quipped: 'Make friends with the earth, for we will be long enough in it!' I find gardening therapeutic, a fascinating occupation and a great way to block out worries. True, it can be frustrating at times, yet it has many compensations – observing the seasons as they change, seeing the mystery of nature at work.

I can find such peace there and believe there is a lot of truth in the old cliché that one is 'nearest to God in the garden'.

In an earlier chapter, I referred to my mother's love of flowers. Father's weak eyesight greatly impeded his enjoyment of nature, although he took a particular interest in bird song. He enjoyed some recordings I had made (although of mediocre quality) of the songs of the blackbird, thrush, robin and others. When he heard these recordings, he remarked that they brought him back to his boyhood in Bruree, Co. Limerick. His clear favourite was the song of the blackbird, reminding me of Francis Ledgewidges' lovely lines:

The blackbird blows his yellow flute so strong

And rolls away the notes in careless glee…

Father, like so many who have poor or no eyesight, often compensated with his acute hearing. At times this was used with devastating effect, especially if he happened to overhear something that perhaps we did not wish him to know.

As my interest in painting developed, I attended exhibitions, especially the annual exhibition in the Royal Hibernian Academy. For a long time previously, I had been taken by the paintings of Frank McKelvey RHA, so much so that I resolved to meet him. A native of Belfast, he was a great deal my senior and was born on 3 June 1895. I wrote to him asking if I might call to see him and he promptly extended an invitation. Phyllis, Síle, Jane and myself set off by train for Belfast where he received us with great courtesy in his studio in Howard Street.

Almost from the first moment of our meeting, we took to each other, and he showed me many examples of his beautiful landscapes. Frank McKelvey seldom came to Dublin, although he was a regular exhibitor at the RHA. We arranged to meet him when he next came, and he and his wife Elizabeth visited us at our home. From then on, we kept up a regular correspondence, interspersed with occasional phone calls. McKelvey was a Protestant but not a great church-goer. He boasted that his friends could be found among those who held divergent political and religious beliefs. He had not the slightest trace of bigotry in his character. While not very politically minded, he voted unionist, but these views never adversely affected the bond of friendship which grew between us.

By the time I came to know him, he was a highly regard artist, with examples of his work in galleries in Ireland, Scotland and America. His work, which is full of poetry and quiet contemplation, is generally associated with rural landscapes of Mayo, Antrim, Down and Donegal. McKelvey's great talent, however, was by no means confined to such painting, as he received countless commissions for portraits of those who were prominent in the unionist tradition. These were always executed with care, skill and competence, with a marked capacity for capturing the likeness of the sitter. He was a magnificent draftsman and an outstanding watercolourist, having done scores of paintings of exquisite delicacy in this difficult medium. His pencil and charcoal drawings are equally refined and outstanding.

Not long after I had first met Frank McKelvey, he decided to close his spacious studio in Howard Street and to build one in the garden of his house in Hollywood, Co. Down. He and his wife Liz invited Phyllis, Síle, Jane and myself to visit them there. McKelvey lived in considerable comfort, and the house, although not large, was beautifully appointed, to say nothing of the large garden. Both he and his wife were great gardeners. He showed us his private collection of pictures, including so many that had not been seen by the public. Pride of place was given to a stunning portrait in oils of his wife. This, he told me, was 'one picture I would never sell'. He then took us out into the garden to see his new, spacious and highly organised studio. He had taken very much to Phyllis and to her delight, presented her with a delightful watercolour as a memento of our visit.

While he was not a frequent visitor to Dublin, he and his wife visited our home whenever they came south. I have special memories of a glorious summer evening in June 1969 when he and Liz had motored to Dublin to attend the RHA exhibition. After dinner, we walked around the garden for a while and he remarked: 'Terry, there are plenty of pictures here.' He then expressed an interest in seeing my own efforts at painting. I brought him to my den, which I rather grandly call 'the studio', a retreat where I keep my paintings, books and the organ. He asked me if I had some watercolours which he could use. I told him they were not of any quality, although I had gouache. 'That will do fine,' he said. 'I would like to give a little demonstration.' He told Jane, who was then ten years of age, to fetch some newspapers and to spread them on the floor. I then produced some reasonable quality paper, a pot of water and a suitable brush. He said: 'I would like to show you how to paint trees, or at least give some impression of them.'

He commenced by making a faint pencil drawing. He then took up the brush, dipped it in the water and flicked it across the newspapers on the floor, loaded the brush with paint and started painting. Almost like magic, a landscape began to appear as he talked of how the trees should be painted. He paused for a moment, looked at a portion of the picture and said: 'I think we should have a ploughed field there.' Again he flicked the brush until it was almost dry and drew its hairs in a downward direction. Instantly, the ploughed field appeared. He then looked up at me and said: 'I think that will do. That will show you what I had in mind.'

Although this little picture took only minutes to paint, it was a true Frank McKelvey with its own peculiar charm. Considering the shortness of the time he spent, the quality of the finished picture was amazing. This picture is one of my most prized memories of the artist and of his enormous talent. That glorious Sunday in early June remains a treasured memory, as the sun cast its golden rays across the azure sky, with the garden full of bird song and the scent of flowers. As the evening shadows lengthened 'on that soft dying day', I was filled with thoughts of hearts at peace, of his friendship and of his art.

It was on that evening that I first mentioned to Frank that his biography should be written. I pointed out that he was so long established as a first-class artist and that it would be a shame if his magnificent life's work were not recorded. He agreed that he would like this done and later supplied me with material, including well-kept notes, newspaper cuttings, and photographs. I undertook this work and completed it, but it remains unpublished, although at least my typescript is there for posterity.

Frank McKelvy's health began to decline, and as the year 1974 approached, it was clear that his days were numbered. He died peacefully on 30 June 1974, and with his passing, Ireland lost a great artist, as I had a dear friend. In the meantime, however, I had become friendly with his son, Frank Junior, who had become a professional painter a number of years previously. He specialised in watercolours, a medium in which he excelled, although he was an equally fine landscape painter in oils. As his paintings began to sell in Dublin and elsewhere, he used the pseudonym Frank Murphy to distinguish him from his celebrated father. Although Frank Jnr had a marked individual trait, his general style, especially in water colours, was very much that of his father. As we were of an age, we had a lot in common. Tragically, this friendship was cut short when Frank McKelvey

Junior died of a heart attack in August 1979 at the age of fifty-four. With his untimely passing, I had lost another good friend and art was the poorer by his loss. Liz lived on for many years and did not die until she was in here 101st year.

By the 1960s, the practice of a solicitor in Dublin began to change. A considerable number of the older generation had died and younger men were taking their place. The tendency towards one-man practices, and even smaller firms with one or more partners, was on the decline. There was a movement towards forming firms into greater grouping with a large number of partners. This increased as the years progressed, but I still have strong reservations as to whether this best serves the profession and, more important, whether it is in the best interests of the client.

As the 1960s were growing towards their close, I realised that I had to make an important decision. One or two medium-sized firms were sending out feelers, but I knew that I would not be happy in a partnership. I recalled what Master Kennedy had said to my mother when I first set up in practice and when there was a question of my forming a partnership. Kennedy could be flippant at times and say sharp things, but some remarks were very much to the point and indeed very shrewd. He said: 'Ah, Mrs de Valera, there is no such thing as true partnership… One partner will always try to outdo or overshadow the other.' Although this is not universally true, it does contain more than a grain of truth.

Paddy Kennedy could occasionally be extreme in his views. As Taxing Master, he once exclaimed that if it were not for the law of libel, he could write a book on what he called 'solicitors to be avoided'. However, the blame for delay and lack of attention cannot always be laid against solicitors. Because much of the justice system is cumbersome, unduly complicated and protracted, it could be strengthened and improved. This would be an advantage, not alone to the public, but likewise to the legal profession. It is only too true, and too frequent, that delays are not caused by the solicitors but by those barristers who 'sit' on cases and hold up proceedings. It is unfair when solicitors have to take the blame for delays caused solely by members of the Bar.

An instant took place in May 1963 which, while it had nothing to do with my practice as a solicitor, I found interesting; others may regard it as macabre. Certainly it aroused my morbid curiosity. I knew that burials had taken place during the 1916 Rising in the once beautiful gardens adjoining Dublin Castle. I understand that some 169 persons were interred there, both military and civilian. When I knew the gardens, they were in an extremely dilapidated condition, no more a large open space covered with grass. One afternoon, I had parked my car in the castle grounds, and was returning to my office, when I noticed activity at the entrance to the former gardens. I asked the caretaker what was happening, and he said that the only remaining bodies, five British army officers who had been killed in the Rising of 1916, were being exhumed to be re-interred in the British War Cemetery in Blackhorse Avenue. This information aroused my curiosity. The caretaker introduced me to a garda superintendent who said he could take me behind the canvas screen which surrounded the graves so that I could see the operations. He did remark, however, that he would not disclose my identity, but let anyone who wished to, think that I was a member of the gardaí.

The following day, accompanied by the superintendent, I went behind the screens. The first thing to meet my eye was a group of men with shovels and picks who were sitting on crude, plain coffins and drinking tea. They were somewhat taken aback by our unexpected appearance. There was another person present, an official from the British War Graves Commission. At the request of the superintendent, one of the coffins was opened. One of the men turned the skull over where I could observe a large hole in the centre of the forehead with a small exit hole at the back. The caretaker had told me that this officer had been shot dead by a sniper. He had already told me that, during the first week of the Rising, he saw this officer being carried out for burial. He was wrapped in a sheet with his head showing a large wound.

The official from the War Graves Commission had himself served in World War II. Curiously, he spoke of the dead officers in the present tense, as if they were still alive. Noting that all five officers were lieutenants, he did not refer to them as 'Lieutenant so and so' but as 'Mister'. He also pointed out that the quick-lime in which the bodies had been buried was still active after fifty years.

It had been an eerie experience to see the remains of these young men who, as the enemy, had lost their lives in the Rising. I reflected too that they had given their lives in the exercise of what they regarded as their duty.

In the summer of 1968, I learned that both taxing masters, Masters Kennedy and O'Reilly, were due to retire soon. I made up my mind to seek an appointment for one of these positions and was appointed Kennedy's successor when he retired in March 1969. Patrick F. O'Reilly, his colleague of some twelve years' service, then became the Senior Master. From the very moment I took up office, he extended a warm welcome and gave me every help and co-operation. I had known him when he was in practice as a solicitor, as well as his wife Dora, who was also a solicitor. His son Barry, now deceased, also joined the profession. Master O'Reilly and I became good friends and he took a paternal interest in my career as Taxing Master, giving me the benefit of his extensive experience. As a Taxing Master, he was considered strict and difficult to convince, while at the same time being absolutely fair. P. F. O'Reilly had strong political views and had once been a Fine Gael senator. He was proud of his family's pro-Parnellite tradition and had been a friend of Michael Collins. When he retired in the summer of 1969, I became Senior Master. He lived close by and we kept up our friendship. Calling to his house one day, I found him alone, sitting amongst his law books. His heart was still very much in the law and his thoughts lingered on his days as Taxing Master. I think he was a little lonely and often came to my home, wishing to be kept up-to-date with all that was happening in the Taxing Master's office. He died suddenly of a heart attack on 5 May 1975. Master Kennedy survived only one year in retirement and died in March 1970. Master O'Hanlon had lived into old age and died in his eighty-first year in November 1967. I very much regret that he had not lived long enough to see me as Taxing Master. I know this would have pleased him as he had taken such an interest and offered me much guidance in the law.

Few people outside the law understand the functions and duty of the Taxing Master. Only a solicitor with at least ten years' experience may be appointed Taxing Master. His function is that of a senior court official of the superior courts, with some additional jurisdiction. The law provides for two masters who serve in quasi-judicial capacity. Each has his own court where he adjudicates and rules on costs, whether arising out of litigation in the superior courts or between solicitor and client. Their decisions can be appealed to the High Court, with further appeal to the Supreme Court on points of law. Their range of activities is highly specialised in dealing with various aspects of law relating to legal costs.

Taxing Masters rely heavily on their former practice as solicitors. As it is a highly specialised field, trained experts known as legal costs accountants conduct the cases which come before them and are instructed by solicitors. Not infrequently, solicitors and barristers also appear and present their cases. The legal costs accountants draw up a detailed bill of costs which, where necessary, are 'taxed' before a taxing master. Legal costs accountants are justly proud of their tradition of expertise and, above all, their integrity which goes to the root of their pursuits.

Having listened to the evidence and law put to them, the Taxing Masters make their decisions and rule accordingly. Like judges, they cannot take any part whatever in politics during their term of office.

Master O'Hanlon, who held office for nearly three decades, applied some valuable maxims to his work. He said that the first duty of a Taxing Master is to protect the pockets out of which the costs are to be paid. As he put it rather graphically: 'Whether it be a widow with ten children or the state herself,' this maxim should apply. He continually stressed that absolute integrity was the essential stuff when dealing with legal costs.

Towards the latter part of my career as Taxing Master, I was disturbed to find a marked change of attitude towards the charging of legal costs, especially among younger lawyers. This was particularly noticeable among members of the Bar whose charges were so different from the charges made by barristers in the earlier part of my career as solicitor.

Unlike my days in practice, it became the norm to charge not what the case was worth, what was fair and reasonable and the true value of the work and services rendered, but rather what the case could bear in financial terms. Sadly, I noticed that attitudes were changing all round, applying even to newly appointed judges who took a decidedly more liberal view than their predecessors. It would be frightening if a position should arise (and it looks like it is fast approaching) whereby only the very poor man, or the very rich one who can afford the cost of litigation, could ensure the enforcement of their rights. The law should be for the benefit of all citizens. It should not be allowed to become a means, as my father once remarked, 'for the benefit of rapacious lawyers'.

If I have been hard on lawyers, other professions cannot escape my long experience. Blame can often be attached to expert witnesses, often those in the medical profession, whose fees far exceed the value and the length of time devoted to the service rendered.

For some strange reason, possibly at the behest of the Department of Finance, the government did not appoint a second Taxing Master immediately on the retirement of Master O'Reilly. I was therefore left to carry the burden of two masters for the next eight months, which proved to be trying and exacting. It was with great joy when I learned that David Bell had been appointed to fill the vacancy. I had known him since my days in practice and knew of his reputation as a first-rate solicitor. He was particularly prominent in the field of criminal law, although his wide knowledge extended far beyond this. I also knew of his rugby prowess and his great interest in the game. In his later years, he was chairman of the referees and continues to take an active interest in the sport.

David Bell was a most desirable colleague and I have an enormous respect for his shrewd judgement and his knowledge of law. He is one of the best known and popular members of the legal profession with the highest standard of integrity. He is fiercely independent and strong-minded. We served together for twenty years, which for me, were the happiest times I had spent in my career in the law. When he was making his farewell speech on the day he retired, he said that in all the years we had worked together, 'not one cross word passed between us'. He was right.

The life of a Taxing Master was quite different to that of practice, and I found it a relief to be released from all the stresses and strains which are so much part of the life of a busy solicitor. I also discovered that I had more time to devote to those pursuits which were denied to me as a practising solicitor. Some clever lawyer of the nineteenth century said: 'Solicitors are the charwomen of the law.' In so many ways, I agree. Solicitors' lives can sometimes be thankless, even dangerous. As Master Kennedy said: 'A solicitor's only real enemy can turn out to be his own client'.

Since my time in practice, it is now permissible for solicitors to advertise (subject to certain conditions). This would have been absolutely unthinkable in my day. A solicitor would have been accused of touting and thus subject to sever censure. Such a regrettable change of attitude is, it seems, a result of the modern doctrine of market forces, a highly dubious concept as far as the law is concerned. It derives from Thatcherism, which itself is a doubtful doctrine at best. In my view, the law is reduced to that of a business and ceases to be a profession. It becomes nothing more than an occupation, wherein the profit motive is the prime, if not the sole, criterion. It has to follow that this must be to injurious to the client's interest which then become secondary. Nor can competition be made a proper standard for it must in turn lead to unfair methods and under-cutting, inevitably resulting in the loss of service and proper dedication to the interest of the client. A solicitor's practice (indeed any other profession) should be based on proven ability, dedication and service to the client.

Another very disturbing concept which emanates from the EU (for which a number of undesirable foreign practices have by stealth already made their way into our daily lives) is the suggestion that those who are not qualified, practising solicitors, should be allowed to carry out or practice specific legal work, which of its nature is highly technical, requiring years of training, experience and practice, and special skill.

What a pity that those who advocate and support such an ill-advised move are not made accountable for all the ill-effects, damage and loss, which such a practice would beget. Would, for instance, you engage a person, who had only very limited and basic knowledge and experience of surgery, to perform and carry out a heart by-pass operation? Those who play with fire deserve to be burnt, but it will not alas be the people who advocate this dangerous proposal as above, who will bear the cost of any loss or damage, but the unfortunate Irish public at large and aggrieved parties. If we are wise, we should not allow these dangerous ignorant foreign concepts ruin or adversely affect our long-tried legal system.

# CHAPTER XVI

*Death of Parents-in-Law*
*Retirement of Father as President*
*Death of My Parents*

The year 1972 turned out to be a sad one with the death of both my parents-in-law. Percival Blake died on 13 January at the age of eighty-six, his death undoubtedly hastened by his wife's illness. They were deeply attached and rarely was a bond of love so strong. Notwithstanding his advanced years, his death came as a bitter blow to Phyllis. There had always been such strong ties between them and she was like him in so many ways, possessed of unsung talents and virtues with a marked degree of unselfishness. I too felt his passing enormously and missed his ever-valued advice, guidance and loveable personality. In everyday matters, particularly in later years, he even had become closer to me than my father.

This loss was soon to be followed by yet another. Phyllis' mother had been in poor health for a considerable period. She died on 25 March 1972 at the age of eighty-four. Sarah Kathleen Blake was a quiet, private person, someone who radiated goodness. She had a deep religious faith and was a thoroughly devoted wife and mother. Phyllis and I missed her greatly.

By this time, my parents were spending their last years in Áras an Uachtaráin and my family continued their regular visits. Síle and Jane were now growing up and beginning to look towards adult life. Síle was showing a liking for history and politics. Jane too had an interest in history but did not share her sister's enthusiasm for politics. Both girls, however, shared their grandparents' love of teaching. They both obtained their degrees and entered the teaching profession.

Síle loved to chat with my father, asking him about the important events in his life, while he took a great interest in her attraction to history and politics. Mother too reminisced with the girls as she did with all her grandchildren.

By June of 1973 my father had completed his second term as president and was due to retire. We all have distinct memories of our last visit to Áras an Uachtaráin while he was still president. Jane had formed a real attachment to the place and was sad that this era was coming to an end. When we came to make our final farewells, I found my mother in her sitting room. She looked up at us and said with a sweet smile, quoting Thomas Moore,: 'Our hearts, like thy waters, be mingled in peace.' Deep down, I knew she had little regret that this phase of her life was coming to an end. She never entirely regarded Áras an Uachtaráin as her home and would not have been there of her own choosing. Yet she had the satisfaction of knowing that she had done her duty to her husband, family and to the nation, as indeed she had always done. Not long before she left Áras an Uachtaráin, I tested her memory. Perhaps her favourite poem of all was Grey's 'Elegy in a Country Churchyard'. She recited the entire poem from memory without a single prompt; she was ninety-five years of age.

My parents spent their retirement at Talbot Lodge attached to Linden Convalescent Home in Blackrock, Co. Dublin.

I was 'silly enough', as Éamon put it, to develop acute appendicitis in June 1975. I was lucky: the surgeon, the late F. X. O'Connell, remarked that it was one of the 'dirtiest appendices' he had ever removed. Father visited me in the old Mater private nursing home. It was his last visit to this place which was so full of memories of his own eye operations, to say nothing of the deaths of Mother and Brian which took place there. When Father came to visit, he was accompanied by his former senior *aide-de-camp* Colonel Sean Brennan. Later, Col Brennan told me that he was greatly disturbed for he thought I would die. Mercifully, I recovered remarkably quickly and was soon able to resume my duties as Taxing Master.

It would indeed be remiss of me if I failed to give special mention of Col Sean Brennan. He had been active in the troubled times as a Fianna boy and was one of the first to join the S Branch in 1932. My father quickly recognised his merits and chose him to be his *aide-de-camp*. He was commissioned a captain in the regular army and remained at my father's side throughout the years, rendering invaluable service and a loyalty quite unrivalled. When my father was president, Sean was promoted to colonel and became his senior ADC.

Sean Brennan was always regarded as part of the family. My mother referred to him as 'our staunch friend'. She had a great affection and respect for him. He was full of common sense, an able organiser, very diplomatic and with a great sense of humour. When I was young, I sometimes approached him to get on the soft side of my father when I wanted something done. He was usually helpful, but if he thought I was pressing my luck too far, he characteristically said: 'Oh, no. The Chief would tick me off if I asked him that.' Yet I always found him a most useful conduit. Sean Brennan died in March 1976, only months after the death of his Chief whom he had revered and served so well.

Two other great Irishmen who served my father throughout the years with particular devotion and dedication were Sean and Maurice Moynihan. Father had a great regard and respect for them and relied upon their ever-willing and shrewd judgement and advice, to say nothing of their unswerving loyalty.

Another person who rendered tremendous service to my father was Kathleen O'Connell. She had been his personal secretary over many years and shared personal dangers with him, even risking her life during the Civil War. Father had complete confidence in her loyalty and dedication to the Irish cause. Her expertise, experience and knowledge of matters political was invaluable, especially as Father's eyesight deteriorated. Even in the most secret and confidential matters, she had become his eyesight. She read heavy and minutely detailed documentation for him and took down speeches or other memoranda which he had dictated. Kathleen O'Connell was warm-hearted, generous and deeply committed to her religious faith. As any good personal secretary, she sometimes had to shield Father from unnecessary enquiries, freeing him to concentrate on matters of State or the party. For this, some have unreasonably criticised her, but knowing my father's heavy workload, she regarded this as her duty.

My father was grieved at her loss when she died in April 1956. Kathleen O'Connell was succeeded by her niece, Marie O'Kelly. Like her aunt, she provided an indispensable service to my father and showed the same loyalty and trust as had her aunt.

By 1973, Mother had reached the age of ninety-five. While her mind was still clear, her health began to fade towards the end of 1974 and she was removed to the old Mater private nursing home. She deteriorated from then on but remained remarkably lucid until very near the end. By Christmas of that year, it was only too clear that she could not last much longer. Mother died at 9.40 p.m. on 7 January 1975. With perfect resignation supported by her unflinching faith, 'her quiet eyes closed; she had another morn than ours.' She was in her ninety-seventh year. My aged father was deeply moved, and the entire family joined him in his grief. We all knew that she was quite irreplaceable.

The requiem mass which took place at the Pro-Cathedral in Dublin was attended by a vast crowd who demonstrated the sincerity of their sorrow at the passing of one so loved and respected by all sections of society both at home and abroad. Liam Cosgrave, then taoiseach, attended the removal of the remains from the Mater and the memorial mass. He too was a Flanagan, my mother and he were distantly related. Since that day, I cannot hear Bach's exquisite 'Jesu, Joy of Man's Desiring' without thinking of that morning and the way in which the choir sang with such feeling. We laid her to rest in the family grave in Glasnevin where she had said that she longed to be re-united with Brian.

I find it so difficult to come to terms with her death, for somehow, she seemed to be always available to consult. I tried to express my emotions and my love in the following lines:

My Mother

Now in death's company you dwell,
Freed from life's irksome, bitter lot,
The weariness, the loss, the pain,
Washed away as by the gentle rain.

Now in the chorus of the Blessed you live,
More pure than light upon the flawless snow,
All you suffered, now your worthy gain,
While earthly thoughts and love of you remain.

By the beginning of August 1975, it became clear that Father too was fading. Our visits to him at Talbot Lodge became more frequent. As the months wore on, it was evident that his end could not be far off.

Early on the morning of 29 August, we were all summoned to his bedside. He lay there quietly with an oxygen mask over his face. The chaplain and Éamon led the assembled family in prayer. As midday approached, the late Dr Bryan Alton, my father's friend and personal physician, moved quietly to the bedside and gently removed the oxygen mask. At seven minutes to midday, my father's breathing ceased. In a very soft voice, Dr Alton looked around and said: 'He is gone.'

If I found it difficult to come to terms with the death of my mother, it was equally so with my father. The news of his death spread rapidly and tributes came pouring in from all corners of the world, from heads of state to the most lowly in society.

The government provided a state funeral. My father's remains were removed from Talbot Lodge on a gun carriage accompanied by the military escort. The requiem mass took place in the Pro-Cathedral. The choir sang and the organist was the late Oliver O'Brien, someone I had known since my childhood. At my suggestion, he even managed to work in a morsel of John Field's music. The service was attended by huge numbers of clergy, members of the government, the opposition, the diplomatic corps, public dignitaries and a vast crowd of people. Outside, thousands awaited the funeral cortege. At the end of the mass, the coffin was borne by eight military policemen. The pall bearers, representing every branch of the defence forces, accompanied the gun carriage. From there, a great procession took place towards Glasnevin. As it made its slow way through the streets, they were lined with dense crowds anxious to pay their final respects amid the solemn music which was played en route.

When the cortege finally arrived at Glasnevin, the coffin was borne to the graveside where full military honours were rendered, including the Last Post and Reveille. Among those lined up were several military attachés from foreign embassies. I could not but notice the British representative, a brigadier, as he stood there at the salute. How odd history can be. It had come a long way from my father's surrender to Captain Hitzen in 1916.

As Father himself would have wished, he had a soldier's farewell.

# CHAPTER XVII

*Death of My Brothers and Sisters*
*My Farewell to the Law and Retirement*

My father had not been long dead when Vivion married for the second time, Veronica (Vera) Rock who had been the personal secretary to P. J. Ruttledge and later to me when I was in practice as a solicitor. She is a person of many talents, so much of my success as a solicitor I owe to her and her devoted service, to say nothing of her powers of organisation and unswerving loyalty.

Some two years later, Síle was completing her degree course in history and politics, to be followed by a course leading to a higher diploma in education. She decided that she wished to take an active interest in politics and first stood for the Dáil in the general election of 1977 at the age of twenty-two. She was successful and then the youngest member of Dáil Éireann. While I did not wish to follow such a career, I was immensely proud that she should follow in the footsteps of her grandfather and that she had inherited many of the traits necessary for such an exacting career. She was later a successful candidate in the European elections, becoming the youngest MEP in Europe at the time. Like so many others in this sphere of politics, she had her ups and downs in this thankless, even cruel, occupation. Her own preference, however, was to return to domestic politics, and an opportunity arose which led to her election in her grandfather's old constituency in Clare which she has served with great dedication and enthusiasm. She was a member of the cabinet and Minister for Arts, Heritage, Gaeltacht and the Islands, a portfolio she enjoyed greatly. Like her grandfather, she has never shirked hard work. A number of years ago, in addition to her pressing work as TD, she qualified as a clinical psychologist. These political genes have also passed to Emer's son Éamon, now Minister of State to the above-mentioned department. After the change of government in 2002, Síle became a Minister of State in the Department of Education and Éamon became a cabinet minister. He too has been a highly successful, dedicated and hard-working TD for Galway.

In 1978, I learned that Ruairi's health was giving cause for concern. Although I knew that he had not been well for some time, I did not realise that it was quite so serious. He was then professor of archaeology in UCD and continued to devote himself to his work with the zeal and enthusiasm so typical of him. By then, his reputation as an expert in his field was not only recognised in Ireland but likewise abroad. In spite of the great stress and discomfort caused by a vascular condition, he would not give in and was due to present one of his sought-after lectures in Enniskillen. The lecture was considered one of his most brilliant, but no sooner had it ended than he collapsed. He was rushed to Enniskillen hospital but was dead on arrival, the result of a massive heart attack. This was Saturday, 28 October 1978. In a matter of a few days, he would have been sixty-two.

The news of his death came as a tremendous shock. Although he was far from his old self in recent days, I had no idea that the illness would prove terminal, especially since he often made light of his complaints.

Éamon drove me and other members of the family to the removal of the remains to Dublin. The funeral took place in Donnybrook, then to the family grave in Glasnevin. As is a family custom, members of the family were pall bearers, including Ruairi's two sons, Éamon and myself. Fittingly, the coffin was borne to the graveside by a number of Ruairi's former colleagues in the university. As the committal service ended, I was approached by a man standing by the graveside. He was gazing down at the newly-laid coffin and explained that he had served as a corporal in Ruairi's platoon in the 2nd battalion. He had not forgotten his commanding officer after all those years and had come to pay his tribute.

Ruairi's love of art and archaeology has continued through his daughter, Eithne, who is an exceptionally talented artist and keen archaeologist.

In so many ways, I have never got over Ruairi's death. He had been my mentor and guide with his shrewd judgement and wise counsel. Síle was also very grieved for he had been her godfather. Ruairi, like Father, was possessed of a shrewd political judgement in his deeply-held principals and his capacity to sum up his fellow man. My mother remarked that Ruairi reminded her so much of his father, while Éamon remarked that he had a mind like G. K. Chesterton.

Ruairi had so many talents. He was most artistic and wrote some beautiful poems, both in Irish and English. He was, however, very shy about these and only showed them to his close circle of friends. I nevertheless harbour the hope that a number of these may yet be published and available to a wider readership.

Ruairi also had a particular capacity for making friends easily. His former students still speak of him with great affection. While he had little former musical education, he was a splendid critic. With his exceptional knowledge of German, he had a true appreciation of the songs of Schubert and Schumann, his particular favourites.

Some years previously, in 1974, I was able to reinforce my love for Co. Wicklow by acquiring a site on which a bungalow was built. It was situated some three miles west of Ashford in the beautiful townland of Aghowl (the degenerate form of the Irish name 'Achadh Úill', the field of the apple tree). It was Síle who suggested its name, taking part of Phyllis' name and the Irish word for apple and thus came up with the name 'Lisual'. There the family spent many summer and other holidays and came to know the county even better than before. There too we made many friends with kindly neighbours. In its way, it became a home from home, and we had the pleasure of laying out and attending the new garden. Phyllis, as usual, displayed her talent in making it a comfortable place in which to live. It was so refreshing to spend time amid unspoiled countryside and all its peace and rural beauty.

Too soon, however, the years passed; the girls grew up and life changed. The time spent there became less and less. Beautiful and restful as it was, our holiday home in Wicklow was rapidly becoming redundant and the sad decision was taken to sell. I felt the break with Co. Wicklow very deeply. In parting with 'Lisual', we had the satisfaction of planting trees in our memory. Phyllis was the first to plant hers. It so happened that I was planting trees the day Ruairi died, so there is at least one tree in memory of him in a place we came to know and love, in that county which had meant so much to me in my childhood and youth.

Vivion's health had never been the best but it deteriorated further towards the end of the 1970s. He spent many long periods in hospital, bravely fighting on, in spite of a losing battle when cancer was diagnosed. He suffered a lot and finally succumbed on 16 February 1982 at the age of seventy-one. As the eldest, he had been the leader in the family, having achieved so much in his life as a distinguished scientist, army officer, successful barrister, politician and a tough businessman. He was fond of music, although he had little training, and loved playing a reed organ which I secured for him many years before. He delighted in playing Handel's 'Dead March from Saul', although not always on the most appropriate occasions or at the most convenient times. His son Éamon remarked that even in the small hours of the morning, the sound of the 'Dead March' could be heard echoing through the house. If ever someone had a party piece, this was it!

Vivion's funeral was both impressive and emotional. Booterstown church was packed to overflowing. Priests from his old school, Blackrock, chanted portions of the office of the dead, as was his wish. The British ambassador of the time was among the mourners and said that he was greatly impressed with the service. As we bore his remains down the aisle, the pall bearers included his son Éamon, my brother Éamon and myself. Appropriately, the music was his beloved 'Dead March', a fitting farewell for his burial in the family grave in Glasnevin.

The year 1982 was one of particular interest to me as it was the bicentenary of the birth of John Field, as well as the centenary of my father's birth. I was anxious to further the remembrance of Field and to take steps to ensure that this occasion would be adequately celebrated, so I was pleased to be approached by RTÉ and informed that a TV programme would be undertaken. My friend, the eminent pianist John O'Connor, now the doyen of Irish pianists, was chosen to perform the music. A series of eight TV programmes was prepared and presented by me, becoming the most comprehensive series to date on the Irish composer. Since then, John O'Connor has done so much with his exquisite playing to spread a love and knowledge of Field's music throughout the world, especially in the USA.

I also felt there should be a lasting memorial for Field and approached the taoiseach, Charles J. Haughey, who showed himself to be very sympathetic and encouraging. A competition was set up among artists for a suitable bust of the composer to be erected in the National Concert Hall. In the event, I was delighted to hear that Yann Renard Goulet had won the competition. During the course of Renard's work, I was able to provide pictorial representations of Field, many of which were little known. These proved to be of great help to him, and he executed a beautiful bust which was unveiled by Mr Haughey. From that time a room in the Concert Hall is called after Field. The pianist on this occasion was Charles Lynch. Earlier in 1979, I had the honour to unveil a plaque commemorating Field's baptism in St Werburgh's church in Dublin.

Other prominent artists whom I have had the privilege to know and count among my friends are Gerard Gillen and Bernadette Greevy. Gerard Gillan has long enjoyed a reputation as a concert organist of international status. He paid me the compliment of asking me to deliver a lecture in Maynooth college on the Irish composer, Philip Cogan, whose life I had reserached.

At around the same time, I met Bernadette Greevy, having admired her unique voice for a considerable time. By then, she too had an international reputation for the excellence of her performances. George Child, the much-respected English concert pianist and friend of Patrick Piggott, told me that he regarded Bernadette's voice superior to that of Kathleen Ferrier whom he had known.

Meanwhile, Síle had become a member of the European parliament and of necessity spent a great deal of time abroad. Jane was now married, leaving Phyllis and me alone in the old home. We continued nevertheless to spend our holidays in 'Lisual' and were enjoying a pleasant break in August 1984 when news came that Máirín had been found dead. She lived alone in her house in Galway, and the news came as a terrible shock. Although I had noticed that she had not been looking well for some time, I had no idea that her life was in danger.

We had always regarded Máirín as a second mother and felt her loss keenly. She was most generous, almost to a fault, and loved giving us presents. She had long fallen in love with the West and had lived there since 1948 when she became professor of botany in University College, Galway. She expressed the wish that she be buried in Galway and these wishes were carried out. Emer chose a fitting text for her tombstone, particularly as Máirín's speciality was marine biology. It was of course in Irish and read: 'I Liontaibh Dé go gCastar Sinn' (In God's nets may we be entwined).

In 1982, through the kind introduction of my friend Tony Behan, I became a member of the Old Dublin Society. This gave me an opportunity to write, deliver and publish papers on subjects close to my heart such as John Field, Sarah Curran's musical interests, the Shears brothers, J.B.S. MacIlwaine RHA (friend of Walter Osbourne RHA) and other subjects too.

The Old Dublin Society has much for which it may be proud. It has been in existence for more than half a century, and throughout this time, many scholars have, through its journal 'Dublin Historical Record', had the opportunity of publishing historical research which otherwise might have been lost or neglected.

Jane's marriage took place in August 1983. It looked like a time of great hope and promise, but turned out to be one of sadness and bitter disappointment for Jane and the family. Jane's son David was born on 6 September 1986, an event which brought a completely new dimension and great joy into the lives of Phyllis and me. Jane and David came to live with us and David soon became the centre of our attention and concern. From a selfish point of view, I found him quite rejuvenating as I tried to keep up with all his lively games and pursuits. In him, I can relive my own happy childhood, entering into the wonderful land of make-believe only known to a child, its dreams, its hopes, its aspirations for a better world which adults seldom realise.

David too has shown his good sense of fun. In the course of writing this book, there were many occasions on which I had to absent myself from playing with him. He once asked me how I was progressing, so I explained. He then said to Jane and his grandmother: 'As far as I can see,

Granny, Grandpa's book is mostly about himself!'

I can only hope that he may grow up and inherit the stoic qualities, courage and determination of his mother. There is the strongest bond of mutual affection between Síle and her nephew David. As for Phyllis who prayed, and I still do, that we will see him grow to a life of health, happiness and success, with his potential developed to the full.

Phyllis and I had just returned home from a holiday in Holland in May 1986 when my nephew Éamon came to tell me that his father, also Éamon, had undergone a serious operation in our absence. He had been taken ill quite suddenly and was promptly admitted to the Mater private nursing home where cancer was diagnosed.

Éamon himself had such a dread of this disease, having experienced its effects throughout his long career in medicine. He was violently opposed to smoking, drank little, was careful about his diet and took regular exercise, yet he too became a victim of this scourge. He was remarkably brave and composed throughout that summer, but as autumn came, it was clear that he was loosing the battle for life. As the end came, he was resigned, relying on his deeply-felt faith. He was surrounded by his wife Sally (since alas dead), his son Éamon and daughter Maire (herself a doctor, and who too is now tragically dead) and he died peacefully in the late evening of 9 December 1986. He had turned seventy-three the previous October.

The extended family felt his loss greatly as he was always on hand to advise on matters medical. Even from his youth, medicine had been the very essence of his life, a calling in which he had been outstandingly successful. His profound knowledge of his specialised field was recognised not only in Ireland but also in America. In addition to his extensive practice, he was also professor of gynaecology in UCD. In his student days, he invariably attained first place with first-class honours in his examinations.

Eamon's only interests outside medicine were reading, tennis, and a little golf. He loved music and sang with a clear tenor voice. He also had a wide knowledge of opera.

The large attendance at his funeral from Donnybrook church showed how much he had been respected. Again, I had the sad duty of being one of the pall bearers. Éamon was laid to rest in a grave immediately adjoining the family plot in Glasnevin cemetery.

Towards the end of the 1980s, my professional life as Taxing Master was coming to a close. When David Bell retired in January 1989, his departure left a void. I missed him greatly, especially the camaraderie which we had built up over the previous twenty years. Thomas K. O'Connor was appointed in David Bell's stead. While we only served together for a short while, I found him a most pleasant, competent and companionable colleague. Unfortunately, he died only a week or two prior to his own retirement in 1996. It was so sad, as he had planned to do so much.

My career in the law came to an end in June 1992 when I reached seventy years of age. The final farewell was somewhat sad. While I never claimed that life in the law was my first love, it had been good to me and in ways, I was sorry to go. Such a life was demanding, however. 'The law is a jealous and demanding mistress,' as an eminent English lawyer once remarked.

If this was the end of my professional career, I hoped to accomplish things in my retirement which were largely denied to me while I practised law. I devoted my time to painting and I tried to apply myself more seriously to this occupation. My friend, Ultan Kennedy, allowed me to exhibit regularly in the prestigious exhibitions which his firm holds in their beautiful gallery in Harcourt Street. I was particularly lucky that a number of my works sold. As I had remarked to his father, Kenneth Kennedy: 'Hope springs eternal.' But I also remember his reply: 'Abandon hope, all ye who enter here!'

In July 1984, the Polish government conferred me with their Order of Merit in recognition of my work on the life and music of Chopin and John Field. Thereafter, I became a frequent guest at the Polish embassy receptions, where I always received a warm welcome. It was there that I first met Yan Vincent Czak, himself a leading authority on the famous ballet dancer, Nijinsky. Yan Czak is also a knowledgeable and respected linguist. Yan Czak has done, and continues to do, tremendous work to further cultural relations between Ireland and Poland.

From our first meeting, Yan took a special interest in my work on both

Chopin and Field. It was through his influence that I was invited to Poland to deliver an hour-long lecture on Field which took place in the Ostrogski Castle in Warsaw, the home and headquarters of the renowned Chopin Society. This lecture took place before a large and distinguished audience on St Patrick's Day 1993 and the event turned out to be one of the most memorable of my life. That night, I was presented with the prestigious Chopin Medal. In turn, I presented the society a framed print of a rare portrait of John Field who, as creator of the nocturne, had been the precursor of Chopin. Earlier that day, Phyllis and I were taken on a private tour of Ostrogski Castle in the company of its director, Albert Grudzinski, where we saw so many souvenirs of the composer. It was so thrilling to see and even touch mementoes of Chopin.

While in Warsaw we visited the apartment which had been the home of Chopin's parents. Later, with Yan and the deputy director of the society, we drove to Zelazowa Wola, the birthplace of Chopin, now a beautifully kept national shrine. We also visited the church of the Holy Cross in Warsaw where there is a shrine that contains Chopin's heart.

On my Polish trip, I was also asked to deliver lectures on my father and the Countess Markievicz, the latter in a school with more than 2,000 pupils and named after the Irish heroine. Before delivering my lecture on my father in the University of Warsaw, I had a long conversation with the rector. He spoke perfect English and told me that this university boasted of teaching sixty different languages. Following my visit, he planned to add Irish to the list.

Later, we journeyed in a splendid express train to Cracow where again, through the influence of Yan, I delivered my lecture on Field at the Music Conservatoire. I found Cracow to be a place of great charm, historic interest and aesthetic beauty, although we were only there for a short time. We visited many famous buildings, including the great cathedral where I had the honour of placing flowers on the tomb of the great Polish patriot, Marshal Jozef Pilsudski, whose life, principals and ideals have been compared to those of my father.

Another day, we drove to the university city of Lublin which had suffered grievously in World War II. The present Pope had once been a professor there.

The Irish ambassador, Richard O'Brien, had been our host throughout our visit, and we stayed at the Irish embassy in Warsaw. Both he and his wife showed us great kindness and did everything they could to make this visit a memory to treasure. Richard O'Brien proved himself to be an excellent ambassador for his country. Earlier, he had taken us on a tour of Warsaw, a city which suffered appallingly during Word War II. With tremendous resilience and dedication, the 'Old Town' was rebuilt, stone by stone, conforming almost exactly to what had been so ruthlessly destroyed in the war. It was almost incredible to see how each building was reconstructed to what they assured me was the smallest detail. This included the great palace which the Germans had blown up by placing no less than ten thousand charges to demolish the building. I was further told that the Poles had cleverly secreted detailed plans of so many of their famous buildings just before or during the early part of the war. This foresight enabled them to carry out their rebuilding and reconstruction so faithfully.

While in Poland, I met many Polish people, including a number of distinguished professors, musicians and artists. I was greatly impressed by their magnificent courage which they have always displayed throughout their long and tragic history, which in many ways so similar to Ireland's. I found them warm-hearted and generous, notwithstanding their trials during the communist regime, to say nothing of the trauma of World War II. Their work, enthusiasm and sheer dedication to the rebuilding of Warsaw is something truly remarkable. However, I was not impressed with the rebuilding of the remainder of the city, with its dreadful tower blocks of flats in the worst Soviet tradition. To me, they were an eyesore on the landscape.

At the time of my visit, the Polish people had just emancipated themselves from communist rule. Although they still suffered many restrictions, their economy was slowly picking up and they were looking forward to the opening of a few supermarkets and the setting up of a Western-style banking system in which the Irish banks were taking an active part. While all this progress and emancipation must be for the best, I hope that they will have the good sense and strength to resist so much of western ways which could not be for their benefit.

Following my visit, I felt greatly honoured to be informed that the Chopin Society had decided to establish a John Field scholarship and to present a medal as part of the prize. This scholarship is confined to Polish citizens and has been successfully held since. I was to be one of the recipients of this prestigious medal. Some time ago, I was elected as an honorary member of the Irish-Polish Society and attend a number of its functions. A further great honour was when I was elected an honorary member of the council of the International Frederic Chopin Society – the first Irishman to receive this honour. One of the most gratifying honours I have received was when the Royal Irish Academy of Music conferred a fellowship on me in 1998, when the academy was celebrating the 150th anniversary of its foundation. This was on the nomination of my good friend John O'Connor.

Save for pneumonia in early childhood and the sudden appendicitis in 1975, I had always been blessed with good health and was full of energy. Suddenly, however, and without any warning, I had two heart attacks, either of which could have proved faithful. Thanks to the skill and dedication of my surgeon, Maurice Neligan, who performed a quadruple by-pass, I made a splendid recovery. I have every reason to be grateful for the interest and undoubted skill which Maurice Neligan and the other doctors and nurses showed and for the enormous advances in modern medicine.

The last year of the twentieth century saw more loss for the family with the deaths of Sally (Éamon's wife), Eithne (Ruairí's wife), and Brian (Emer's husband). Of the original family, only Emer and I remain.

Throughout these pages, I have endeavoured to tell my story and treat of those who, in one way or another, have touched or influenced my life. Vastly more important, I mention instances and events which formed a vital part in the life of my parents. I have also written of the valiant and heroic, and a number who possessed exceptional talents and gifts, achieving international fame in their various spheres of activity, whether in politics, the arts or other callings.

Mention has been made too of lesser mortals who have, nevertheless, each in their own way, by their lives, actions and brave deeds, enriched the life of the Irish nation.

As for my father, he holds a unique position with his world-wide fame and stature, long since recognised as one of the greatest statesmen of the twentieth century. Try as his detractors may, nothing can diminish his integrity, his sincerity, his courage and his unselfish devotion to his beloved country. All this has been demonstrated clearly throughout his long life.

My mother too played her part so well in a supporting role, without ever once deviating one iota from her deeply-held convictions and constant loyalty, her husband, family and the country she so loved.

I have now reached the end of my chronicle and can think of no better way of completing my story than to return to Robert Emmet, whose name I have known since my early childhood. Emmet's famous and eloquent speech from the dock ranks amongst the finest in the English language. It prompted Lord Byron to say that 'Robert Emmet spoke not for man, but to time and eternity'.

On completing his speech, Emmet added three short words to his masterpiece which I, in all humility now borrow – 'I have done'.

# EPILOGUE

I had thought that when I had written the concluding words of the last chapter, my task was then complete. Little did I know that when I had written those final words, I was about to suffer a grievous loss with the sudden and quite unexpected death of my beloved wife, Phyllis. It is so difficult to write of her passing, having been so happily married for over fifty-one years, known her for almost sixty, and seen her in childhood for upwards to seventy. For me, this void can never be filled.

I have, however, tried to express my sorrow and grief in the following lines (however inadequate), with which I wish to complete my work.

My Wife Phyllis, In Memoriam

The scythe of death has swathed the corn of life,
And laid it low on earth's receiving layer,
Oh! dear wife, to be with you at rest,
And kill the pain of loss which racks my breast.

The many happy years we spent together,
While through life's long labours striven,
But you are now at peace with God,
In His eternal heaven.

Soon my path must lead me to the grave,
And bid farewell to life, this vale of tears,
Then neither time, nor space can ere again sever
Our reunion in paradise for ever.

# BIBLIOGRAPHY
# PRIMARY SOURCES & REFERENCES

Bruce Arnold, *Orpen: Mirror to the Age*, Johnathan Cape, London, 1981

Edward J. Bourke, *Shipwrecks of the Irish Coast*, self-published, Dublin 15, 1994

Tim Pat Coogan, *De Valera: Long Fellow, Long Shadow*, Hutchinson, London, 1993

Terry de Valera, 'John Field (1782-1837)', *Dublin Historical Record*, Old Dublin Society, Vol. XXXV No.4, September 1982

Terry de Valera, 'Letters of the Sheares Brothers', *Dublin Historical Record*, Old Dublin Society, Vol. XLIII No.2, autumn 1990

Terry de Valera, 'Sarah Curran's Musical Interests', *Dublin Historical Record*, Old Dublin Society, Vol. XXVIII No.1, December 1984

John P. Duggan, *A History of the Irish Army*, Gill & MacMillan, Dublin, 1991

John P. Duggan, *Neutral Ireland and The Third Reich*, Lilliput Press, Dublin, 1989

Sean P. Farragher CSSp, *Dev and his Alma Mater*, Paraclete Press, Dublin & London, 1984

Nicholas Harman, *Dunkirk*, Coronet Books, 1980

The Earl of Longford and Thomas P. O'Neill, *Eamon de Valera*, Gill & MacMillan, Dublin, 1970

Dorothy MacArdle, *The Irish Republic*, Farrar, Strausau, Giroux, New York, 1965 and other editions

Donal MacCarron, *Landfall Ireland*, Colourpoint Books, Newtownards, Co. Down

Terence MacSwiney, *Principles of Freedom*, The Talbot Press, Dublin 1921

Maurice Moynihan, ed., *Speeches and Statements by Eamon de Valera*, Gill & MacMillan, Dublin, 1980

Madeline O'Rourke, *Air Spectaculars*, Glendale, 1989

Sir William Orpen RA, *The Onlooker in France 1917-1919*, Willams & Norgate Ltd, London, 1921

Sir William Orpen RA, *Stories of Old Ireland and Myself*, Willams & Norgate Ltd, London, 1924

A. A. Quigley, *Green is My Sky*, Avoca Publications, 1983

Hazel P. Smyth, *The Turn of the Road*, Pale Publishing, 1994


Bunreacht na hÉireann

Documents in the custody of the Franciscan Friars and University College Dublin

Articles, reports in various newspapers

Private, confidential family papers and records

Personal notes, diaries and records

# INDEX